NOTHING OVER TRUTH

MICHAEL R BRADLEY

Tribute to Lizzie Mae Bradley

Your presence made me a better man.
When I look for serenity you are the drop of water under the arc of
a rainbow. Your strength never allowed me to quit and your smile
allows me to love.
I thank the gods for allowing me to know your spirit.

4

As a human phenomenon, however, freedom is all too human. Human freedom is finite freedom. Man is not free from conditions. But he is free to take a stand in regard to them. The conditions do not completely condition him. Within limits it is up to him whether or not he succumbs and surrenders to the conditions. He may as well rise above them and by so doing open up and enter the human dimension. Ultimately, man is not subject to the conditions that confront him; rather, these conditions are subject to his decisions. Wittingly or unwittingly, he decided whether he will face up or give in, whether or not he will let himself be determined by the conditions.

༄ ༄
Viktor Frankl

ACKNOWLEDGEMENTS

My existence requires that I give special thanks to Linda Hensley for her dauntless belief in my right to life beyond the experience of shackles. I also want to thank Dr. Rachel N. Hastings of 4th Stage Publications for the depths of her awareness, and the Soledad Scholars participants from Southwestern College, for their input in making this project a reality.

Much thanks to my sisters, Michelle Wright, Tara Taylor, and Angela (Peaches) Wright for never turning their back on my truth. To my brothers, Darwin Williams, Cleo 'Macc' Calloway, Maurice 'Pie Face' Alexander, Henry Bratton, Sr. & Jr., Charles 'C-Dog' Stewart, Kari 'Killo-Watt' Watson, Virgil 'Tike' Byars, Kenneth Farmer Jr., Jonathan 'Tray' Ware, Emile 'Enfant 1' Allen, Tristan 'Slick' Lopez, Warren 'Eyes' Collins, Kenneth 'Kareem" Berry', and Lamont 'Domino' Boone, for keeping the concept of family alive.

I want to give a special thanks to Dr. Isaac Slaughter for ushering in the unraveling of my confusion. Also, Dr. Stuart Rosenberg for reassuring me of the validity of my shared experiences. The positive childhood influence of Charles Burnett made me realize I could actually accomplish the challenge of writing a book, thank you. I also want to thank Dr. Robert McMahon for introducing me to existential philosophies and inner-peace, which has transformed suffering into strength.

There is an endless list of those who I have not mentioned although our encounters enriched my life, 'I love ya.' To those that I perceived their existence as a waste of human life, you made me stronger....

Michael Bradley, April 2015

I woke this morning dressed in two white prison jumpsuits and a pair of undershorts. Each jumpsuit was taped at the waist, thigh and ankle. The inside jumpsuit was

placed on me correctly, while the outside jumpsuit was reversed.

I was then shackled at the ankles. A chain wrapped around my waist and linked through a pair of handcuffs. I would remain like this for fifteen days. The tape so tight that my body could not stand erect. My cell was modified to accommodate a process called *Potty Watch,* where the sink and toilet were taped closed with cardboard and the water shut off to my cell. My bunk was a concrete slab. All I was afforded was a thin, plastic mattress.

It is January 2012. Winter has finally decided to show up. My shoulders, upper back and forearms are completely exposed to 20 degree Northern California weather. I am located in the part of the prison that has no heat, yet expensive computers occupy and grow dust on every desk at Folsom.

I am forced to urinate in a bottle and to defecate at least three times in a bucket used for floor wax. Due process had fled. There are no appeals, no showers, no letters, no visits, nor toothbrushes. All human rights are suspended until I submit.

Then comes, *The Sadist,* with the full backing of the United States Government behind her. She is offended that some mere convict would hesitate in following her commands. After all, she is a prison guard. Prison guards in the United States make more money annually than many people with college degrees. She is the girl that was bullied because of the possibility of inbreeding. Now she can return the favor. She knows the darkness of degradation and humiliation.

7

Life is great to her because all she has to do is tap into the hatred that has festered in her since childhood. She understands the conundrum of Hitler's Third Reich guards and feels empowered by spitting on corpses. The ills of a society weren't determined by her, yet she is more than happy to follow this established conduct. It was God-sent that her self-esteem issues and economic throes were reconciled at the expense of another. These days she finds *hate* invigorating.

She also understand that she isn't alone. So she entertains like-minded people with sadistic techniques. It is 25 degrees in my cell and I am shivering. Even the guards are cold with the protection of knit caps, gloves, thermals and heavy jackets. The nurse wants to take my vitals, during my only opportunity to urinate. Every thread of clothing that I have on is draped around my ankles and shackles. *The Sadist* turns on an industrial-sized fan. Clearly, I was dealing with a sadist in all her glory while other sadists were quietly triumphant. I saw courage in the eyes of a couple of other guards. But I also understood staff should never disagree with each other in front of inmates.

My resistance grew. I questioned the purpose of *Potty Watch*. Is it to humiliate me or to make me submit? I once remember reading a Martin Luther King, Jr. quote, "*He who passively accepts evil is as much involved in it as he who helps to perpetrate it. He who accepts evil without protesting against it is really cooperating with it.*"

On the average it took seven staff to watch me urinate and record my vitals. The next morning, a 6'7" guard was assigned to me. He is a stoic, by the book individual, which was fine with me. I just wanted to do this as fast as possible so I could resume shielding myself against the cold with my mattress. While he was instructing me on which move to make next, there was a constant chorus of chatter in the background. These competing suggestions only impeded the process. After being told to pull up my undershorts, I reached down and was startled by the sound of the snap of a baton. When I turned towards the noise, I witnessed the guard assigned to watch me push back a female guard. She was about to strike me. Supposedly, she didn't hear anyone tell me to reach down. I am 210 pounds and the blow of a 5'2", 130 pound female could not kill me but caused me to wonder about what personal issues had her prepared to strike me without cause?

Later, I had a relaxed encounter with a gun enthusiast, martial arts expert who was about my same age. I had been in the system a decade before he became a guard yet we understood that there was only one decision that changed our place in life. He wasn't shy about sharing his accomplishments (S.W.A.T., D.E.A. and I.S.U.). The day ended with civil gentlemanly departing exchanges.

The very next day he was told of a semi-accident I had as a result of medication given to make me defecate. This same man went into a tirade about sodomizing me, sticking his fingers up my rectum to retrieve something that wasn't there. He gyrated his hips. I was amazed by his actions. Immediately, his supervisor stepped in wanting reassurances from me that I would not retaliate. In 35 years of incarceration I have never had a man speak of my rectum. His supervisor offered several insincere apologies. The guards will push and submit an inmate to many types of mental warfare. There are some things a man will die for! As Frederick Douglas states, *"Find out just what any people will quietly submit to and you have found out the exact measure of injustice and wrong which will be imposed upon them, and these will continue till they are resisted with either words or blows, or with both."*

I don't think a day has passed in the last 37 years that I don't self analyze my adolescent circumstances and question how I volunteered for modern day slavery or a life of living hell. Sometimes, I see myself in today's youth, yet other times I find it interesting how some of them get so mentally twisted. Being a former gang member myself, I can identify with the feeling of disenfranchisement as a result of a dysfunctional family.

Prisons are for punitive purposes only. Today if an inmate receives an education, he pursues and acquires that himself, against the sentiments of those who promulgate the idea that no inmate is redeemable. If you enjoy a nice meal, your sanity should be checked. To afford staff pay raises food cost was reduced and one method of achieving that was to introduce unfermented soybean to our diet. Like education, any program thought to be a benefit to prisoners has been eliminated or so restricted that the gesture is meaningless. They are just decorations like the word rehabilitation.

Some days I struggle to justify breathing. The abandonment of people who need me equates to my greatest pains. Very few days go by where I don't wonder about a God who allows me to be of sound mind and body just to experience this nightmare. The venom of my captors, accompanied by carcasses of men destroyed long ago eat at my soul. To live, deprived of dignity and without a soul is even more frightening than death itself.

I remember when I could not sleep because I had found in a book something that I never realized while I was free. I learned that knowledge transcends into marketable skills. I also became aware that a diversity of lifestyles existed outside my neighborhood. The combination of marketable skills and life choices were the golden key to freedom. During those years I watched very little television because it interfered with my studying. I came to realize that my own worst enemy was myself. The strongest of shackles are those we gullibly allow to manifest in our minds which in turn enslaves our spirits and denies us the realization of our full potential.

At moments I find myself searching for space not occupied by scar tissue. My mind dances with cold and frightened children escaping from slavery. I am valued as livestock, my human potential ignored. I maintain a place of solace for those who have paroled and successfully integrated back into society. Unconsciously, I brush upon earned but never realized dreams.

There are children that I would have loved to have fathered. Loves that had the potential to be great and love stories made. I lost legitimate career opportunities that offered purpose and untold riches. I could have been a meaningful father, husband, brother, uncle, and friend. Instead my life is valued as testament of how wrong the human spirit can be.   Existentialism helps me qualify happenstance by design.   Agendas and philosophies are meant to crush the spirit of a child, leaving the mind to be trained as a pet parrot.

If I am permitted, it is logical to conclude that day needs night.   Throughout America there are untold people like me who intentionally had the cancer of drugs, gangs and immorality placed in their lives.   It is a good bet that curiosity of man could be used to kill millions. With all his splendor, man loves plants and defenseless animals. But I find it bewildering how man will accept pseudonyms placed on fellow humans without considering that the code word insinuates justifiable homicide. Television provided him with a boogey man. I bear the scars of no mercy!

> "We have to do with the past only as we can make it useful to the present and the future."
>
> ❧ ❧
>
> Frederick Douglas

The gestation from which my life springs denotes evil, narcissism, racism, chauvinism, and how many can live an impotent existence, never feeling adequate as a human being. This is a reflection of imps and how the stones of evil can have a lasting effect on generations to come.

Hell met me at conception, from that moment on struggle and hardship have been my fate. This journey is seasoned with ignorance, injustice, unconditional love, hate, and an acute awareness of self. Tears have showered the flowers of my existence and the only genuine peace I have known was found in my darkest hour. In this life, death has become my most trusted ally in ending humiliation, bigotry, and indifference of my days. When my love decided to go on vacation it took the luster of life with it, and I was left with hypocrisy, deceit, and gloom. I found myself introduced to throat shackles and back in slavery being comforted by the bosoms of dead ancestors, family, friends as death beckoned me proclaiming to be the antidote to my torment, furnishing images of dead loved ones and a sense of serenity in my soul.

Today death is part of my decision making process. Am I willing to stand by the actions that determine who I am for eternity? I trust her unequivocally as my adviser in deciding my next move on whether or not I want my next string of words to be the last thing that I express to someone I care about. She is a constant reminder that my next move may be my last, and that I might have to stand on them for eternity. My life is entwined intimately with hell. All I have to do is open my eyes to find myself surrounded by folks I do not like. By those who are acting out roles of master and slaves, sadist and masochist, with broken minds and spirits. These walking cadavers kneel to those who pretend to possess moral, legal and intellectual superiority. I have absolutely no desire to spend eternity stained with the stench of man's deceptive foolishness.

A man has to know himself and most importantly must be truthful with himself to bring about change. Only an idiot has any faith in his ability to deceive death with pretentiousness of hollow impersonations of faulty images. I have to accept that I was fathered by a little man's need to relieve the frustrations of being inept as a human being through an orgasmic experience when he took my mother's pussy. On May 16, 1958 I was born in Los Angeles as the result of a grown man's loveless thirst for the flesh of a confused, thirteen year old girl who's desperate cries for help resulted in the birth of an unplanned and unwanted child. Some men maintain a strained relationship with responsibility, having no inclinations of what it is to be a man, which makes it easy for a coward to flee and become a burdensome fixture in the shattered life of those that witnessed his affection.

Misfortune snatched my mother's world by the throat when she was eleven years old causing her to spend most of her life dealing with the repercussions of bad decisions in men caused by happenstance with the death of her mother. My grandmother died in 1955 from lymphatic cancer. She was married with two children. Her first husband was killed in World War II, a couple of years later she wed another soldier, a real American hero who accepted the role of father and later grandfather as well as any man could. It's been said that my grandmother earned extra money during the war by allowing cosmetic and pharmaceutical companies to experiment and perform research of their products on her. Grandma was a guinea pig, which left her scarred on the inside and out. After the war she was diagnosed with cancer and unfortunately she had signed a waiver of responsibility. Her suffering and eventual death wounded my family.

Some people just don't seem able to handle death well and my mother was no exception. I happened along during a period in her life that peer acceptance and partying held a much greater value to her than rearing a child. She was having babies when most teenagers were enjoying the innocence of adolescence and was determined not to allow the inconvenience of having children to interfere with whatever fun she was having. When adventure lie elsewhere she was off and running with not much concern for babysitters. Sometimes these escapades required days of her undivided attention and we were left to fend for ourselves. By the time she was seventeen she had three children and no parts of a man. Finally, realizing that she couldn't take care of one child, much less three, she accepted the strong advice of family to have her tubes tied. She finally did her part to stop unwanted pregnancies.

Her life tells a story of a girl attracted to men that couldn't care less about her. Street nigga's, gangsters, an assortment of broken characters attracted her affection like insects being drawn to sweet smelling poison. She was soft and gave her affection to the seedy and wanna be bad boys. She admired the ones who were going to die young, or dance in penitentiaries until their spirits were broke. Her fixation with being the pussy on their plate occasionally erased any thought of how her children would eat or manage alone. These departures from responsibility created conflict between us and animosity because I chose to contact someone to assist us in her absence. Still in diapers there were times when my siblings and I ventured outside to search for our mother and were subsequently rescued by total strangers. Of course, she resented her neglect being exposed. At the age of four I knew hunger, not because there was a lack of food in the house but having someone there to prepare it was the problem.

By the age of four, I had a little brother and a baby sister and I possessed an unconscious awareness of my role. I was the oldest and a protective cord arose within me that placed itself in opposition to the good times my mother sought. This was the beginning of a conscious molding. My survival was developing into something that required my personal attention. Innocence was being lost to keep me from drowning in the sewage of neglect and subsequent rejection that comprised the world that I knew. To keep afloat in a world that ignored my tears and ridiculed my screams for help I began to lose the humanity that accompanied me through the birth canal and an indifference began to erect itself as a shield against life.

The lack of knowledge limited my choices. I could have rolled over and been a coward, human waste, waiting to become another man's carnage, or I could learn to fight. Being deprived of love and compassion fuels a need to be cared for. Being vulnerable taught me quickly how to protect myself and my family against whatever predators that might be invited inside my home or lay within the quagmire of my cage. Being the eldest of three children and taking the lead in whatever we had to do to survive was my role, like it or not.

My innocence was being stolen before I even got to kindergarten. Out of necessity I began seeking the ingredients of what it took to become a man, hoping that manhood would erase my pain. Neglect makes it apparent what you don't have. When adult good times took food out of my stomach, and the streets were rendering parenting, how I got what I wanted did not make a lot of difference to me.

There were times when scrounging through empty cupboards filled with scrimmaging roaches looking for a meal was normal for me. Reality makes surviving right and hunger wrong when the refrigerator is bare. I have sat in dismay when my voyages only reaped a mayonnaise sandwich with a teaspoon of sugar as a treat. It's not for me to question individuals who are capable of rolling over and accepting whatever life gives them. My fight just started at a young age.

My soul has been placed in peril against my circumstances for as long as I can remember. As a child my penchant for surviving sentenced me to the role of underdog when it conflicted with my mother's ceaseless need to satisfy herself. I was always the Indian in a cowboy movie, the robber in a cop show. Life aligned me with the underdogs; this tragedy is not something that I chose.

Where there is no opposition people will do what they feel like doing. So revealing not being fed and prolonged absences created the perfect environment for an ass whipping and the ability of being resented. Right just like wrong has its justifications. I equated dealing with pain instead of running away from it as some kind of manly act. Early in life I became immune to ass whipping, crying about being beaten became more humiliating than being whipped. I came from my mother's womb, loved her, and assumed that she loved me. Love can often be confusing and everything you love doesn't necessarily love you back. She wasn't prepared to be a parent. Some days I agonized over what went wrong and why hell is more alluring than my life, pondering that my dilemma shines light on how obscure the meaning of love can be.

My mother definitely had her faults, which I have come to understand and in being prepared for death, forgive. On the other hand I question that I am my father's son. It's hard to believe that I could be the product of disdainful trash. There is absolutely no comparison between him and I in any way. I am unsure if he even possessed a soul. As his son I never witnessed anything in him beyond superficial masks that were designed to hide him being impotent as a man. If there was anything of value in his existence I never witnessed it. My encounter with him left my soul stench with the smell of shit that I unfortunately stepped in. I have no sympathy for my father. I do regret allowing his presence to rob me of what could have been a beautiful existence.

My father was the first man in life that I anticipated killing. Unlike enemies, bitch-made friends, injustice and others who I momentarily held in disregard I consciously chose not to forgive that punk. I still can find no justification for him. They called him "Snake," and at an early age I somehow understood and appreciated the nature of mongooses. His reptilian presence trashed my innocence to some degree leaving huge amounts of debris that cluttered my journey with bullshit, distrust, and anger, dulling my sense of humanity. As a man it's embarrassing even knowing him. The saying "moma's baby, daddy's maybe," would be a dream come true for me if it turned out that I wasn't his son. As a child it was discernible that the man in me was greater than anything he could ever hope to be. He wouldn't have lasted long on the path my life has taken. The streets that embraced me had no respect for his kind, nor are these penitentiaries tolerable of such human waste. His irresponsibility and predaceous demeanor only apply to the weak and vulnerable. He is my model of what it is to be small and inadequate. Oppression is a double edged sword that impedes values in some, while birthing principles and respect from others. To avoid hardship and possible death some sink into the valleys of their lowest self, exacting a coward's revenge on all they touch. He was no exception, but his impact upon me created a powerful chasm within me of insecurity that fueled a willingness to utilize a deadly hand as a remedy to conflict.

Even though his presence was menacing, I strangely still sought to satisfy that father son relationship in me. I looked the demon in the eye and never saw anything that I recognized as similar between us, love or a father. What I found was emptiness. Eventually the whole father son relationship thing didn't matter; the streets became my surrogate father.

I tend to believe he was the catalyst of the dangerous destructive games I have played. What repels me from some men are character traits I recognized in him. What I admire in others is normally what he lacked. Mistakenly dysfunctional circumstances caused me to want to be something other than a bastard child. So I played that game of wanting to be accepted by those whose irresponsible actions gave me life. It didn't take long before I realized I was better off without him. He liked the concept of a son and enjoyed using me as a prop in his theatrical rendition of being nothing of substance.   I have felt more appreciated by enemies than I did by him.

I have imprinted on my brain the image of a bug-eyed, thick mustached, short muscular man who one day volunteered to take all of us to a Thrifty Drugstore, on Vermont Ave and 31st Street. My mother probably attempted to use her three kids as a safeguard in taking the trip.   But while my siblings and I sat in the back seat of an old car,   pandemonium erupted in the front seat.   In broad daylight, this carefree trip to the store turned into another disillusioning incident as the sounds of my mother's face being slapped echoed through the car. He was oblivious to my siblings crying and her pleas as he beat her in a sexual frenzy. My mother, kicking, swinging and screaming is one of those episodes that you don't forget easily.   Nor did her admissions ever escape my consciousness as she conceded to his attack,   "You sorry bastard, you'll rape me in front of my kids." Some things, I just don't forget.

At the age of four, I still was open to love and the acceptance of a parent. He wore the title of father fraudulently, we never had a semblance of connection, no trust, and the whole relationship was suspect.   While he assumed that I was a thoughtless child the damage had already been done to my psyche. Warnings were implanted. Confusion and fear became a major role in our relationship until he was accurately identified as just another parasite in a world where youthful fantasies and innocence looked for something meaningful.

My father came around because my house was a hangout spot for a local street gang known as the *Rebel Rousers*.   Self-aggrandizing and trying to be amusing to gangsters, my welfare was not his concern. I was once told by a member of the *Rebel Rouser,* Lil Joe not to expect much from my father. He understood my disappointment before I had a true concept of what human garbage was.

In my neighborhood the streets are lined with tall palm trees and most homes were three bedroom houses so there was no shortage of kids running around.   In the presence of others he played the role of proud father. I lived on Halldale Ave, at 37th Street and walking past my home was the easiest route to take between Foshay Jr. High School and neighboring Denker Park. Normally, there was an abundance of kids going to and from these two competing recreational centers.

This idiot that I had to reconcile as being my father goaded me into chasing this boy past my house with a knife. Most understood that whatever hostility I demonstrated to them was the result of being egged on by adults. Others foolishly allowed childish follies to be the seed to animosity, as we grew older. By the time that I had received my first bicycle, I had been given a switchblade and with that the path of violence was a means to feel a sense of belonging. Fear played a masterful role in the ravine of ignorance which motivated me and I utilized it for the entertainment of adults around me without realizing what was being taken from my humanity.

I wasn't five years old yet, still hadn't entered kindergarten when my father was doing work down the street from my house as an independent painter. Even though our relationship was marred with ambivalence, all I knew of him beyond our biological connection was what he wasn't doing for me in terms of support. Somehow showing interest in me meant something regardless of the repugnant sentiments that filled my heart. I wanted to impress him and became efficient with helping him paint houses, clean up work areas and running whatever errands he requested of me. Being in his presence satisfied something in me. My parental figures had always been fleeing objects in my life, so being with either one was comforting to a point.

We were working down the street from my great-grandmother's house. The sounds of children that I knew penetrated the walls of this empty house we were in, as I assisted this idiot. I was four years old working like a damn slave and the fool had the audacity to grow irritated with me. This was coming from a man who I was repeatedly reminded of by my mother, had never purchased a diaper or a pair of shoes for me, but he wanted me to go in the back room and pull down my pants so he could beat me. I didn't see that as his role. Outside of the title, he was a stranger and the sporadic appearances didn't qualify him for all that. I became frightened and questioned his motivations for wanting to whip me for no apparent reason.

What justifications he was trying to provide wasn't going to be well received in my house. My uncle had far more of a right to beat me than this idiot I was still trying to get comfortable being around. I was connected to him through some questionable act that I couldn't quite grasp. He seemed not to fully comprehend that he was the subject of scorn by those I loved.

He tried to rationalize that what he wanted to do to me would somehow determine whether I was a punk or not, but we had to keep it a secret between him and I. As he checked the sounds outside he stressed a covenant of secrecy. All this was strange and unnerving to me as when I got out of line in my house they popped me immediately and didn't care who knew it. He stepped out to check a noise and I decided to pull my pants down for my father and let him whip my ass if that's what it took for him to be a father. When he returned from checking the source of some noise I pulled my pants down as requested. He instructed me to lie down on some old mattress, I did so expecting the sting of a belt to end this test of my courage. I looked back and the fool was pulling his pants down and rubbing Vaseline on his dick. Sadly, several things were destroyed right then and there before I accepted that something was drastically wrong with this father-son relationship and began to get up threatening to tell my great grandmother what he was trying to do. He attempted to pen me down, saying, "Boy if you were my son you would let me do this without crying or running to tell someone like a punk." I panicked and he became more frustrated with continuous squirming. He didn't hit me, he just tried to manhandle and intimidate me with his mouth as he tried to penetrate me. He cared nothing about my frustration or the tears that escaped from my eyes as he tried to fuck me. His only apparent concern was that I keep what was transpiring a secret between us.

I slipped out of his grasp and we scrambled about the room as he tried to corner me with his pants down around his ankles. His lack of mobility allowed me to get out of the room. The house was empty of furniture and only the back room had shades on the window so once we entered the main house what was going on could be witnessed by anybody passing by. At some point, I got my pants fastened around my waist. He cornered me in the living room and grabbed me by the collar of my shirt and was trying to physically drag me to the area we had just left. This was damaging to my psyche, hurtful, then anger showed up and I just wanted to hurt him.

I was too big for him to pick up and my squirming made it difficult for him to control the situation without just beating me with his fist. Frightened and angry, I threatened to tell that he was trying to fuck me. He had given me a souvenir, a switchblade knife that I proudly toted around as evidence that my father had in fact given me something, which was contrary to popular opinion. Somehow this knife popped in my hand and he backed off to assess the situation. This moment seemed to have lasted a lifetime but finally noise from kids playing in front of the house penetrated our standoff.

Often I wish that I would have made him kill me because right then and there he was dead in my eyes as he collected himself. At this point yelling would have drawn curious onlookers who were directly outside this house looking for something to do. I was too ashamed to scream at that point and he looked puzzled as to what came next. I took that opportunity to leave the house physically intact but wounded in ways that I did not completely understand the ramifications of this dehumanizing afternoon with my father until I was a grown man.

This singular act directed me down a path that fostered the use of violent as a means to demonstrate my manhood. The wrong tone in someone's voice, or tough looks could easily trigger a cycle of violence. That moment created issues that had nothing to do with those I would later encounter who fell victim to violence unjustifiably.

He rained a poisonous mist in my life than disappeared. I didn't miss him, and whatever rare appearances he made were tainted with hostility. I maintained our secret out of shame, not because of sympathy for him. Three or four years later he started coming around again, but by then he was already dead to me. Anxiety and mistrust occupied his space in my life. Some didn't recognize or intentionally overlooked how despicable he was and naively tried to push me into forging a relationship with a piece of shit. They didn't understand his ominous meaning to me. We never spoke on his attempt to fuck me but we shared a truth so there was no persistent pursuit to pollute my space.

I developed a real interest in the tales of men who no one dared to bother. I revered the most feared and respected in my environment. I listened to them intensely for guidance. I stand for what I stand for in the world that would love to strip me of integrity.

My father utilized drugs, violence and humiliation for control and that only lasted as long as the dope had affect. He treated people to cocaine just to get them hooked on heroin. Eventually his own tools captured him. His need to control made him a dope fiend, "Idiot." The circle he frequented cared about as much about him as he did about them. Had to be a lonely world. He was despised not loved. The punk died owing me some money, and his family wanted me to bury him. The Los Angeles County Coroner's Office cremated him, I couldn't care less about his ashes. I do need my money, though.

When I get to the other side it's going to be embarrassing to acknowledge that I even knew my father in this life. As his son I regret not killing him and I hope these words torment him in whatever hell he occupies.

My mother made me feel like an inconvenience to be discarded at the first available opportunity. Her man, "Big Yard" implanted pride, love and manhood to my sense of self while still being a young child. Without his voice I became indifferent and empathy was misinterpreted as weakness.

I started kindergarten at 75th Street Elementary School. At that time we lived directly in front of Fremont High School in some white apartments. Life was normal and he was teaching me what I had to do to survive. Fighting was a means to being accepted by my family, a way to earn respect within a culture driven by oppression. My family did not have a lot of money, but men who had earned their respect with their hands surrounded me. Fighting to win made you a man and instilled pride. Being a poor coward wasn't admired and has to be a sad life.

> *Our society suffers from our lack of connection to each other and our collective lack of meaning in our lives. Homelessness, depression, drug abuse, alcoholism, road rage, and gun violence all have at their roots a lack of spiritual wisdom.*
>
> ༄ ༅
>
> *Melvin Morse, M.D.*

Big Yard was from Watts and ran with a notorious click called the *Farmers*. He is the only man in my life that the title of father fits. In my eyes he always exemplified what a man was supposed to be.

At this point my life evolved around childish endeavors like affording candy, going to the movies, and playing with neighborhood kids. This Sunday afternoon, I had already unsuccessfully exhausted all my avenues to obtain funds intended for the movies. Big Yard and a friend of his were sitting in his 1959 powder blue Cadillac talking and looking at what I suspect to be a porn magazine. I approached from the driver's side and peered into the car curious about what they were trying to hide from me as I made my plea for some money. He pulled all the money he had out of his pocket which only amounted to two or three dollars and without complaining gave me a couple of dollars and apologized for not having more.

He was a laid back, cool dude who only associated with a small group of friends. He sported a large Afro haircut, owned a couple of pairs of Stacy Adam's Biskets shoes, a couple of leather coats, a Studson hat, along with a few pair of black straight blacks and that was it. He seemed not to want much more. His wealth was abundant in his character, not his possessions. He was a proud man who defined himself on his own terms.

In this world I have come to know all kind of deception. Religious predators, political prostitutes, sleepwalkers who navigate life without a single genuine thought, men who would murder you for the opportunity to kiss a woman's feet even though she is oblivious to their existence. Weak men seek artificial power through association and materialism. Some are indifferent and have been wounded in ways that deny them access to their own humanity. While others allow their spirits to be drowned in drugs and alcohol. Success is subjective to one's perspective. The lives of rich men can be meaningless when the price of the riches is one's soul. The pure soul of a poor man always outweighs the pretentious soul of a rich man.

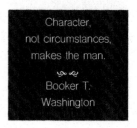

Character, not circumstances, makes the man.

ꙮ ꙮ

Booker T. Washington

As a man, I can still trust what Big Yard taught me even though life has made me a cynic. He would resort to violence in the absence of any other reasonable solution, yet he was compassionate. He is the only man that I can dare call father, any other person who held my mother's affection was a parasite transporting filth from one location to the other. If I learned anything from him that was bad or led me to the penitentiary it wasn't from a lack of his love. Big Yard is without blame for the tragedy of my existence. He wasn't conscious of how diabolical men were during that time of my life. I only stumbled over obstacles intentionally placed in my path that were designed for my demise by a society that pretentiously claimed to love thy brother.

His family lived in a corner house on 99th Towne Avenue. His mother, grandmother and occasionally his younger brother who attended U.C.L.A. resided there. He enjoyed taking us fishing and these predawn excursions provided calm in the mist of my chaos. When money was tight he would try to teach me the art of killing and skinning rabbits that his family raised in their backyard. He sincerely tried to make the best out of what little he had.

No man wants his son to grow up to be soft. If that occurs he has to accept him as he is but that's not the preference of most men. His sentiments lay closer to a belief that fighters had a better chance of surviving the trials of this life. He had no natural children and I believe that his lessons to me were a demonstration of his love and not sport. He stressed fighting to win as an art form and losing was punishable.

I started attending kindergarten while living with him and I probably got into innocent mischief. There were a few boys who stayed around the corner from us who I played with and we squabbled from time to time like boys do. We were all about the same age and probably liked each other to some degree. Once I made the mistake of coming home complaining about a fight that I had with one of these boys. Sharing that information wasn't the sensible thing for me to do because from then on it was without question that I had better not lose another fight regardless of the size of my opponent because winning was something men learned to tap into their souls to achieve. Size made no difference when you find the fight inside of yourself, he would say.

We played hot hands for reflexes and he showed me different punches and where to place my feet when throwing them. He was a boxing enthusiast who made it a point to differentiate fighting styles to me. I enjoyed the well meaning attention and I construed his message to be a mandate not to come back into that house whining about getting my ass kicked.

Unfortunately, one day I found myself playing on a beautiful blue Los Angeles day. The sun was bright in the sky and a few clouds added awe to the experience of being alive. Teenagers attending Fremont High School were going about their business of hanging out in front of the school. Some were showing off their cars, while others were picking up girls and I had the audacity to go into my apartment seeking sympathy over a disappointing playtime and to speak of my plight. I was ordered to go to my room and stay there until further notice for acting like a punk. I did not get fed dinner that night.

Every day the donut man would pull his truck into the driveway of our apartment because kids tended to congregate in this open area playing while being easily observed by parents. When the donut man parked we scurried to locate parents for nickels and dimes to purchase donuts and other sweet treats. I hadn't been told that donuts and pastries were no longer part of my life. I have had a vicious sweet tooth all of my life and was dismayed when I ran to my mother seeking change for these treats and found the signature of disgust written across her face. The look was more threatening than the use of her profanity laced mouth. Big Yard's reprimand could be seen in her face as she left the apartment to buy pastries for herself and my siblings. When she came back into the apartment I was told to go into my bedroom and shut the door. The only TV we owned sat in the living room. I can still remember laying on my bed pissed off at everybody because they were enjoying donuts as I glared at the walls. My mind contemplated what I had to do and I was determined to realize bakery bliss again along with being an accepted member of my own household.

I had never ran or cowered before a threat in my life. My problem came from seeking comfort after a battle. Men learn to suck it up and that was the lesson that I was learning. It was clear to me what I had to do...win. In the following days when it was time to go out to play I didn't have to be told to kick someone's ass when I left the house because the rewards and punishments were clear to me. With Big Yard and his friends watching I didn't need to be provoked to attack one of my playmates for something that he had done because the battle to be accepted was already going on in my head. I didn't always feel like I won the fight because concealing my own discomfort was the manly thing to do and satisfying my family with my performance in seeking their approval was more important than any annoyance of being bruised.

Seemingly everything was all right. I was with my family and those circumstances were the only world I knew. Big Yard cared about me and I knew it. He frequently took me with him to visit family and friends. He never said, but I knew he was proud of me like any father would be of his son. He never pitted me against another child, he was just adamant that I win when confronted. My fears became an attribute that I learned to handle once I made up my mind to swing as hard and fast as I possibly could at the first indication of disrespect. The rest would take care of itself.

My innocence had been soiled and I childishly pursued manhood believing that arrival would provide a peace of mind. People liked me because I was respectful, quiet and knew how to keep my mouth shut. I enjoyed that acceptance and in a short period of time I assumingly had figured out the level of aggression necessary to appease my folks.

Next door to the apartment that we were living in there was a church that I never attended. Adjacent to that was a laundry mat and the area in front and behind these buildings served as our playground. Our apartment was upstairs and had a balcony parallel to our front door. That balcony was like a control center because we received the majority of our commands from that location. Approval or displeasure was nodded from that spectators box and I was conscious of my actions when in eyesight.

There was no animosity in these childhood games. My issues were private and confusing to me. To keep the peace at home I played rough and competitive with these kids. Naturally one of these kids stood out as my foe. He had several brothers all around the same age as us. One of his brothers was a couple of years older who hung out with us. It didn't take long before he and I were locked into a cycle of competition with one another, none of which left me comfortable with the decisive victory that I needed for my home life. His size advantage unnerved me for a moment. The altercations between he and I became my motivation to invest more of myself to winning.

There was no grass in the area we played in. One afternoon I was having a bad day and losing meant too much. The rule was to always get off first because that first blow might be the deciding punch. So without provocation I socked this boy in the face on a couple of occasions. I was motivated not to go back into the house with a defeat hanging over my head. He came to expect unwarranted attacks and his reaction to my punches lessened. He was no longer stunned by my strategy. So after a few week I reassessed my situation and I picked up a red brick of average size and flung it upside his bald head. To my surprise the blow caused blood to immediately spurt from his head. All of us were stunned as the red fluid began gushing from his head onto his white t-shirt, the sight inadvertently transform the significance of a day at play. The situation alarmed me as the screams of other kids indicting me echoed in my moment of silence. I didn't intend the severity of his wound, my actions were thoughtless, I just wanted to hit him harder than he was hitting me. I was concerned for him but it was too late to withdraw the now lifeless brick, so we all scurried for our homes.

The news of what had happened reached home before I did. Big Yard gave me a not to worry look as my mother ranted and raved about everything wrong with her life. I hid in my bedroom worrying about my punishment instead of the lack of humanity that I was exhibiting. I seemed to be removed from the whole scene. My pain and confusion rested in a vessel outside of myself. I was tormented not about the boy's condition, but over the pending storm that swirled outside my bedroom for cracking this boy upside the head with a brick. On many occasions I had been firmly instructed that when getting my ass whipped, to pick up whatever was close to me and hit someone with it or be prepared to get my ass whipped when I got home. I had done exactly what I had been told to do, yet the situation had an ominous feeling to it.

I was in my room voluntarily as my little brother and sister came in and out, harassing me about my troubles. Later that evening the boy's parents knocked on our door. I cracked my bedroom door to listen to what was being said about me. My whole family was in the living room along with the boy's parents and they were explaining his injury, their frightful trip to the hospital and the associated cost. I was called out of my room to apologize, which fearfully I did. Big Yard told the boy's parents that he would pay the hospital bill, apologized himself for what had happened and then they left.

Shit hit the fan after they left. My mother went into an emotional tirade and made a futile attempt at whipping me. Big Yard kept her at bay. The real pain and permanent scar came from her willful rejection of me. I could have easily taken an ass whipping and within days it would have been forgotten with no hard feelings. But she was vehement about wanting me out of her house. I would have taken a hundred ass whippings rather than live with the void in my heart created by the fact that my own mother didn't want or love me. My mother was cute and her looks carried her through life. I wouldn't contribute the attribute of being strong-willed to her character but she was unyielding in her decision to get me out of her house.

I have never understood why I was cast out. I acted straight from the playbook they gave me. I was wrong as a human but true to the rhetoric taught to me. I would have assumed that as soon as the boy's parents were gone that my folks would have showered me with gifts for following their instructions on conduct in these types of situations. Instead, my world became twisted and confusing. I was tossed out without a logical explanation.

Just because we have a mouth doesn't mean we should use it. Some days I am dismayed by all the tough talk and hatred spouted by men who don't really mean it. They walk around the penitentiary disparaging themselves with the rationale of imbeciles. Reasoning that calling themselves disrespectful names, like niggas and their moma's bitches, may take the sting out when called that by others. You would have to be a bubbling idiot to accept that logic. I am not going to degrade myself or allow someone else to belittle me with a melodic cadence provided and funded by slave masters. My ignorance had me shackled. I am a modern slave and my days are being stolen by the rich for profit. But I know better than to allow the cancer of hate to reside in me, especially against those that it should be my duty to protect. We have killers that have never killed. Bad boys without the credentials of a fair fight. Pretenders who associate with the real for validation and then muddy the arena they play in. The codes of the streets promote dehumanizing ethics to those looking for guidance. Words are basically worthless. They only possess value when being acted upon. Talk allows people to sound tough especially when words are depicting a hypothetical situation.

Many people including my family forge the ethics of gangsters while spouting the codes of men. The problem is that only a few live by it and those who do end up wanted by the police or in my case I was thrown out of the house by my mother. I was raised to act like a man. My role models loved winners. The rhetoric of the streets is like the Bible, full of gaps. Tough talk leaves out foresight and reasoning. A win in trivial circumstances can quite well ruin you for life. I have been a prized piece in a few different theaters but while others can claim to know bravery through loose association I sit pitifully with nothing but my principles. Of course, my understanding is shattered; everybody is not playing by the same rules. If the philosophy of men were an accepted creed, respect would be the foundation to our existence. Instead manipulation and deception is what carried the day. You can't believe the hype, it sounds good but the reality of it can be devastating. I felt deprived of family, tricked and as though I was unwanted by both parents. Rhetoric eroded the sense of a family bond, causing it to become fragile. I had issues of abandonment and dealt with loneliness while surrounded by many.

Check what goes into your mind because under close examination what you are being told by people close to you may well be worthless and nothing good may come from it. Men who stand on principles understand the value of respect, love, and knowledge. Those who pretend to be men deal in deceit and tough talk. Their advice is useless and will only assist you into an early grave or the penitentiary.

Slavery: ....that slow poison, which is daily contaminating the minds and morals of our people. Every gentleman here is born a petty tyrant. Practiced in acts of despotism and cruelty, we become callous to the dictates of humanity and all the finer feelings of the soul. Taught to regard a part of our own species in the most abject and contemptible degree below us, we lose that idea of the dignity of man which the hand of nature had implanted in us, for great and useful purposes.

ço ৯

George Mason, July 1773
Virginia Constitutional Convention

It never was enough to just accept being in the penitentiary. I needed to understand why the gates of hell were so readily available to me. This question was best answered by my history and an honest exploration of my soul.

My own mother didn't want or love me anymore, which caused me to grow to understand the attributes of rejection and it's friend, loneliness. It hurt watching her come and go. For a long time I begged for her to forgive me for whatever transgressions she utilized as justification for abandoning me. My pleas fell on deaf ears. Being excluded from her activities real or imaginary birthed a deep pain within me. It took years for me to accept her rejection and stop trying to be accepted by her. Sadness stole my voice, carefree was gone, and innocence was a folly not afforded to children that were being assaulted by life.

I was sent to stay with my Great-Grandmother whom I had spent a lot of time with in the first years of my life. So much time had been spent with her that she was the only person I ever called Moma. Moma had to be in her mid-sixties when I was born, was retired and now in her seventies raising another child. What she lacked in youthful physical ability she over compensated with in an absolute love for me! Often I wish that I had been mindful then and during adolescence that our physical existence comes to an end at some point. She was in her end life cycle and showered me with a love that would last for eternity. I was dealing with issues a child shouldn't have to deal with but even that is no excuse for hurting the only person on this planet who truly loved me, without exception. The path I took had to hurt her heart.

I was enrolled in 37th Street Elementary School to finish kindergarten after being rejected by my mother, wounded and stumbling but my life continued. Moma was all for me defending myself when necessary but fighting had nothing to do with her criterion for being a good child. She respected men who worked hard to support a family, so I found odd jobs around the neighborhood. I worked at a corner store named Charlie's, cut grass, shined shoes, delivered newspapers and at one point I became pretty handy working on cars due to a job I had working at an auto mechanic shop. I wanted for nothing, she dressed me like a walking mannequin from a Broadway Department store window.

Moma was born in 1892, in Sunflower, Mississippi, and was of mixed blood, Cherokee and African. One of her parents had been a real slave, although she seemed not to know either well. Later in life, I stumbled across an explanation as to why she never acknowledged her parents by simply reading the book, *The Miseducation of the Negro* by G. Carter Woodson that described her unusual parental omission. She had a firsthand accounting of a mindset that allowed a race of people to be bartered, bought or sold like a tool in someone's garage. She stood on the remnants of a history that I barely comprehended, 'A Jim Crow South.'

A lady that they fondly referred to as "Auntie," raised Moma. She was a honey-colored former slave herself who housed, cared for, and educated herself and a group of other children, whose parents had been sold, died or driven away. Her tone could denote defiance that was fueled by pain and hardship. This sweet little lady that I cherished was from the south, Sunflower, Mississippi, aka as "Death County." According to Wikipedia, this was "due to the presence of Mississippi State Prison at Parchman."

As a child she grew accustomed to witnessing dead Black men hanging from trees, blue and swollen along roads she had to travel on for simple errands. She was extremely cautious about the potential viciousness of white people and was guarded with most encounters. When I was sent to stay with her she still had two living sisters. The eldest was named Viola and the youngest was Amanda. Their life cycle was coming to an end and they often reflected on the past. They stayed true to their experiences, their reality was filled with an abundance of occurrences that played over and over in their minds. Both had a history of being preferred because of their light skin color. The degrading instrument of rape had conceived them. All three had legitimate cause to hate the caretakers of oppression.

We frequently travelled by RTD bus to visit Moma's sisters who lived on 51st and Hooper Avenue. Often we carried bags of food with us, not that they needed anything to eat, these were special items that reminded them of home, such as, raisin bread, sponge cakes, and other hard to find delicacies.

By 1965, all three were in their seventies and Viola was dying, which partially restricted her to bed. Understandably Moma spent as much time as she could with her dying sister and they sat in Viola's bedroom talking and reflecting on the past. Occasionally touching on sensitive areas that caused all of them to just sit and reflect quietly. Amanda was a petite soft-spoken elderly lady who was radiant with youthful beauty. I sometimes wondered about her mental faculties especially when observing the amazing love she showered on her dog, Fido. The dog was cared for like a human. His food was cooked, he slept on a sofa and even had beer with his meals. While rotting away in the penitentiary, I fantasized about being treated as well as that dog. The majority of meals prepared behind these walls would not be fit for consumption by her dog.

All of these women had worked hard throughout their lives, owned property and were financially comfortable in their retirement. Amanda's skin was the lightest of the three sisters and she had spent most of her life deceiving people about her ethnicity. She had passed for a white person so much that she could mimic most dialects from across the country, which they all found amusing. Amanda had worked for the mob boss Al Capone's auntie for over twenty-five years, who lived in a mansion on Adams Blvd, right off of Western Avenue. On occasion we would pass by that location and she would point out where she had spent much of her life working as a maid. Each of their homes was furnished with beautifully hand carved chest of drawers, china cabinets, bureaus, lamps and plush blankets given to them by Al Capone's auntie. They often spoke rather fondly of her.

Viola, Amanda, and Moma had a brother they had not seen in years whose memory they clung to. He appeared to be the spirit of what allowed them to remain patient and work twenty-hour days, in their quest for equality in a society that they were cautious of. There was a quiet sorrow that was reflected in recounts of the episode that separated them from their brother early in life. Chilly, was the second eldest of the four kids and when they recounted memories of him there was something very suspenseful in the unfolding of a closely, guarded family secret. They questioned the wisdom of the lady who raised them in a stinging way that I wasn't meant to understand.

Viola owned the house that we visited, a duplex next door and an ice cream parlor at the corner of 51st Street and Hooper Avenue. She was bedridden but her mind was fully active and she could recall moments long ago in the past with clarity and humor. Obviously, Viola was the matriarch of the three and would engage them in play, imitating voices of individuals in their past. The house seemed stuffy with a stench of sweat-soiled fabric. The house set close to the street and cars could be heard as they busily went up and down Hooper Avenue. A Baptist Church sat catty-corner from her house and on Sundays their singing could be heard from the churchgoers.

Lying in a bed stuffed with pillows, Viola would impersonate Auntie's southern vernacular normally after her sisters had performed whatever personal maintenance task or household cleaning they came to do. During these moments they shared experiences that were beyond my understanding. I sat in a comfortable chair quietly out of their way as they shared touching moments gathered around her bed. Viola was dying and they positioned themselves close enough to her bed to allow themselves precious gentle last touches as they discussed family affairs of the living and dead. Obviously, they were acutely conscious of death's presence in the room, he was giving Viola another opportunity to demonstrate her beauty.

Life had shown these three Queens the lowest of human nature, greed, racism, sexual deviants dressed in nobility. Yet, instead of drowning in sorrow or bitterness they welcomed the opportunity to confront their oppressors in hell and to meet death light heartedly, if not frolicsome, changing their mood with playful body language and joy in their tones. Maybe fear of never being able to see one another alive again caused them to want to spend their last encounters with each other in merriment.

In a childish, melodramatic tone Moma spoke playfully of the serious nature of their lives. These were lessons and a time to keep my mouth shut. These scenes were confusing to me but of utmost importance to them and being a defining point in their lives.

Moma started by begging in a childish voice saying, "Let's leave here, lets get away from these mean white devils." Viola had turned her head in a dismissive manner as my great grandmother spoke. Amanda continued to rub Viola's hand softly. In a low harsh sapient voice, absent of her frailty and crisp with strength Viola spoke assuming the voice of Auntie, "You little children belong to God and you ain't leaving here. You ain't going anywhere." In a dramatic gesture they held their heads down signifying a boundless respect. "You children haven't lived long enough to know what these white folks are capable of doing to you."

Moma said, "Auntie we free, but we still go around here letting these old crackers treat us like slaves. Most of these colored folks around here act like slaves too. We can go

36

anywhere we want to, there's work in New York, or out to California. White folks in other places can't be any worse than these backward ones around here." Amanda spoke, "They don't like me Auntie, they are full of just pure meanness."

Moma spoke, "We been down here with these spiteful people that hate us for no reason at all, just cause we black and the nicer we be the meaner they get, there's no reason for it."

Amanda continued, "They hate Chilly because he loves us. We girls need to get away from these sorry so n' so's. If we go somewhere else we can pass by acting like them if we want because of what they forced our mama to do. I hate them!"

"The Colonel and the rest of those men try to do whatever they want with us, ain't nobody gonna say nothing. When he caught Amanda in the fields out behind the house, he practically scared her to death, she was just a baby, didn't know nothing about those things," Moma said. Viola and Amanda sat shaking their heads as if they were a thousand miles away. I remained silent. Then Moma continued, "She didn't know what to do back there, she was just scared, that's all, like a rabbit."

I assumed that the Colonel was wealthy, owned property and livestock in the town they were born in. The abolishment of slavery had no affect upon the feelings of entitlement due to the color of one's skin. If one plays righteous, he will always find those willing to take on the role of docile, allowing themselves to be treated like slaves.

Moma added, "The Colonel made her take off all her clothes." I looked at Amanda trying to imagine why someone would want to see this old lady naked. Mama said, "A child shouldn't know how to make a baby at that age. The Colonel put a nasty smirk on his face and said, 'You gonna learn how to give a decent white man some more niggra's around here."

Moma said, "We girls just hid in the bushes by the trees so he couldn't see us. We didn't want him to find us to, besides, knowing that we were there wasn't going to stop him anyway. Auntie, he just sat on the back of that old horse of his and watched her as she trembled and stood there naked trying to shield her little self with her forearm. She stood silent while tears ran from her eyes. Auntie, now, Amanda don't talk much anymore. She plays with us just fine, but she is scared all the time because of the Colonel and the rest of them men, really scared."

This incident in their past caused Amanda to tremble in remembrance of southern hospitality. They never ceased touching each other's hands as they reminisced. Someone had opened the windows for fresh air and the breeze made the drapes dance as the sun played intermittently within the room, as I remained guardian of my chair and held fast listening to their story.

She continued, "Those other white men that come around here ain't no better than him. She's only ten years old, ain't even a woman yet, her bleed ain't even come yet, they have done some things to her already that niggras and white folks are ashamed to speak about." Viola moved around in her bed indicating that she was acting out the role of Auntie. She just sat there and we could see the flush of blood rising in her light skin. Moma paused, then continued, "The Colonel stayed on his horse just glaring at her, for what seemed like forever. Then he took his old rag from his back pocket and wiped his old greasy fat face and the top of his baldhead. He stuck his hands under his fat belly, reaching inside his trousers like he was getting himself ready to do his business to her. Amanda just stared at the ground, too scared to look up, too scared to run. She just stood there with tears running down her face. Auntie, we sat there frozen in those bushes wanting to do something, but anything that we might have tried to do would have probably made it worse, so we didn't do nothing."

As this story was being recreated my elders and saviors continued to tenderly caress each other's hands as loving sisters who were reliving a defining episode in their lives. "The Colonel kept staring at her like he couldn't figure out what was on his mind," Moma said. "Then he got off that big red horse and walked closer to Amanda still pulling on his private parts. Amanda never looked up. He pinched his nostrils with two fingers and blew, and like a nasty ole man he used his other hand to clean his nose. Snot clung to his fingers as he tried to sling it away. Then he walked over to Amanda, grabbing her by her three braids and started cleaning his old nasty sticky fingers in her hair as if he was trying to massage her scalp. She didn't say a word."

I sat glued to my chair watching these three women as they unknowingly educated me to my family history and an obvious secret. In a distant, nasally voice Amanda attempted to depict the tone and demeanor of the Colonel saying, "Are you scared gal?" Amanda lowered her head as she replayed some act of submission, her sisters looked on without replying. "You know that you niggras still belong to good white people before the eyes of God."

Moma spoke, "Auntie, he pulled her over to his side. She was so tiny compared to him and rubbed her like he was capable of being nice to her. She was still trembling. He walked her over to the side of his horse and told her to rub the horse's hind leg. She did what he said, and then he made her grab that horse's private parts. She started petting it, like we pet our dog, then he told her to pull on that horse's privates like we get milk from that old cow. The Colonel put an evil grin on his face when the horse's private parts started growing. It got real big and he had to calm that old horse down. He told her to grab it with both hands and she started pulling on it like she was told. She pulled it back and forth for a longtime with tears running down her face. He unbuttoned his worn out work trousers. The stench from him was so bad we almost choked in the bushes where we hid nearby. We could see his pale, pinkish, fat belly and the stains in his nasty white cotton underwear. His privates were hanging out. Amanda was almost completely under the horse crying. She couldn't really see what he was doing as he started pulling himself. He threw the rings to the horse around a tree and started walking towards her. The Colonel pulled her from up under the horse and walked her to the back of the horse. While he was guiding her he had a tight grip on her arm, his breeches fell to his ankles and he didn't bother to pull them up. Instead he grabbed the horse's tail, which was hitting him and Amanda. Auntie, he made her put her mouth on that horse's ass. He told her to lick it. She was trembling and acted like she didn't even hear him, she was just crying. Then he grabbed her by the hair and smashed her face into that horse's ass, he held the tail with his other hand. Auntie, we couldn't see her face anymore, just the back of her head. Every couple of minutes he would, as mean as a hungry possum snatch her head back, she was choking, trying to get some air. Then he would bury her face back in that old horse's ass again. We could hear the muffled screams as he put his privates inside of Amanda's buttocks. Her shrilling sounded far off like she wasn't even there. His fat belly was all over her back, I couldn't figure out how she was standing or breathing as he humped on her like a dog. Then I just couldn't watch anymore. I turned around and cried looking towards the house until he rode off. Auntie, all the pity and caring for in the world ain't gonna help us or Amanda as long as we stay around these evil people, we need to leave these parts."

Sitting in the penitentiary legitimizes a retrospective yearning to want to understand why my existence has been a virtual hell when the gift of life should have been an opportunity to experience heaven. My aunties spoke of an era where the most intelligent minds in the country lent their energy to methods of humiliation, dehumanizing practices, annihilating spirits for the sole purpose of greed. Wealth protected itself against losing a coin. Atrocious circumstances were unleashed upon my ancestors for the power of the almighty dollar and not because of anything they deserved or had done. Pimps wanted their money and didn't care whose ass it came out of. Author and historian, Chancellor Williams states, "The real object of worship turned out to be neither Jesus Christ nor his father, God, but western man and western civilization."

Our English compatriots exercised another kind of social differentiation system that comprised wealth and status as a barometer to one's character, not ethnicity. This practice of placing one's neighbors into specific social stratum is known as the caste system. This particular method gave no real advantage to race and Caucasians were viewed similarly to those of African descent and subject to subservient treatment and indentured servitude. So instead of risking the threat of a united populace against the few who relished in wealth, they intentionally divided Americans along racial lines, which offered vast opportunity to lower class whites for their allegiance in the dehumanization of Blacks.

Sociologist Loic Wacquants wrote, "Racial division was a consequence, not a precondition of slavery, but once it was instituted it became detached from its initial function and acquired a social potency all its own. After the death of slavery, the idea of race lived on."

My forebearers spelled out words hoping that I didn't understand the meaning. They adopted a jubilant tone but the pain could still be felt. Viola began reflecting on a conversation she once had about leaving the south with Auntie. She had worked in the home of a white family. The father terrorized Black families in the area to validate his superiority, even though a Black woman washed, cooked, cared for his children and shared his wife's intimacies and sorrows. Being the eldest of her siblings, motivated her to sacrifice her body to his desires while she acted out the role of a house servant believing that her willingness to please him would divert attention from those she loved.

Once while sharing a moment of closeness with the wife who was only a step or two beyond being a slave herself, Viola thought to speak on a known but unspoken fact about a man they both shared intimately. They both agreed on how mean he could be and Viola went on to talk to his wife about a time when he had violated her as a young girl. "She shivered and waved her hands in the air, as if indicating to everyone in the room that the temperature had somehow changed."

Viola said, "Mister tell me to go out back and fetch something for him. I didn't question what people tell me to do I just do it. You know he was bigger than me but I didn't think nothing of it until he came back there himself and make me take off all my clothes. I

41

knew what he meant to do but I didn't want any trouble. He made me lie down on some filthy rags back there and he took me. When he finished he left his stuff all over my private hairs, then he poured some dirty water on me to clean me. I was a virgin and that dirty water made me sick, I thought that I was going to die." The wife took a heavy wooden stirring spoon and beat Viola for her admissions. On her deathbed she was expressing being dismayed over how another woman that was barely escaping the throes of abuse by a slight twist of fate could be so unsympathetic. If it weren't for the presence of Blacks the white woman would have been oppressed, bartered and sold. Some to maintain their slim advantage pretended not to be next in line as a subject of servitude.

Moma and my great aunties kept alive the mystical presence of their male sibling by showering me with tenderness and foreboding. I failed to comprehend the deliverance of my ancestral history. They constantly tried to instill caution in me. To question the whys of a good deed and to understand the seeds of a bad one. I was told that Chilly was too proud for his own good. It was clearly understood that they would rather have him alive and wounded than dead with his pride. The sun was shining outside but Chilly's horrid legacy painted a different picture of this color blind society. Being the beneficiary of his spirit, I always took note when his presence touched my predecessors. His story was of great significance to me because it resonated the spiritual yearning within me. It represented the peaceful souls of people who worshipped god's creation and lacked the trait of true evil. I have always felt a spiritual hand stirring within me, even during moments of turmoil. Pride has definitely proven to be the fuel of rebelliousness and personal faults throughout my life.

An inventory of my ancestral legacy made obvious an innate need for personal pride. The mere fact that I could analyze psychological citations as they applied to my history highlighted the probability that others have used their intellect against me.

The story of my family history was never lost on deaf ears. I hear and see little men at work all the time. You don't have to share the intellect of great scientists and philosophers like Imhotep and Dr. Cheikh Anta Diop to understand the nature of morally corrupt little people who seek external power because of the emptiness in their hearts. I see it everyday in prison amongst guards and inmates alike. What a man lacks internally he will seek externally. Racial bigotry and gender bias speaks to what a man is not. We hate from fear not strength. The very act of abusing others reflects a moral deficit. It doesn't make you a bigger man to sit in safety and subjugate others because of your race or gender. Behind these walls external power is meaningless, elegant words lose their value and thinking you are superior because of your race or gender may not save your ass because no one gives a damn about things men adorn themselves with. External power is allusive and may not support you when you are forced to stand alone.

I have sat in these penitentiaries a long time witnessing the selection of victims by those who profess to be bad, or society determined that they were bad. Political whores who adopted the path of least resistance to base their career upon have harmed me. Inmates will prey upon the weakest amongst them, will take another man's ass just to degrade him, stripping him of membership in the fraternity of men. Some have tattooed "Trust No Bitch," on their

> *Deeds of violence in our society are performed largely by those trying to establish their self-esteem, to defend their self-image, and to demonstrate that they, too, are significant.*
>
> ❧ ❧
> *Rollo May*

chest. While others may select regional or ethnic traits to render a group or individual's prey, strangely some groups fall right into the roles of prey after playing tough in their community.

Men of questionable fortitude universally pursued the physical and psychological war that was waged on my family. I wonder if there will be any steel in their eyes when we meet in hell. Will they be so righteous when confronted with truth about how they actually lived their lives? To some the death and degradation of my family will probably be no more significant than rain drops falling into an ocean of carnage. It has been said that in the end we'll have to stand on our deeds and actions. I hope they are consciously prepared to stand on the deeds and actions generated by their insecurities.

It doesn't take a lot of courage to team up with the majority to victimize the minority. Nor does one need principles to seek out the physically weak amongst us to prey upon, because that is the true nature of a coward. You are not going to garner any respect with me by catering to the powers of the moment because the path of the powerless is too difficult. Those who are tough surrounded by their homeboys won't be so fearless standing alone.

History accompanies me in my loneliness and love and friendship is not a pursuit of mine in the penitentiary. There is relief in understanding the centuries of my ancestors being persecuted. Who am I to cry about the perils of slavery when ignorance allowed me to volunteer for modern slavery renamed as the prison industry. I have to admire the proud souls of Africans that chose to be stomach fillers of sharks rather than become slaves on American soil.

My Great Uncle and I entwined spiritually in essence of the love that we shared for these precious women in our life. He was protective when a Black man was supposed to be docile. By the time he was twelve years old that protective cord was starting to lace a rope around his neck. They lived in a prison town, where Mississippi State Penitentiary at Parchman was located. The place was known as Death County. I was probably safer dealing with the racism of the Los Angeles Police Department than Sunflower, Mississippi especially during the times that my family still lived there. The town was run by a bunch of good ol' boys, 'Confederate Soldiers', whom lost the civil war but fought to maintain their customs at home. The value of a racist is not based on his own character, but on belonging to something perceived to be powerful. My uncle warned men away from harming friends, and then walked away probably feeling good about himself. The same situation repeated itself only a few days later, and he reacted the same. Only this time it was one of his sisters who found herself being preyed upon by some good ol' boys and this time he was more aggressive with his stick.

The boy was twelve years old and his chin was starting to rise from unknown pride, a sense of a death defying dignity that resides in the core of some people unconsciously. All the kids slept in one room and were fast asleep when nightriders showed up seeking the presence of a child. Grown men on horses with torches brutally dragged Chilly from his house, into the night, which caused the women and children left behind to streak with fear. They used torches to keep crying women and children at bay and occasionally the butt of a shotgun jolted a hysterical member of my family back into line. Dressed only in nightgowns they followed Chilly as men who wore sheets over their heads into the night were dragging him off. Eventually they found a young weeping willow tree in the darkness and tied him to it. My family stood and watched as they beat a twelve-year-old boy as though he was a man with the sole objective of intimidating all the others. Shrieking at the boy one of the nightrider's said, "You crazy niggra boy, you don't mess with a white man's business, we do what we want to a niggra philly." Then another of these good ol' boys stabbed him in his left shoulder twisting the blade for a reaction He screamed and the rest of the onlookers went berserk under a cold southern night sky in fear of his death. Falling unconscious probably saved his life.

My family's problems weren't over. White men wanted to rejoice over the burial of a Black child . Thinking they had killed another child made them feel manly. When that didn't occur the smartest amongst them sought another opportunity to terrorize a group of women and kids. On a freezing night a couple of weeks after stabbing my great uncle these good ole boys came back for more fun and excitement at my family's expense. Daunting him and tormenting the rest of the family they took him back to the same weeping willow tree they had beat him on for amusement. This time they tossed a rope over one of the tree's lower branches and placed its noose around his young neck, stating, "Niggra boy we gonna finish the job this time." Seventy years later I could hear the cries in their voice as they abandoned their fear dressed only in nightgowns trying to save their brother's life. The boy weighed so little that one of them picked him up while another placed a rope around his neck allowing him to dangle just a couple of feet above ground. The commotion and pleading had drawn the attention of neighbors who in the absence of fear milled towards his dangling body.

He survived the purveyors of evils follies a second time. But the combination of being stabbed, only to be lynched days later brought to realization his smallness. The presence of a powerful love allowed my ancestors to temporarily overcome the fear of a southern hospitality that castrated men for merely sustaining themselves and their families through honest means gave him a third chance at life.

My family planned to flee as soon as he recovered and they hid him in a variety of places trying to keep the news of his survival a secret. They possessed an enormous amount of respect for Auntie while their life lie in peril and sought her approval to save themselves from the good ole south.

Auntie was sympathetic saying, "White folks are the same all around the world. Whether it be in the south, east, north or west, they are just as bad as they are down here in the south. They act a little bit more sophisticated than these no-good red-crackers around here, but they all the same. I been in this south all my life, I was born a slave and was lost in a stupid gambling game. Never knew my real people and horses sometimes ate before I did. That's how much they cared for me. After all the man still come see me at night, he felt nothing for me and was always cold."

Moma said, "That's why we need to go, most of these people around here act like rabid animals."

I remember Auntie saying, "I seen your parents work themselves to death, just hoping things would get better. I am taking care of you children because of what I know can happen, don't tell me about animals." This matriarch had witnessed the slaughter of beloved friends and family for trivial issues. As she saw it, her main obligation was to care for the wounded of America's holocaust, people of color and allow God to tend to the dead.

Again Auntie said, "You girls have worked yourself with talk of these nasty crackers and of being better off elsewhere. I heard that before and each time we end up worse off. Now you want to go out west, California maybe, thinking those crackers out there will treat you better than they do here. I don't know what's beyond Sunflower, Mississippi and neither do you. I do know that it's always better dealing with an evil that you know, than one you don't know."

Moma said, "They gonna kill that boy, he just don't know how to be scared."

Auntie said, "They gonna kill him anyway. That boy has way too much pride for his own good. I love that boy with all of my heart, but you can't stop the sun from rising and he no different. I show him extra attention because it pains his soul to live like this. It ain't natural by far. That boy came out your momma's womb kicking and he ain't stopped yet. In these parts they always kill the likes of him and I have told him so a thousand times. The boy way too proud, ain't scared enough and will probably get killed before he understands the way things simply are in this country."

While they begin making preparations to escape, Chilly disappeared scarring their souls until their dying days. Whether he left on his own volition or against his will remains a mystery.

Auntie had been born into slavery in the mid-1840's and did what she could to make life a little bit more bearable for those in her care. She never talked much about the deep-seated pain that she knew from life's experiences. Instead she looked to God and the heavens for solace. Over the years people had just come to know her as Auntie. Her true biological connections are unknown. She fed, sheltered and cared for each child equally and I never heard mention that any of these children whom she raised were of her own flesh. Her child rearing approach consisted of hard-work and discipline, fueled by an overt fear of white people that was based upon the many long physically exhausting and soul wrenching years of sadist bigotry that she knew first hand. Degradation, humiliation, bestiality, molestation and rape in the fashion that one breeds dogs was her experience. These volumes of family history shattered once God given innocence, which she fought to cling to before allowing herself to drown in the sewage of an era.

The doctrine of deception that had been instilled within Auntie by whatever means had her believing that suffering and submission to God and man were some how part of God's plan. As though her worthiness to enter heaven's gates needed to be tested by partaking in the practices of savages against her. This mindset represented either docility towards life, or a denial of the realization of demons feasting upon her soul. The basic comforts of life were denied to her yet she stood strong as a temple of hope, smiling in the face of despair. Within her, the flames had to burn deep over happenstances from minds whose sole intent was to oppress and gain status through declaring a carnal wrath of mortal destruction based upon outright silliness. Her soul had to beg for mercy, having little to no defense in the sizzling skillet of earthly imperfections. I wonder if she considered herself a martyr in the stove of a southern hell's indecencies. She was tenacious with a shining strength but was unable to protect herself or anyone else against the atrocities of the times. She chose a convenient concept of passivity to cope with the aggression of savages and tried to pass this twisted perception of existence off on to the fertile minds she nurtured.

Obviously her colossal fear of masters, their rules and their God wasn't totally unjustified. It was a fear passed down through the survivors of slave blocks and those who made the voyage to America witnessing loved ones become shark bait. Those who possessed the keys to hell hold a clear advantage over its hostages. One is made to feel unsafe and unsure when demons will attack. When God given understanding and natural inclinations stand in conflict with lawful conduct, some choose to submit to avoid the torturous ways of greedy pale monsters.

Through this lady I am empowered with the understanding that my family came to this country as free adventurers, Africans, Mediterranean Moors, Bantu and worked to establish their craft successfully. They were worldly people but after building a foundation and contributing to the groundwork of America they ended up being collateral damage between two elite financial institutions. One side wanted to unite all the lower-class citizens against the elite Plantation owners and seize land from Native American to his benefit. This is known as the Bacon Rebellion of 1675. Plantation owners reacted by brilliantly dividing the lower class with racial bribes and eventually passed laws that established slavery based upon the color of one's skin. According to Michelle Alexander's book, The New Jim Crow, "Under the terms of our country's founding documents, slaves were defined as three-fifths human, not a real, whole human being. Upon this racist fiction rests the entire structure of American democracy." The struggle between two power elites resulted in laws that robbed, murdered and sold people of color into slavery.

Some learned to submit relying on God for relief, while others perished with their dignity. Those who chose to submit were often worked until death in fields yieldings profits for their captors.   Auntie worked around the house, in the kitchen, was trusted with her slave master's children, whom she cared for in spite of their parent's brutality towards her. She prepared meals for those who were working in the fields. Not many years after being delivered from her mother's womb she came to understand that her mother had been used for breeding to enlarge the master's stock of laborers. Her mother was allotted in these births a few days to breast feed, then back to work until another pregnancy prevented her from performing a full day's work. She tried to comfort her children during the evening hoping that a piece of her wouldn't be sold.   She knew her mother's tears, screams and pains of hopelessness. By the age of six she had adjusted to the menial role of someone being born into slavery.

As a result of these circumstances my family fled Sunflower, Mississippi to Jackson, Mississippi, then to Kansas City, Missouri as refugees fleeing Southern atrocities before finally coming to rest in Los Angeles, California in 1917. They have remained in the same neighborhood until this day.

> When there is no
> enemy within
> the enemy outside
> cannot hurt you.
>
> ❧
> African Proverb

Whatever my cousin Albert was running from or to, he did it with genuine enthusiasm. The man embraced hard labor with the same ardent passion he had for romancing women. He was law abiding, respectful, but seemingly only responsible for himself. Sometimes I ponder on what skeletons might have played in his sub consciousness that pushed him to leave good women and jobs instantly. Was he running, or just in search of something? I loved and respected him. But as a man I wonder about those who have no loyalty to anything beyond the pursuit of pleasure.

Dispirited, I entertained the tears of a clown missing the chaos of the circus like an outcast. Nightfall chased away playmates, television and homework replaced the unexpected and occasional flashes of turmoil with calm. As I was being loved by Moma, I still clung to the bond of my mother and siblings. Early on I was plagued with obvious pains of feeling abandoned by my immediate biological ties. Even though Moma showered me with affection, my Angel had long ago run out of energy to participate in youthful mischief. Life's experiences had settled the inquisitiveness of existence for her, and she was more purposeful and loaded with understanding than with the tenets of frolic.

I imagined children playing until they were exhausted with never ending excitement in their homes, while Moma provided a peaceful environment. I looked forward to visitation of family and friends, their tales and character would instantly disrupt my melancholic feelings of rejection. On most days by the time the sun had fallen I had already eaten dinner. Homework was challenging because her knowledge came from live experiences, not books. She went to work as a child and I am unsure of what grade she actually completed in school. Questions of old math versus new math and grammar dilemmas became the source for asserting myself in school. If I asked a question it was because we just didn't know. Occasionally, neighbors and friends of the family would help me with my homework. If I wanted the accolades that came with good grades than it was imperative that I grasp the concept of what was being taught while I was in class. After dinner and homework I would bathe, get dressed for bed. We normally watched T.V., while she enjoyed a game of solitaire with me laying on a comfortable artistic throw rug eating ice cream or pastries. Life was so still that she could be engaged one moment and asleep the next.

On a normally quiet evening our world was interrupted by pandemonium. Someone was on the front porch running amuck as though he was trying to feel Moma's wrath. Wildly knocking on the front door, loudly laughing and repeatedly saying, "Woman there is a pretty Negro at your door, and you better hurry up and open this door before I leave." Then came more impatient knocks with continued chuckling. I beamed and life was altered.

Albert rushed into our home like a gush of early morning sea breeze and full of life. The man was definitely exciting, personable and armed with adventurous tales from around the world. He was family, a cousin, the exact particulars of his blood connection I never knew. He injected adrenaline into the ordinary, excited my mind with enthusiasm and his presence was equal to waking up on Christmas morning and finding gifts under the tree. During this period of his life he was working as a merchant seaman and each port offered the opportunity to collect postcards and take photographs, which afforded me views from around the world. The material that he sent was once the source of pride for a current affairs assignment at school. This time he brought a friend, Rob with him who was as personable and as funny as he was. They were in love with life and bustled to tell their tales.

Moma had often referred to Albert as a womanizer and he did everything he could to give validity to her pronouncements. He was a medium built man who was always neatly dressed and groomed. He was courteous and polite to everybody. I never witnessed him angry or threatening in any way. He was welcome anytime in our home and knew it. I never knew him not to have a decent job and a brilliant smile. He loved cloudy days, bragged about his ocean swimming abilities and enjoyed the tranquility of fishing.

One afternoon I milled around the house probably bored and finally landed in a comfortable chair next to the couch. Moma sat playing cards and talking on the phone to someone about Albert. I liked him so I paid close attention to her characterization of him saying, "That boy has brought every woman under the sun to my house. Black ones, white ones, Indians who still lived on the reservations and he loves those Asian girls, especially the Filipino kind. I have tried to tell him that he needs to quit running around before it gets him killed. But he don't listen. More than one woman has come around here claiming to be his wife and calling me like I am trying to hide that crazy so in so. If he would only settle down he would be a good man for any woman."

My entire collection of photographs that he sent from abroad and within the states were of his big smile and women of multi-ethnic backgrounds. Moma had been chastising him about the women in his life, so we took a walk to a local store and he told me, "Lil' Mike, all kinds of women love me and I love them. Sometimes they don't even speak English and I can barely say a word in their language. But we find a way to communicate anyway. People in this world like to hate other people for nothing because it's easier than caring about one another. You will never hurt anyone by simply loving them regardless of what somebody has to say about it. Moma's scared for me, that's why I love that woman."

As a child Albert's stories ignited my imagination. His stories gave me cause to wonder about the galaxy, foreign shores, and giant waves on never ending oceans of water. He would describe waves taller than any building I could imagine. Sitting on my front porch there was a view of downtown Los Angeles, and the Hollywood sign. To emphasize his narration he would take me on to the porch, point at downtown Los Angeles and say, "Those buildings over there ain't nothing compared to the waves that I have sailed over. We could be standing right here just like we are and water tall as that building could be coming right at us. You can't run, all we could do is brace ourselves for a hell of a ride." He was full of theatrics and would grab limbs of trees in our front yard to hold on to, planting his feet and rocking for dear life. We could spend the entire day together without him running out of stories and lessons naming every star in the Milky Way. He believed that he could navigate his way around the world and back just by using the stars to guide him.

He gave life to old pirate ships, World War II fighter ships and cargo places as big as football fields inside of ships. I was told not to believe everything that he had to say by Moma when I inquired about details of one of his stories. Moma said, "He got more stories than you got teeth, and if you believe everything that he has to say then you'll end up being a bigger fool than he is." Her sentiments tickled him and he encouraged my questions even more and never attempted to dissuade me from my wonderment of his life.

He had women at his beck and call plus a stalker or two lingering around. He often requested that I wait until he got home to do my homework, which made fun out of a chore. Albert stressed acquiring the ability to read as though it was a privilege once denied to him. He tortured his own ears by bribing me to read out loud in front of him and would send me on a mission to find the correct spelling and definition of words that I am sure he already knew the definition and spelling of. He told me, "Lil' Mike, don't let anybody tell you what you can't do. Outside of Moma, if someone tells you that you can't do something because you are not smart enough or because you're Black then you do it anyway just to prove them wrong. You can read, now all that you have to do is get a good education and you won't have to use your back like I do to make a living. I got a quick mind but when I was your age I had to go to work to survive and I didn't get the education that I wish I had now. Plus it's a whole lot easier for you these days. When I was a boy, white folks didn't want us going to school and made it hard for us to attend if you wasn't well-to-do, which we weren't."

He had stories about Southern racism and Northern men ready to kill him over messing with their women, which he shared with a bit of amusement. His tales about adventures as a merchant seaman were the most intriguing to me. Albert was animated recalling the times when he first joined the merchant marines and how no one wanted him there. "Them old white boys were making all the good money. It was okay for us to unload ships in the docks but the real money was made when you go out to sea. I needed the money and didn't see why I should allow them to make all that money—which you can't even spend while at sea. Plus, if someone was willing to give me the work, I wasn't going to be frightened away from taking the job. Even though most brothers didn't want to work where they obviously wasn't wanted. Then here I came." His smiles would widen as though he was about to laugh. "I was Black and beautiful and I knew it. Never have been ashamed to let other people know that I knew it." He humored himself with that statement.

If nothing else, penitentiaries provide ample opportunity to read and this statement by Martin Luther King reminds me of Albert, "The ultimate measure of a man is not where he stands in moments of comforts and convenience but where he stands at times of challenges and controversy." He dared to flaunt a sense of pride and dignity when he was supposed to be sheepish and downtrodden.

Several of his stories made me fearful about his welfare. He recounted, "Lil Mike, I was stationed on a ship and them crackers wanted me off so bad that they could taste it. Like it foamed from their mouths. It makes me feel awful to see hatred towards me or anybody else burn so deep within a man's eyes that don't even know me. I can stand up for myself with the best of them, but I prefer simple times with a woman or being with my family. I always have had a lot of energy so when I am aboard ship I tried to keep myself busy working, that's why people like me working for them. Being out to sea can be boring and makes you think about not signing up again. I'm not really a gambler but out there on that ocean I would throw bottle caps for money just to stay busy. I had a few dollars to give away but instead of losing I won big. Kept playing just to allow some of them boys to win their money back because I didn't' want to sit around twirlin' my thumbs."

He drew a picture of ships larger than football fields floating on water with no land in sight. He sat in my home as a Prince but described being surrounded by racists that in my mind seemed monstrous. His experiences inferenced fear as the catalyst of bravery. I stayed hungry for what he had to say even though my participation was just to listen in disbelief of a world I knew little about.

He said, "Boy by the time we were about to dock somewhere I would be on the verge of going crazy. Felt like I was in prison or something and boy some men possessed more attitude than a woman during her time of the month. By the time we spotted land all I wanted to do was be with a woman and would be the first one running to wherever someone of the opposite sex was at." Smirking with a proud confidence on his face, he said, "Don't believe all that stuff about what a Black man ain't, because he is all any other man is and in some cases a lot more."

He sent me to get some pictures that he had mailed to me while he was out to sea. Each group of photographs depicted a different woman or groups of people in various foreign locations around the world. Each picture held its own fascinating story.

Moma's reluctance to participate in conversations about women was somehow viewed as charming by us but in actuality she didn't want to hear it and would say, "Most of what Albert has to say is foolishness and he's lucky it hasn't got him killed." It was of no surprise when she would busy herself with some task or tell us to take our conversations somewhere else. When time permitted it, he would talk and on occasion his colorful depictions of his prodigious odyssey rendered me unconscious, leaving me vaguely remembering changing into my pajamas and getting into bed.

Albert separated one photo away from the others, looked at it for a while and said, "I used to hang this by my bunk on the ship." He and this female wore big smiles as though nothing else in the world bothered them. She was Scandinavian and he called her his wife. I didn't make much of that because he often referred to his lady friends as his wife and a couple of women actually showed up at our home claiming to be his wife. The woman in the photo he referred to as Red and they stood on a giant rock overlooking a cloudy shoreline in some foreign country. This exposition with threatening rain clouds and challenging peril only represented a brief moment in his life but framed my image of him.

Albert shared a story of distant lands where people loved you because you were American and paid little attention to the color of your skin. After being at sea for months he was filled with loneliness and a need to relax with a beautiful woman. Racial divide and pettiness that existed on the ship followed him and the other men of color on shore.

It didn't take long to find the warmth that he was looking for so he danced, drank and joked with anyone willing to listen. His attention was directed towards the females that he longed to share a moment with. One caught his eye and became special for an evening. He craved time alone and soon she danced to his desires.

It's quite possible that she was a prostitute but he was inclined to treat her like a queen. They interacted like men and women often do, playfully and wanton. His colleagues spent their leisure time observing his pursuit of pleasure with a taint of hostility. While he adored the smell of a woman they saw the color of his skin as a violation of a sacred back home law where Blacks wouldn't dare woo a white woman in public. Instead of unwinding from the stress of endless hours spent at sea, they entertained racist creeds and penis envy to override common sense and civility.

Nature took it's natural course and he found himself in her bed satisfied with himself but still full of energy, the night was still young and he decided to return to the festivities only to find resentment, anger and disparaging comments fueled by alcohol filling the air about him and the woman who honored him with her essence. He wasn't an aggressive man so he ignored comments that made him a, "nigga boy," that don't know his true place. As beautiful as 'Red' was bigotry had reduced her to a two bit whore from the mouths of his colleagues. He was a peaceful man who fought against allowing the blatant disrespect to steal from a good time.

The Black merchant seaman that travelled with him had warned him about the trouble brewing over him chasing women. He brushed it off because the touch of a woman was his joy and to him it didn't matter whether it was love or a professional courtesy. Red understood prejudices but these were strangers and their sentiments meant nothing to her. Albert said, "This woman hasn't done anything but show me a good time and if they want to hate me because I am Black and pretty than let them go right ahead. It's not going to stop me from doing what I like doing. They wear the frowns of men that would like to kill me and regardless of what her occupation is there's no reason to be disrespectful. Red is a real jewel and pretty enough to marry." He smiled saying, "I spent my honeymoon there with her."

When he got back aboard the ship he might as well have been on the yard at Folsom State Prison, because shit was about to hit the fan due to pettiness and insecurities. Paying no attention to it wasn't going to prevent confrontation. He tried to busy himself with work but could smell their hatred caused by being intimate with a white woman. Controversy isolated him, which caused him to long for what they hated. He reacted to snide comments with a smile. While living in Boston, Massachusetts he had trained to be prizefighter but the use of violence just wasn't part of his make-up and he viewed it as a last option, a sport that should be enjoyed without emotions. He would ball his fist up in a Jack Johnson type of fighting stance, smile and reflect on a career that he had abandoned to see the world.

Albert had problems in a few places about chasing women which seemed to bring life to him as though she was the first woman he had ever seen. All of this scared Moma, who often reacted with an unusual anger or dismissiveness about his conduct. Her warnings were deflected with humor, even though situations had occurred that forced him to leave town on more than one occasion before someone's jealousy killed him. He knew the taste of a variety of flowers and found intrigue in his quest to enjoy the forbidden ones. Even though he loved Moma he was grown and normally his thirst was quenched far beyond her presence.   Her disapproval was obviously out of concern for his well-being and made him love Moma even more.

Albert and my great grandmother knew of a few near death experiences he caused with his taste for women but the ship episode appeared to stand out amongst those excursions with death.   He understood the ease in which he could have been tossed overboard at sea and the fact that sharks have never been known to reject dark meat when a meal presented itself.

Walking through the penitentiary can be a hellish situation, there is always the possibility that you don't see what's behind the mask.   Everybody plays their roles pretending to be genuine to character but you can't always believe the act. I remember Albert telling me about working below deck and how the normal jokes and smiles, bravado and tough exteriors had vanished in the face of adversity. That's not unlike prison, where men are prone to flock to the ideology of the majority, seeking refuge in the opinions of the brainless, thinking intelligence stems from the spiritual dead.

The good deeds in some showed me something bad in others. I was still a good boy but wrongly craving grown-up things to garner respect. Indifference started to take hold around this time in my life. What you felt about me, I probably felt the same about you.

Albert knew fear but didn't allow it to be his guidepost. Nervous laughter and threats of being dragged off, tarred and feathered wasn't going to be the reason for being another man's buffoon. He was satisfied with having a couple of brothers to watch his back, thinking that he should be able to deal with anything in front of him. Then he got orders that his position was changed to a top deck assignment. He was aware that things were about to get bad because Blacks were not normally afforded the cushier jobs unless requested by a superior for some menial if not humiliating task.

Albert had signed up to work and work hard for the money, not to shine shoes or be a manservant. When he was ordered to the top deck all understood that he had a problem playing the boy in a man's theatre. The weather was as bad as it can get and hateful crackers made the top deck the last place he wanted to be. But he was getting paid to do a job, which he intended to do despite the circumstances, believing that his personal affairs shouldn't have any impact on how he made a living.

The first couple of nights were hell but without incident. He was by himself and trusted nothing that moved. The rain and wind was throwing him around like a feather and he feared accidentally going overboard more than being thrown overboard by the crew. He joked about the thought of needing to eat more. He said a storm seemed to be following the ship that made the hairs on the

> There is no passion to be found in playing small, in settling for a life that is less than the one you are capable of living.
>
> ∽ ∾
> Nelson Mandela

back of his neck stand up like a scared dog. Something wasn't right and he started jumping from the sounds of the winds.

Albert was sitting down on some sandbags on the top deck when he noticed two white boys coming his way. His stomach got uneasy so he reached for a pack of Pall Mall cigarettes in his pocket, pulled one out and lit it trying to act like he was paying them no mind at all. Watchful he looked off into the distant sky in avoidance, hoping they would recognize that he didn't want any trouble and would go on about their business. He wanted to believe that whom he slept with was insignificant in comparison to the storm that chased them. Right then a small baseball bat appeared in the hands of one of the men. He should have been watching but he was struck on the side of the face. They had come to handle their business and throw him over the side of the boat. They hit him so hard the first time that he actually didn't know what was going on. He was stunned and when he finally came to his senses he was slumped in one of their arms bleeding and felt like shitting on himself but something inside of him made the decision not to die, right then.

He wore a scar from the incident but was more wounded by his moment of rage. Albert never saw any use in hurting other people but when struck across the face he abandoned that principle and was willing to kill. He grabbed an axe handle and exacted punishment upon the two men for reasons not of his own.

Albert's friend, Rob had been smiling and following the conversation but hadn't said much. Actually, the floor belonged to Albert in relating the reason for the presence of a scar on his face. Surely Moma would want to know how that happened along with an understanding of what was learned by such foolishness.

Finally Albert's friend Rob spoke, "He almost killed those two crackers. The Captain was the one who set him up to be killed. Thank God we were in foreign territory. Here in the United States he would be in jail for the way them white boys looked after Albert got a hold of them. We finally made land in Guam where they could care less about a white man. It was reported and they looked real bad and, of course, Albert was made out to be the bad guy. They took him to the station when I came to check on him and gave him some cigarettes and checked on what else he needed. They were in there treating him like a celebrity or something and he was lying about knowing Joe Louis and Muhammad Ali personally. Then I knew that he was really crazy and just started laughing with the rest of them."

The Chief of their police force was a short, wide man who had fists that looked like balled bricks. He dismissed the charges believing that a fight between a Black man and two white men was a fair fight. Albert humored his way right out of a foreign jail and thought of the Chief of Police as a friend.

By the time Albert showed up at our home he wanted to clean everything in sight, even though Moma kept a clean house, so his efforts offended her somehow. Being that housework was thought of as primarily a concern of women, my main responsibility was yard work, so him busying himself by thoroughly cleaning the house didn't bother me at all. Every time he showed up he would sneak a bundle of money in her pocket and slide me a fifty dollar bill. I loved that man. He was one of the most considerate men I have ever known. When time permitted he found ways to entertain me with outings to the movies, the zoo, fishing and amusement parks. I never heard the man say an ill word about anyone and obviously there were some around us that he could have disparaged in all honesty for their pursuit of nonsense. He viewed hard work as a key component of manhood. He loved travelling, finding wonderment in all things and people, believed that humor and being conscientious would allow people to know him and look beyond the color of his skin. I never witnessed any insecurities in Albert that a lot of those who profess to be a man while hiding behind masks of deception exhibit.

Undoubtedly he loved women and maybe to a fault. The only criticisms I ever heard were of his philandering disposition and disregard for racial creeds that impeded his thirst to realize the humbling mystery that lies within the souls of most women. It could have been human nature that motivated him to appreciate the sweetness of forbidden fruit. Whatever the catalyst may have been for his desire to experience life through the intimate passion of another human being he wasn't going to allow the mindless ideology of color to refrain him. Obviously for those who wanted to possess him permanently his free spirited nature was an impediment to achieving their goals. It would be next to impossible to deny that any family or person who was embraced by him wouldn't be enriched by the experience. I would trade in the majority of men I have encountered in this life to know him as a friend, father, and in-law of any kind. He was a good man, responsible, compassionate and an excellent role model. He was touched by a sense of humanity and goodness as a derivative of his own soul, and refused to adhere to the voices of evil that deceptively promoted prejudices. Although, I have often wondered about what demons prevented him from putting his hat down somewhere and raising a family.

It has to be a huge adrenaline boost to the ego when you're capable of putting the masses to sleep mentally, to witness them parrot your rhetoric while sleepwalking, and still capable of giving you a forty hour work week. Evil probably dances to that reality.

I enjoyed Albert's presence and it was understood that eventually he would leave again with whereabouts unknown until he sent postcards and pictures. In his absence ladies would phone and stop by our house inquiring about his whereabouts and safety. Naturally, Moma wished that he would find a good woman and settle down. When he departed, trailed by our love, life returned to normal.

Immediately following his leaving, Moma speculated with concern about his inability to sit in one place for long. I tried to imagine him in locations that he had described to me through his storytelling. For a few days his aura still lingered in the air, but as the excitement died down I became ill with what appeared to be grief. I didn't want to go to school and preferred to lie around the house in self-pity and eventually feeling bad produced symptoms of a bad cold or the flu.   A verifiable temperature sent Moma straight into overdrive with conventional remedies, such as, children's aspirin, orange juice, Vick's vapor rubbed on my chest and I didn't even have to go get in my bed because she wrapped me in blankets on the couch next to her bedroom door. I felt her rewrapping me all night.   Going outside wasn't even an issue, as I was too sick to complain.   Whatever had a hold on me wouldn't allow soup to stay on my stomach and my temperature stayed about 105 degrees.

After a few days of trying to cure me herself, her concern became palpable and she phoned my mother to come get me and take me to see a doctor.   I guess my mother was busy playing cards or recovering from a hangover or something because I lay on that couch watching television, too weak to care about what was on the screen. Moma's irritation with my mother grew to levels that alarmed me as she continued to call my mother demanding that she take me to see a doctor. My mother would appease her with lies, saying that she was on her way, probably assuming that the true nature of my illness was to come back to her household with her and my siblings. Moma's frustration with my condition and my mother's unwillingness to get me some medical assistance lined her face with worry. Her anger sharpened her tone considerably when speaking to my mother about getting me to a doctor. Several days passed and my mother just could not bring herself to interrupt whatever activities she found that were more important than my health. The tension that arose from Moma being adamant about her getting me to a doctor caused me to want to recuperate as fast as possible and remove myself from the center of discord, but I was too weak to will myself out of my predicament.

Neighbors came in and out of our house wanting to know if there was anything that they could do for me and ran errands replenishing what would stay on my stomach, oranges and orange juice. Moma stayed by my side and covered for my mother by telling individuals that she was on her way.   It had to be embarrassing knowing that most of our neighbors missed very little of what transpired on that block, a no show by my mother with me unusually sick would be noted by the very same people who came by to visit and ended up evaluating my health.

Moma was in her seventies and nursing me as well as anyone could. She never learned to drive and rode a bus wherever she needed to go. She was visibly shaken by whatever evil she viewed lurking within me. She voiced anger and begged for my mother to tend to her ill son. I guess she was too busy being cute or caught up in the soap opera of the trifling bitches that she called friends. Therefore, my conclusion was that my well being meant very little to her. I lay there calmly weakened by death's presence not comprehending the circumstances, as my innocence took another blow.

After damn near a week of laying on the couch helpless, my mother finally showed up wearing that familiar mask of being upset over an obligation she incurred when she allowed her panties to be pulled down. If being a parent was such a troublesome ordeal she should have fought harder, screamed and forced the punk to kill her instead of appearing irritated by a brief encounter with responsibility. My mother first took me to her house, then called the doctor's office, which was across the street from where she was living on Manchester and McKinley. The doctor must have told her to bring me over immediately because neither of us had the opportunity to take off our coats.

It only took two or three minutes to walk from my mother's house to the doctor's office and half of that was spent avoiding traffic that ran down Manchester Blvd. Yet she appeared oblivious to the harm done to our relationship. There was something about that whole affair that demoted my biological mother to something just below what one perceives as undying love between a mother and child. In this instance my great grandmother became the source of a love that will never die.

There were several people sitting in the waiting room when we entered the doctor's office, mostly women and their children, who sat quietly awaiting their turn. We signed in and took a seat and within moments people who had been sitting there waiting when we entered the doctor's office suggested that I be seen first. I guess I looked contagious.   I expected at least a couple hours wait to be seen but someone obviously approached the receptionist and I was seen within five minutes of entering the doctor's office.

I entered the examination room of a Black doctor, took a seat on his table and he began the routine of checking my vitals and inquiring as to how long I had been in that condition.   My mother had a difficult time answering his questions without making herself look bad.   He never broke stride with his examination   or questioning of her.   He maintained his composure and was professional but his tone revealed a truth that frightened me.   His demeanor shook my mother up also.   All of a sudden she wanted to get out of there.   He told her that he was putting me in the hospital.   She wanted to go back home and wait on the ambulance but he refused to allow me to leave the doctor's office.   She fled momentarily to make a phone call.   The doctor and a nurse discussed amongst themselves what justification she could have for not bringing me to the doctor's office sooner when she lived right across the street.   He knew her because she frequently sought to renew prescriptions for barbituates, which were a popular drug of choice in the 1960s, and he assumed that I lived with her.   His concern for my condition and his irritation with her scared me.   I had no idea what going into the hospital meant, by the time the sounds of a screaming ambulance siren penetrated the walls of his office I was more frightened than sick, and would have preferred being sent home with a pill over the screeching of an ambulance siren and the unknown that awaited me.

I had somehow contracted viral meningitis and had no idea what that meant.   I didn't realize right then that my existence was going to be riddled with hardship and awareness of those whose life would have been easier if I were dead.   We all have our demons. Being rejected, alone and locked-up caused me to relive my pain a thousand times.   Someday suffering and I would become close friends, and death would be viewed as a dependable cure to my pain.

I left the examining room on an ambulance gurney confused by the sight of the nice people that allowed me to go in front of them to see the doctor now shielding their faces as I was wheeled by. Right then I was a little boy being loaded into the back of an ambulance, unsettled by the urgency of the moment and racing down Manchester Blvd, westward to the Harbor freeway with sirens blaring and tears in my eyes.

I had no understanding of death and by the time my great grandmother arrived at the hospital her concern caused me to be fearful of the unknown. Of course, she was distraught over my health, which only saddened me. She made me promise to get better. What bothered her most was the idea that I could have died while waiting for someone to take me to a doctor. She promised that we would never wait on anyone again, as arduous as that was we never did.

A doctor questioned about where I could have contracted the meningitis virus assuming that I hadn't travelled abroad. I guess that ailment is more common in third world countries than here in the United States. I still loved Albert but all the exhilarating play and tussling exposed me to something that had the potential to kill me. I underwent spinal tap procedures and remained hospitalized for a few months.

Getting sick was a game changer and I was perfectly happy living with my great grandmother and the feeling of rejection turned into an acceptance of being detached from the flock. After I was released from the hospital I had doctor's appointments every week which seemed to go on forever, regardless of the weather. It steals a little of your humanity when reality shows you how little some people care about you. During this phase of my life some things became less important and the voices of some were softened if not completely silenced. Making these appointments to Los Angeles County General Hospital weekly was a task that forced me to see some people differently. Being accepted by parents lost it luster.

As did the words that came out of their mouth, and all other gestures were taken with a grain of salt because unbeknownst to them their actions were doing a marvelous job at allowing me to start seeing them for who they were.

Moma would have me up before 4:30am, feed me, and then we would walk to the bus stop on Denker Ave and Jefferson Blvd, always being there before a scheduled 5:30 am bus. At that leg in our journey we never saw the sun. I seriously didn't appreciate her being forced to walk the streets in the dark. In a rough, high crime community where you don't want to be caught slipping at seven years old as I wasn't enough protection for her. We didn't really trust the police around our neighborhood, because they have a history of playing with several different hands. We had to catch at least four different buses just to get to the hospital, which was located in East Los Angeles and at the time that might as well have been in a foreign country to me. I was from the west side and hadn't ventured far at all out of my neighborhood. Moma was over seventy years old at the time and we had to endure pre dawn weather and jumping on and off buses. At the time my community was ninety-nine percent African American and where we had to venture it was ninety-nine percent Hispanic. I was a child and didn't understand the cultural differences, which made me, dislike the mission even more. I resented making those trips but had no say so in the matter. Moma was determined to have me at the doctor's office regardless of my sentiments and we never missed an appointment. Internally, the tree of my indifference started to grow branches.

Maybe if I had experienced the same things she had, I wouldn't have felt so wrong about burdening her with the responsibility of my care. She never complained about getting me to the hospital even though sometimes she was pained by arthritis and struggled with high blood pressure because she lacked the strict discipline when it came to seasoning her food with salt and salted pork. When it rained we huddled in doorways to protect ourselves or found shelter inside of stores browsing until the weather cleared up. She was strong but the hardship she encountered as a result of my illness never sat well with me.

That experience provided a source of resentment within me that lurked in the back of my mind when certain individuals were in my presence. Psychology speaks about breaking points. This episode was probably mine. It became easy to take the wrong turns when fueled with rejection, indifference, and a willingness to utilize violence as a path to manhood. I had difficulty accepting what some people had to say. This was partially based on all the times that we returned home tired and wet after a day of putting up with all kinds of inconsiderate people. I can still feel the resentment I entertained when we returned home to find people hanging out in front of our house with their cars parked in our driveway, or on the street directly in front our house. Moma was a woman with wide wings, kept a pantry stocked for anyone needing food. She walked to the store with a handcart purchasing food that she made available to anyone that stopped by. I was taught to respect my elders but during this period in my life I was losing any genuine obligation to do so. I didn't feel personally threatened by any one. At seven years old, my opinion of some was starting to sink so low that I started to become delusional feeling that the man in me could equal some of the adults I encountered. Foolishly, I started pursuing manhood, seeking out the characteristics of a man from those that I respected with a child's mindset. My humanity was damaged not by the boogey-man or the Klu Klux Klan but by my own parents. The rhetoric of the streets held more credence than of those that should have been nurturing and protecting in their guidance of me. I began to stumble down a path that left me barely breathing all the way to the penitentiary. We are a sum total of our actions.

I am a spiritual man who never really connected with organized religion. There has always been a problem denying my truth for another man's perspective. Especially when their words don't add up right and are filled with hypocrisy.

> Religion is the organization of spirituality that transformed into something that became the handmaiden of conquerors. Nearly all religions were brought to people and imposed on by conquerors, and used as the framework to control their minds.
>
> ༄ ༈
>
> John Henrik Clarke

On a brisk Sunday morning the Santa Ana winds had done their job and blown the smog away. Clinging pots could be heard as families went that extra step in preparing breakfast. Those who enjoyed raising pigeons let them fly on Sunday mornings in competition with each other to the benefit of spectators who viewed the birds acrobatic stumbling. Along with the observers of talented fowl, Sunday mornings on Denker Ave., at 35th Street also included the presence of spiritual followers. The ambiance of holiness was present and delivered weekly by a parade of the latest fashions. The King and his loyal congregation stood in righteousness. Those who preferred to witness the freedom of the birds shared street talk in preference to going to church.

Hanging out at the park was exciting and provided the opportunity to bond with your community through sports, dominoes, joking and horseplay that may lead to a fight. Our community church donated unbridled soulful transmissions that could be heard coming from the hearts of rejoicing churchgoers who bellowed serenely in harmony alongside the sounds of laughter and chirping birds.

I was eight years old with a sweet tooth and on Sundays usually ventured to a local market to satisfy my cravings in the midst of singing, loud preaching and jubilant applauding, which fed my curiosity. Spiritual singing seized a chord in me and I wondered about women exiting the church who professed a spiritual presence after being touched by God through a spell-binding sermon. The congregation would stand on the stairs of the church talking and waving fans that depicted the picture of Jesus on it even when it was cool outside.. Directly across the street from the church there was a park whose patrons stood watching the parade, judging, bad mouthing church people and probably secretly wanting to know God.

Moma encouraged me to pray. She gave life to spirits, believed in the concept of heaven, hell, good and evil, however, her life experiences were void of miracles and what she had achieved was the result of sacrifice and hard work. Religion was introduced to me right along with the meaning of Christmas and Easter. In the heart of my great grandmother spirituality clearly had a deeper meaning to her as it was tied to dead loved ones and spirits that she had witnessed do their dance in life. I was encouraged to go to church in hopes of finding something decent to help build the man I was going to become one day. I treated the adventure like an outing filled with curiosity that I engaged in with other neighborhood kids.

At this time in my life, two separate Baptist ministers and their families lived within a few houses of my own, with children in my same general age group, so naturally we mingled at times. There were also a couple of other families in my immediate vicinity who sent their kids to a nearby Catholic school, *Holy Name.* Then came the local Holy Roller who we called Grandma. She waved her Bible like a machete and had a lot to say about everybody. She was raising three grandchildren that I sometimes associated with and was as fanatical about her Jesus as she was about keeping the secret of loving good booze. In spite of having a man to share her bed, her aura dominated their household, which created an eerie atmosphere without cheer, or laughter and they seemed to be in fear of her.

At one point, I played with children from families that wore deep religious indoctrination within their homes as a badge of honor. The Chambers lived a few houses from me and they had a couple of sons. We were neighbors and there wasn't anything special about our activities. We competed and then went our separate ways. Their father being a preacher had little affect on our jaunts throughout the neighborhood and only in the presence of their parents did I give any consideration to the vocation of the father. At that time the heavyweight boxer Archie Moore was training a few people at a nearby gym and was endeared by many in the community. We spent a large part of our day pounding each other until someone was humiliated by a low tolerance for pain or the result of snot and blood running from their nose due to a lucky punch. The preacher's kids liked hitting, but didn't like getting hit. Both boys had a tendency to cry when losing and allowed the opinions of spectators to rob them of a competitive spirit and return them to just being the preacher's sons.

Reverend Chambers was a medium built, honey colored man in his early forties who shined as the result of a few small financial accomplishments. Out of curiosity I attended one of his church sermons long enough to hear him state, "God has a little black book with everybody in the church's name on it. He knows who is deserving, he knows who is just here to show off their new clothes. I present myself to you dressed immaculately as an example of God's rewards. You, who falter in your faith, suffer with shortcomings, spiritually and materially. Know God, know the truth and you'll become familiar with his prosperity." In church, my attention wandered from him to the crying and possessed individuals who made his congregation lively. He stayed dressed for the occasion like a real pimp. During the era of Vietnam and social unrest. While directly across the street from his church Black defiance against authority was being promoted and culturally accepted by the community at large. But he never crossed the street with what he epitomized, "One could achieve, if one only believed." Those words had little to do with saving souls, they were about getting some cash, which appeared to be the cornerstone of his beliefs.

As a child I listened without the benefit of an alternative truth and those who held power appeared right until I was told differently. I wanted to please those who loved me and going to church wasn't a bad look. Plus the whole experience was new with a bit of excitement. I watched the man

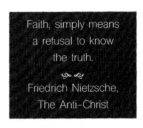

Faith, simply means a refusal to know the truth.

Friedrich Nietzsche, The Anti-Christ

on the pulpit, felt the love and regrets of his children and couldn't escape the criticism of the non-churchgoing community. I was open to knowing Jesus, but my life held a lot of unknowns, darkness, and every noble title wasn't necessarily honorable when I peeped beyond the façade.

Relatives of the Chambers owned a local market that gave almost everyone a limited line of credit at least once. They owned a few houses in the neighborhood and one of them worked at a local Black owned bank that sought community investment. But kids can be mean and being uppity might not protect you from an ass whipping by your peers. The Reverend's boys didn't get out much and preferred the safety of home. Being that I only lived a couple of houses away I was a regular for a while in childhood games. We boxed, threw balls around and shared stories. Their family discord came and went along with rumors of the Reverend's sexual appetite that was flaunted around the church and used by children to dwarf the stature of the Reverend's kids. Their mother wore a gold chain with a crucifix around her neck and rubbed it like a genie rubbing on a bottle. She kept her house pensive and clean and when company entered their home she would be found sitting at the dining room table patting her Bible as though she was looking for understanding while directing traffic in her home. Like his congregation, she remained loyal to him and shrugged off his indiscretions.

The whispers of infatuated women kept adding sustenance to his philandering. He didn't help his reputation any by embracing the attractive women of his congregation publicly with passionate hugs. He was a touchy, feely kind of guy who enjoyed speaking with a tone of sincerity and his arms wrapped tightly around a member of his flock's waist. Things went on in and around the park 24 hours a day, where as church activity was mostly limited to Sunday morning and was a source of entertainment depending on who was narrating their moments.

One Sunday morning a group of us were standing in the park observing the coming and goings of everything on the block – particularly the church people as we waited for little league baseball games to begin. As usual parishioners began to exit the church and mosey around the stairs, onto the street and remaining true to form the Reverend kept his arms around something beautiful as he spoke. The church stood on ground that was dominated by the young Black males of the community, known as the Rebel Rousers. Their edicts or moral conviction had a literal impact upon the community where Jesus was an abstract concept, if not the handiwork of a pimp. The Rebel Rousers were what would be considered today a 1950's and 1960's street gang. But during the tumultuous 1960's they were the protectors of our community. Shank, was a Rebel Rouser and what he proclaimed was commonly held as truth saying, "Little dude, you're still too young to get your little dick licked, but remember what I am telling you. Never allow a slick acting country preacher like that in your house with your woman when you're not around. He'll eat your food, fuck your woman, drink all your alcohol and on Sundays he will take your money. Listen to what I am telling you because when you get older it will save you a broad and some money." At the time his advice was kind of amusing and the only significance it had to me was related to the money that Moma was giving me to donate. Shank had brought into real doubt whether I should be giving that church my money. The information he shared about sex was useless to me at that point in life, but his cynical view created a skepticism within me that incited my need for junk food against that moment of embarrassment when I allowed the coffers to pass me by without donating.

Between the holy ghost that caused some to go crazy with entertaining spasms and the gossip mill that discredited Christianity, the preacher unknowingly validated a lack of interest in his God by visiting the church in a limousine while most of his congregation straggled up on foot. The presence of the limousine was exciting but if he had that much money he sure didn't need mine. I was confused by his ability to pass by the elderly and children with a broad smile, never offering a ride to any of them. During these times Denker Park possessed the feel of a large family. Everybody was a cousin that somehow fed, fought, nurtured, socialized and was ready to die for one another without rewards. Friedrich Nietzsche states, "When a man has a holy life-task, as for instance to improve, save, or deliver mankind, when a man bears God his breast, and is the mouthpiece of imperatives from another world, with such a mission he stands beyond the pale of all merely reasonable valuations. He is even sanctified by such a taste, and is already the type of a higher order." The preacher clearly felt anointed by God, but his conduct was subject to be evaluated like anyone else, which caused his faith to come into question.

Reverend Chambers' church was located in South Central, Los Angeles with medium to low income families, yet he was adamant about parishioners digging deep into their pockets to upgrade his lifestyle and move him to the suburbs so he could be more comfortable doing the Lord's work. It didn't take long for me to realize that the Lord didn't need my quarters as desperately as I did. I continued to feel guilty while allowing the collection bowl to pass me by as he delivered a sermon that implied that the more you gave, the closer one would be to God. He lived well in comparison to the average member of his congregation. He had a gift in making people feel a part of his prosperity. Instead of giving the church the money my grandmother had given me, I would wait until later and spend it at the store, which his family member owned across the street from the church. That made the most sense to me and junk food provided me with God's happiness, which was more in the realm of my understanding than what he could achieve with it in his pockets. There were moments that his words played into my consciousness and I felt as though I was being watched as to my donating a piece of the bounty I had received for attending church.

> *Where the Mystery is the deepest is the gate of all that is subtle and wonderful.*
>
> ❧ ❧
> *Lao-tzu*

In the back of the church there were several backrooms, one of which was used to store cases of red wine that would be watered down and served as the blood of Christ to spirit filled churchgoers. The exit door to the back of the church faced the side entrance to Denker Park and everyone knew that right inside that room cases of red wine sat there for the taking. It appeared to be an agreement to take only what you need because I never saw anyone take more than 2 or 3 bottles when cases were stacked 6 or 7 boxes high. Going into the back of the church to acquire a couple of bottles of wine was a right of passage for little homies, which made Little League baseball games, dominoes, and barbecues much more lively.

We had those who pretended to be morally upright hiding behind their perception of God with ranting and indignation which only pushed us further away. Then there were those who sat with the potential for righteousness, self-destructing and seeking the truth that didn't belong to the morally upright. Both groups occupied the bleachers at the park cheering on their favorite teams enjoying the gaiety and arousal of the spirits that wine could invoke. Occasionally, some switched teams as a result of heightened spirituality, church girls choosing to love gang members in defiance and gang members growing weary of fighting electing to embrace the solace of love from someone within the church, even when it seemed to dull the spirits. People sang, drank, joked and made advancements towards one another. I enjoyed the festivities and the sense of community. Occasionally, things would occur where someone was forced to speak with God after being shot, stabbed, or beaten for mistakes made of his own volition. Naturally, God had the final call about right, wrong, life and death.

Our beloved Preacher finally made enough money off the community to pick up and run to the land of affluent African-Americans. Little was lost. I never witnessed any love in his home that as a man I would like to assimilate, nor am I privy to any information of his that somehow dispelled the image of the community I was raised in a community known as the *Dirty Thirties*. People had their opinions about him and his church. My interests were elsewhere, so I really didn't care.

On Arlington Ave, at Adams Blvd, sat a double plateau hill known as *Arlington Double*. This hill was a local adrenaline fix and great exercise. I would peddle up and down this hill until I was exhausted, ducking busy traffic becoming physically worn out. I must have been about 9 years old and in love with an apple crate green Schwinn bicycle my moma had purchased for me that I rode constantly. That bike caused me to venture too far from home sometimes and was the reason I lost track of time. I would return home to find myself the subject of worry because I couldn't be found. The punishment equaled my transgressions and was the price of freedom.

It was late afternoon and time to start heading home or at least be in the vicinity when dinner was ready. Again, I had a day full of thrill seeking just by riding up and down Arlington Double. Our day was completed after one more stop at a liquor store on Western Ave at Adams Blvd to buy cans of apple beer. So after one more trip down the mountain we raced towards the liquor store going as fast as we humanly could. An alley joined Adams Blvd and 27th Street with the liquor store on one end and the Founders Bank on the other. The Chambers family members worked in the bank and lived on my block and as soon as we reached the alley we turned recklessly into it immediately spotting a black limousine parked in an apartment stall. We began to race in its direction expecting to find someone famous inside visiting the area, like the Godfather of Soul, James Brown who was helping promote Grace's Kitchen and Flash Records stores during this period of time. This is Los Angeles, California and everybody wanted to be a star so limousines were everywhere, which offered interesting conversations. It could have been Little Richard in the limousine instead of being in his flamboyant pink Cadillac. Instead of someone famous occupying this vehicle we recognized Reverend Chambers and he wasn't someone that warranted rushing home to speak about. He had moved his family out of the neighborhood and their presence was of little concern to anyone that I knew of. The sons' existence was based upon the material wealth of the father, which is worthless to those who require nothing from them.

I was already committed to investigating the limousine by the time I recognized the Reverend and was lured deeper into intrigue by the presence of a white female in the back of the limo with him. It was too late to turn around so I slowed my bike to take a look and signaled the others to be quiet and approach cautiously. The sounds from the hustle and bustle of Western Ave traffic probably shielded our approach because he seemed not to notice the obvious noise that we were making. The sun cast a shadow over a limousine that was too big to fit into a parking stall and the reverend was wrapped up in desire of a busty blonde whose exposed breasts stole my attention. He was oblivious to our presence and gaping to suckle upon the flesh of her titties. Her powder blue blouse was open to the waist and he had her pinned against the ceiling in the backseat and she rode him in full view of a small crowd. We did nothing to interfere with his display of pleasure. Initially there was some shock and then we settled into being voyeurs and lay our bikes down to observe as people moved about the parking lot unaware of what we were up to. We nudged each other in play and then he appeared to open his eyes looking directly at us, but didn't see at all or at least he had no reaction to us at all. But his looking in our direction was enough to cause us to grab our bikes and race home.

Outside of an occasional outing with a girlfriend I never went back to his church or any other church again. He disciplined his sons with, "Do as I say but not as I do," theories. That may have satisfied his sons but what I saw was a need for getting money and chasing women, not inspiring a belief in Jesus. He continued to preach across the street from the park, enjoyed the apparent prosperity of being a gifted minister and for me the illicit activities that took place in the park became more important.

For whatever reason, Shank liked badmouthing the reverend and some of his followers. He worked five days a week in some kind of construction job. After work he got something to drink and came to the park to talk shit to everybody while still dirty from work with callous swollen hands that he didn't mind putting on you. He was the Big Homie so it was your job to be accepted by him, he could care less about what you thought. A couple of days later we were in the back of the park describing what we had seen in the back of the limo. He beamed with attentiveness saying, "Boy I love Moma, but I don't understand why she sent you to that tricky slick talking Poot-Butt church anyway. Life is crazy, good men are getting killed by Darryl Gates and his police boys everyday, others waking up in prison. Then we have them sorry ass fakes at that church hiding behind the word of a white man's God placing guilt on everybody else's shoulders for not kissing that white man's ass. All along they chasing pussy and trying to get some money like everybody else. We fight for ourselves and fight for them crackers who will kill us at the drop of a hat. Eventually what's in the dark will come to the light, we all have to answer for who we are."

The Preacher's sons grew up to be not much more than their daddy and like him never ventured across the street from where they collected their money. Father and sons never enjoyed the respect of the community due to their alliance to God. The sons married and had children but their wives grew to love the neighborhood and left the security of marriage for the arms of gang members. Damn, the Deacon and the Preacher started publicly fighting over church money. Wives and mistresses sat in the same congregation as the husband fostering speculation about ménage a trois being sanctioned by the church. The church sat on a corner that became infamous for violence, immorality, drugs and is the birthplace of one of the nations most notorious street gangs. The parishioner's love for self never crossed the street to love thy brother. They ignored the problems and dysfunction of the community while procuring their ticket to the promise land. It has definitely crossed my mind what life would have looked like if those who professed to love God had loved their neighbor. The Preacher raped the community morally with his hypocrisy and financially by only investing in his own prosperity. What should have been a pillar of strength symbolized disarray and carefully crafted deception never intended to empower a community with the greatness of God.

He preached from a Bible that was conjured up to subjugate, enslave and cause the masses to be submissive. He didn't teach a Black Truth at all and used circus gimmicks to blind and confuse the community about beauty and power within all of us. He didn't speak of God-like qualities that knowledge of Isis and Osiris reveals. Instead he enjoyed parroting, deception that gives value to superficial aims to substantiate an existence content with accepting the non God like part of our lower nature. Putting the God that resides within us to sleep. Its been said that Osiris sits at the gates of death and will judge us all with the weight of an ostrich feather.

Down on 37th Street where the trees hang over the asphalt some country people resided and they sure loved Jesus. I didn't know what was going on in the houses of those religious people. Whatever it was I decided early on that they could keep it.

Reverend Robinson was a storefront, small town, country preacher who was out of his league in the city of Los Angeles trying to pimp the words of the Bible.

> Osiris said, I set up a ladder to Heaven among the Gods, I am a divine being among them.
>
> ❧
>
> Erich Neumann, 'The Origins and History of Consciousness!'

Reverend Robinson had converted a secondhand store on Western Avenue at 38th Street into a church. His family would exit their home like a little drill team squad and march in pairs to the amusement of onlookers as he drove slowly alongside them in his old Cadillac. The characters that attended his church were also foreign to me. Their attire and mannerisms seemed to be inspired from an old 1920's movie. Young and old glided down the street in a frightened but graceful stroll that depicted something I had no knowledge of. I assumed that they were fleeing the horrors of small town southern brutality that had instilled a slave like caution into their demeanor and they still didn't trust the apparent freedom of the city. His congregation was invisible to the rest of the community and his family was barely allowed outside. When they did surface there was something off balance with their interactions among other children. He didn't believe in sparing the rod and kids were frightened of him.

There were six kids in that family, four girls and two boys. The youngest boy, Robert was a little older than me. He was odd and drew the ridicule of other kids on the block. He rarely played with any of us and stayed in the house a lot. He didn't participate in the normal activities. Nor did he enjoy the toys the rest of us possessed like footballs, baseball gloves and bikes. He drew vicious criticism for not wearing underwear. When he was caught outside the joke was on him and he was constantly bullied. His childhood couldn't have been that pretty. I don't blame him for avoiding us, because a lot of mean things were said to him personally about his family.

At this time there were several tight knit Asian families in the neighborhood. All of them work hard in trying to preserve their culture along with making a living. Children will be children and when the opportunity presented itself we intermingled. There was an Asian boy, Tommy who played with us at times. He lived a couple of houses away from the Robinson family, so Robert was his closest contact to boys his age. Tommy had a sister named Valerie who knew martial arts and didn't mind the rough and tumble at all. She was capable of kissing you, then beating you up. She practiced yoga in her backyard and influenced a couple of other girls to do the same. It's not good for your image to get your ass kicked by a cute petite girl so she was given a certain amount of respect and if she liked you it was done on her terms.

Once she came and told us that she had caught the Christian boy, Robert trying to kiss her brother and that her brother had told her that he had played with his dick and wanted Tommy to screw him in the butt. That information triggered a neighborhood obsession with catching them in the act and intensified the ridicule Robert already received. Whenever they were spotted we made a game out of watching them and turned into spies lurking in bushes, roof tops and small holes in fences. Busting them in the act became our aim.

Robert was a peanut head boy with a fascination for small animals. Probably all animals that ran through our neighborhood were someone's pet that had no real fear of humans. It was early evening and the sun had already fallen from the sky as we gathered and succumbed to mischief. I only lived a short distance away but nightfall still set off an alarm that it was time to get home and any other thought was delusional and self-defeating.

Somehow, I allowed the suspense of a pitch-black alley and the potential of every threatening echo that arose from the darkness to keep me from breaking ranks and putting my ass in jeopardy. A rock fight began and we tossed stones at one another until the noise that we were making startled us. We fully expected someone to come out and run us off at any minute but no one seemed to be bothered by us. We must have been bored with taunting Robert because he moved amongst us without being harassed, cuddling a cat. Somebody had a cigarette and was attempting to light it, while the rest of us stood around anxiously watching and wondering if it was feasible to puff on it. We were silent in anticipation of the cigarette being passed around as Robert continued to caress the cat. He had the cat in his arms who was perfectly content with the attention it was receiving.

I was standing in this alley with the Cole brothers who probably suffered from ADHD because they were bad way beyond their years. They lived directly across the street from the Robinson's and told stories about having sex with Robert's sister before any of us were biologically capable of having an orgasm. As this cigarette was being passed around one of the brothers named Dane said, "Hey punk, go in the house and tell your sister to come here, I know daddy ain't home." Robert said nothing just kept petting the cat.

The other brother named Steve said, "His whole family is weird, I think their daddy is fucking all of them. They can't even come out when he's at home. They break out that house like they are in jail. His sister lets anybody fuck her, I think their daddy is fucking her too. I know that somebody in that house is."

These two brothers were the first juvenile delinquents that I ever knew. They were creoles and lacked any self-control. They were bad, but more of a threat to themselves than anyone else and eventually they would collide with life to their own detriment. There were about ten Cole's that lived within a few houses of each other and often fighting one of them meant fighting all of them. We clashed, made up and in time their tales of jail and intrigue meant nothing to me.   Their father wasn't much different than them and seemed to always be in the middle of throwing a tantrum.

Unbeknownst to anyone standing in the alley and while we were focused on watching the brothers pass their cigarette back and forth Robert had pulled a can of lighter fluid out of his pocket, doused the cat with it and was attempting to light the cat on fire when Dane yelled, "What is that crazy punk doing?   Man, I ain't gonna get blamed for that bullshit."   By the time Dane was finished with his sentence the cat was on fire with a screech that shattered the calm of darkness.   Pandemonium set in as the cat was attempting to escape but was blinded by fire, which caused it to run in every direction looking for a path or hole in a fence to get away.   The blue flames fully engulfed the cat and it was running amongst us aimlessly screeching from pain that frightened all of us and someone yelled, "Get that punk."   I was trying to stay out of the cats way as it scrimmaged to get the hell out of there.

A little mischievousness was acceptable but this would get my ass whipped and there was something evil about it that caused me to feel ashamed of being present to witness that kind of cruelty. I scurried for my own safety concerned with denying any involvement of being there.   The cat had gone berserk and was attacking whatever it touched as it continued to search for a hole in the fence and voiced its pain.   We were petrified and finally the cat found a hole in the fence and disappeared.

Within moments Robert began his career of getting his ass whipped with deep-seated determination.   The chaos of kicking his ass was generating too much noise in what was typically stillness and the disruption of that silence allowed him to escape into his backyard just to get his ass kicked another day.

The cat belonged to an older Filipino couple who lived across from me who had a few cats.   Eventually they found the cat dead in their backyard, nothing was ever said about how he died. We never told and they never approached anyone with the dead cat.   Robert had officially become a pariah who was subject to whatever cruelty that kids could conjure up and the dynamics of their strict Christian home became the subject of scrutiny. I never figured out what type of excitement he achieved by setting the cat on fire. That act only made his situation worse, he was tormented and rumors about incest and homosexuality painted their home. The parades to and from church only added to vicious speculation about the depravity of their beliefs. Believing in their God had been a hard life. Especially when those beliefs put you at odds with the rest of your community.

The Cole brothers had a white German Shepard named King who jumped high fences and fought against other dogs regularly. One afternoon we were patrolling the neighborhood looking for some kind of mischief to get into. King had already done his fighting earlier in the morning and wasn't expected to fight anymore unless we ran into a real challenge. An old white man lived on the corner of 37th Place and Normandie Avenue, who raised pigeons that could be seen all over the telephone wires and the roof of his home most of the time. He just fed them and didn't make them compete, but anyone could clap their hands and the birds would often perform for us on their own. The dogs and pigeons had grown tired of us and we were getting tired of each other, as well as wandering around the neighborhood. Our last plot before disbanding was to steal fruit off a neighbor's tree. We entered the same alley where the cat was burned with the purpose of raiding a peach tree. While plotting our approach, we spotted Robert and Tommy going into an empty garage that was used by some for illicit activities like smoking and taking girls into. Most of us knew every crack in this particular garage and how it was constructed which invited experimenting with the forbidden and exploring the unknowns in secrecy.

We immediately raced over fences to get in position to see what they were up to. Anyone approaching from the alley could be seen from both directions and that's what made the hide out perfect for those trying to get away with something. We also knew where somebody had to be situated in the garage if he was intent on keeping an eye out for someone coming, so we avoided walking down this unlit and unpaved alley. Soon we were alongside the structure looking for the cracks in the garage to peek through. Our reconnaissance had rejuvenated an uneventful day and was in full motion as everyone readied themself to gaze into the dwelling and discern what they were doing. At first sight, Robert had Tommy's pants unzipped and was playing with his swipe. We fought to keep quiet and started pushing each other. After a few minutes of struggling amongst ourselves to conceal our presence, we erupted in laughter. Both of them got bit by the dog, beat up and chased down the alley. In life I have learned that people without true identity are prone to assimilate delusional characters that denies them inner peace. I doubt that boy ever came to embrace his authentic nature.

Witnessing a man die internally is dismaying to the viewer. Whatever tools he utilizes for his own demise is perplexing to those witnessing his out of sync dance in life.

Do not go gentle into the good night, rage, rage against the dying of the light.

Dylan Thomas

The community was startled by the bizarre behavior of a community member. Down the street from where I lived there was a cleaners and a little market that sat in the middle of the neighborhood and not on the main streets, which made their location convenient for the locals. An old Black man owned the cleaners and was full of what he described as saged principles in handling the clothes of his customers. He was a likeable person who tried to develop a personal relationship with his customers. I doubt that he dry-cleaned and assumed that he used softer detergents on fragile garments, starching according to his prescribed assessment of your needs. Dropping off and picking up clothes was always accompanied with a conversation. He stressed that doing laundry and shining shoes were respectable occupations if the people you served appreciated what you did. A lot of what he had to say didn't sink in.

Next door to the cleaners there was a small community grocery store called, *Charlie's*, named after the store owner. Charlie and his wife both worked in the store and occasionally other family members helped out. He always employed someone from the neighborhood and often allowed more than one at a time to help out with whatever work he could find for them within the store. Most people who worked there lived within a few houses of the store so he was tied to the community in spite of being a Filipino in a predominately Black area. The man was nice to me and a mentor. He kept a notepad behind the counter to keep track of who owed him. I was a kid with my own credit line in his store and don't remember a time when he didn't encourage me either to come in and work for pay or to do some menial task to pay for something that I wanted. He might have worked out a deal with my great grandmother behind my back because I got paid when she needed to run some errands instead of being dragged along or needing a babysitter. The man had our telephone number and sometimes called wanting me to come help him out in the store and would report me throwing my middle finger at someone or telling someone fuck you regardless if they deserved it or not.

Charlie resolved petty disputes and thefts without involving the police. Once I committed the cardinal sin of coming to that store with a twenty-dollar bill that I wasn't supposed to have. I bounced my happy ass into that store not considering how much money I had or what change to expect. They let me buy everything that caught my eye and with my dream of junk food heaven fulfilled I still hadn't spent over two dollars. No sooner had I departed that store they called my house and told my great grandmother what had just transpired. As soon as I stepped into my house, Moma wanted to know what I had bought and proceeded to royally kick my ass. By the time she was through I retrieved the candy and remaining money that I had hid outside and never thought about doing that again. Lesson learned.

Most mornings after I completed breakfast and tended to whatever menial task I had to perform around the house, I could not wait to get outside. I raced up and down the street on my bicycle taking notice of everything in my path and searching for any indication of anything or anyone that sought my attention until I found someone to play with. It was still kind of early in the morning and everybody wasn't out yet so I was entertaining myself with the rhythm of my bicycle, just meandering around when I noticed Robert's older brother come of the front door of his home and head directly to Charlie's market. He smoked a lot and buying cigarettes was a regular occurrence. I knew who he was but I was apprehensive about the whole family and continued doing what I was doing while shadowing him all the way to the store without engaging him in small talk. I raced by the entrance of the store and went out the driveway back into the street. A few moments later I heard shots being fired. The burst of gunfire shattered a sedate morning, shocking the silence and bringing all the senses into play. Immediately, I stopped my bicycle and focused my attention to what was transpiring in the store. The idiot backed out the store gun still in hand and fired one more shot back into the store. I leaped off my bike and took cover as though he were shooting at me. Then, he briskly walked six houses down the street and went into the front door of his home in full view of all the neighbors whose attention had been drawn by the sound of gunfire. This was a quiet area where consistent loud noise wasn't appreciated and occasionally a raggedy car with a modified muffler would disturb the peace. People were coming out of their homes trying to figure out what was going on which wasn't hard to do.

All this transpired within the *Rebel Rousers* territory and they considered themselves the protectors of the community even against the police. It was clearly understood as law that you didn't victimize your own community by stealing, raping or robbing each other. The penalty may cause you to never be seen again and they were gathering to consider what revenge to exact. Their reach even stretched inside of the jail. Robert's brother had shot Charlie in the stomach, and even though he was not part of the neighborhood gang, they knew that ol' Darryl Gates and the boys would be coming through prepared to beat, harass and ready to haul in whomever they determined as suspicious looking.

As Charlie's wife cried and tended to his wounds it was like a carnival outside with the whole neighborhood in attendance looking dismayed, gossiping about the good Christian family and what had transpired. Most people couldn't figure out how someone could be that stupid to do something like that in their own front yard. Undoubtedly, people resented the overtly racist tactics of L.A. Police Department, but were also afraid of the anger building within the crowd that had found the boy and his beliefs guilty of violating the peace. Some proscribed to allowing the police to take him to jail, others advocated killing him right there in front of God and the world. Either way he and that pompadour he wore were in trouble.

An ambulance took Charlie to the hospital. He survived from the physical wounds but his openness suffered from the attack. The Minister's family remained aloof and the source of suspicion.

By the time puberty set in on their daughter she was wearing a comical amount of make-up on her face. She would escape from their home like a prisoner of war content with having sex then disappearing back into their asylum, for lack of anything else to do. They held my curiosity and I acquired a seat directly across the street from the Robinson's to keep an eye on strange occurrences. The porch I sat on belonged to Grandma, the other religious fanatic, who was extremely self-righteous and judgmental.

Grandma was about sixty years old but still clung to a southern 1920's persona. She had a boyfriend who was voiceless and three grandchildren that she raised who were a little bit slow in speaking and mannerisms. Their presence easily went unnoticed in the crowd of neighboring children that lived close by. For a few days we played intensely with each other and they invited me to go to church with them. Just to get out the house I was eager to go have fun with them. Grandma made it a point to ask Moma personally if I could go and she agreed. I ate dinner, bathed and was ready to go to church. It was playtime as we drove to a church on 55th Street and Central Ave. Grandma did her typical rattling on about God and being a good Christian as we jostled one another in the backseat of the old Cadillac that she drove. I paid little attention to what she talked about because she seemed to talk all the time and my attention span wasn't that long. I vaguely remember her questioning me if I had ever been baptized. I hadn't and told her so, plus I had no understanding of what any of it meant because it really wasn't significant in my home where who you were was a lot more important than titles you wore.

By the time we arrived at the church Grandma was in a frenzy that tonight was the night I get saved. It all sounded kind of exciting to me, her grandchildren had all been baptized and made it sound fun. There were a lot of people attending the church that night and the energy of the crowd helped coerce me into going along with becoming a Christian.

With enthusiasm Grandma made arrangements for me to be baptized and like a spectator I sat listening to people speak at the alter for awhile, then she took me in the back of the church where I changed clothes. Within minutes they had me back in front of the full congregation, only at that point did I become anxious about what to expect. The pastor walked me to a pool built within the church, said some words that I have no recollection of and tried to drown me in some dirty water that I didn't appreciate the sight of. Once he brought my head back up from under this filthy looking bath water, the applause of the church made it all became exciting, just another fun adventure for me.

Even though I felt like I needed a bath, I couldn't wait to get into the house to tell Moma about the events of the evening, thinking that my conversion to Christianity was a good thing somehow. The story of my adventure immediately made Moma mad and angry beyond any display I had ever seen before. Whatever cheer that accompanied me home after being baptized broke and ran in the face of her reaction. She wasn't mad at me at all but was definitely entertaining some uncharacteristically animus thoughts. If she would have been a few years younger I really believe she would have pursued kicking Grandma's ass. Now, I felt violated by being manipulated into making decisions that were beyond my scope of understanding.

I had to take another bath to remove the residue of the dirty water off me, which amounted to three baths in less than four hours. I was a one bath a day type of child. Moma was highly upset that the woman had taken me to church and baptized me without asking for permission from anyone who knew me. She felt that it was her decision alone. For the next few days Moma and others were angered over the church lady's lack of respect or consideration that I was someone's child and not a feather in her cap.   Now my Moma's role turned into keeping women that frequented our home from walking down to Grandma's house and slapping her face, which several had wanted to do. I stayed away from her grandkids from then on and like the Robinson's they didn't come out much anyway. My early childhood with religious people left me skeptical of the whole institution.

Shank could be brutal with what he perceived as the truth and especially in his conviction that Reverend Chambers was a pimp wearing a gold necklace with a cross on it and made fun of me for the change I donated to his church.   He imagined way more sinister motivation from Reverend Robinson even though he never associated with anyone in the community.   At twelve and thirteen years of age his daughter was climbing through windows to get out the house caked in make-up, in heat like a dog and it didn't matter who got on top of her.   The cat-burning boy vanished. The idiot who robbed a market within a stone's throw of his home turned into a pathetic impersonation of a jailhouse woman.   Grandma in all her righteousness knew nothing of the soul.   The spirits within her home were dead, free thinking and laughter had been chained to despair without probable cause.   I don't know if her grandkids ever found the courage to live.

Everyday I sit on these stoops wondering where I went wrong?   Why has God showed me so much suffering?   I wanted to be happy like everybody else but it just didn't play out like that. If it's actually true that Christianity and Islam were invaders upon the African continent and designed to subjugate and enslave its people through deception and murder,   what lasting good can come from a lie?   What happens when one walks into judgment empowered by fraudulent beliefs? Does truth or pity condemn you? Existentialists believe that God resides in all that have the courage to look inwardly for truth and deciding one's own humanity. Today, I am closer to the human being I was prior to my ancestors being conquered, than I am to any modern day religion.

> *I started hustling and they couldn't tell me nothing, fronting in the hood trying to be somebody, my soul was empty and I was searching for something, tried to be good, to keep from trouble, living too fast, trying to make good on a hustle, sometimes it gets rough. 'Coming where I'm from'."*
>
> Anthony Hamilton

I witnessed my Uncle Zeke go from a hard working and compassionate man to a pimp. I knew his playfulness and I knew his love. It was sadly disconcerting to observe his demise.

I was ten years old and life was becoming treacherous with potential menaces resting comfortably behind every shifty smile. Things weren't so carefree anymore, the volume of my voice lowered, slowing the cadence of my speech and I was becoming comfortable with distrust. As intrinsically unsettling as it may be for the soul, disenfranchisement is achieved through the tentacles of oppression and naturally cultivates acceptance of unethical conduct, immortality, substance abuse and violence. True morals and a deep-rooted sense of humanity has never been obtained through degradation and deception. My circumstances manipulated one's psyche. Many attempted to evade physical threats and death just to surrender to the fate of mental stagnation and suffering spirits. The destruction of a hope often fosters a mindset of accepting repairable personal imperfections. There is something fraudulent about an existence that settles for lower self-ambitions instead of searching within for God-like qualities. We may not be in a position to fight untruths and demeaning circumstances but when we quiet our minds our true nature will reveal our truth. A clear conscious and a healthy mindset is not predicated upon hate driven by external factors.

The innocence of a child was pathetically losing to the demands of reality. Foolishly, I wanted to belong to a family or village beyond the realm of Moma's love. At that point, I should have boarded the doors and clung to her bosom. I had no concept of the depth and tenacity of suffering. I allowed a moment of loneliness to turn into a life in the damn penitentiary filled with nothing of meaning beyond what it is to waste an existence. I played on several fronts before succumbing to the pitfalls of the game. The lack of knowledge allowed helplessness to transcend into hopelessness.

I was bedazzled by the darkness and lured into streets that accepted me without being condescending, at a time in my life that I needed an outlet for a confusing energy that teetered around my diaphragm. My mind was turning in every direction in hopes of catching sight of myself. When I felt alone belonging to something seemed natural, and vitally important even when it was shadowed by danger. I yielded to the spirit of defiance from those seeking freedom, and adopted their convictions as my own. Where ever wisdom is in short supply there will be an abundance of excuses for a crumbling environment and self-hatred. For a while getting outside the sedateness of my home was a thrill, unleashed adrenalin that fixed my soul. I was delusional and believed that happiness was something I could obtain in the streets. I couldn't wait to get to where it was happening. Obviously failing to realize that peace of mind is an internal pursuit, not achievable through external factors. The solace in a title belongs to the title not the person. Although the role we play in substantiating images that mask our true identity may guide us to a truth about ourselves, if we survive and don't die in the process. It was some time before I understood that some were chosen for the game, while others gravitated towards it through misfortune. People are lured away from home everyday by the promise of success and fulfillment by valueless things that shine in the dark. I know those who masquerade in slum jewelry seeking girls with low self-esteem who willingly lend their bodies to sexual conquest with strangers. These girls allow themselves to be bamboozled into believing that a man's desire to please himself through an orgasmic explosion meant that he somehow could discern a relationship between the two.   When the only thing that was shared was sexual energy. Hoes are created from the stockpile of females who use sex to befriend men in hopes of filling some spiritual void.   Obviously the streets are not designed for everybody to win, as attested to by the multitudes that lie in graveyards across the country before reaching the prime of their lives.   Those who lay rotting in this country's asinine penal institutions can statistically affirm these thoughts.

Like a baby I falsely assumed that happiness was suppose to be part of my sojourn. I started suppressing fear in spite of the presence of realistic lethal dangers.   When the soul is needy, darkness prevails.   It didn't take long before infamous alleys and notorious corners were part of my itinerary.   The neighborhood provided me with a list of people who accepted me when my soul was in turmoil over being rejected by my own family. Sadly very few made it past the obstacles placed intentionally in our path. Some never experienced puberty before they were physically, mentally or spiritually destroyed.

Through means that are deplorable to the consciousness some have relinquished the possibility of peace in the hereafter to seize power in the presence and willfully use it to delegate others to inferior roles in the theatre of life. The streets are also cognizant of the fact that one's station in life and apparent misfortune is not necessarily acts of God.   Survivors study the recesses, behind curtains, and lend an eye to the hand that exists in the shadows attempting to determine their plight in life. When purity wanders through this world with her virginity in hand, she is subject to find a pimp who has the audacity to determine that her sexuality would be grossly misplaced if utilized to experience love. His vocation is dependent upon the presence of romance, which he soon wages against a small inconsequential favor that true love can't refuse and now

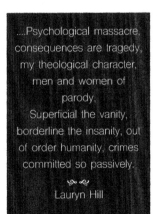

...Psychological massacre, consequences are tragedy, my theological character, men and women of parody, Superficial the vanity, borderline the insanity, out of order humanity, crimes committed so passively.

Lauryn Hill

her womb is a goldmine, a commodity to sustain his meager existence.

Them pimp boys come through these penitentiaries not as spry as they were amongst prostitutes. When a man chooses to be a purveyor of sexual desires he is playing dangerously with his own manhood. Society has minimized him to the lowest amongst us, there is nothing honorable or courageous about a man who utilizes his energy to contemplate satisfying another man's sexual desires. Most of them slither through here with obvious feminine insights about pleasing other men. It's definitely not the same game dealing with men as it is dealing with women, the meanness of a gorilla pimp is worthless when he has to deal with men. Ironically, in the same fashion that they are disparaged amongst men in society, they criticize women. In the process of transference of their mother's nipple to that of another nurturer reveals a sense of entitlement, which nullifies the gist of what it is to be a man.

It would have been a better plan to encourage men to thrive to their full potential instead of trying to keep him small because of personal insecurities and penis envy. Evil has to be present for ingenious debasing and inhumane thoughts to spring from one's mind. When a group or culture partakes in those thoughts they become as worthless as the demonic principles they stand by regardless of titles or status. As fate would have it, I was exposed to good men who temporarily wore the masks of defeat as a means to succeed in an ungodly world.

My mother's older brother, Zeke was a talented machinist, married to a lovely woman named Yvonne. Like many African American males his identity was lost in the degrading fabrication conjured up by enemies of his self-esteem. He burned to connect with his authentic self, and mistakenly allowed defiance to fuel a spirit against all forms of oppression. He tragically misconceived love and morals as weakness. My uncle also fell victim to demonic grandiose delusions of a man and allowed his ego to attack his soul.   Bad decisions internally wounded a beautiful human being, forcing him to self-medicate with alcohol until his dying days.

When I was a child the man used to assemble elaborate wooden push carts for me by fastening together three boards, clamping metal axles to them and spray painting the whole contraption before putting store bought wheels on it.   I cherished that effort.   I was pushed and pushed others up and down the street until exhausted.

Zeke worked at a machinist shop in East Los Angeles on Alameda Blvd. and   17th Street and I enjoyed going to work with him.   My curiosity was fed by being surrounded by a bunch of huge machinery that I had no idea what service it actually performed.   He was a hard worker and liked on his job.   The Jewish man he worked for seemed to enjoy my presence and found little things for me to busy myself with which made my day interesting.   My uncle grew up also being a *Rebel Rouser*, and possessed a penchant for fighting.   The man would get on his knees and we would box and wrestle until I had enough.   My only train ride and visit to the San Diego Zoo was with him.   He played like a kid making that journey exciting from start to finish.   The man must have been a little crazy.   We enjoyed the exhilaration of watching the scenery go by while standing between train cars.   He probably had more fun on the train rides than I did.

I couldn't have been six or seven years old when I learned to drive a car.   He would sit me in his lap and allow me to steer his car down city streets as he accelerated and braked the vehicle because my legs were too short to reach the pedals.   I knew that he didn't have all the sense in the world but he was my uncle.

He was of average size, looks, and intelligence.   He should have been happy to have a good job and a beautiful wife who was a registered nurse.   Between the two of them he was afforded the ability to buy a brand new Cadillac and dress how he saw fit.   Then all of a sudden a machinist decided to be a pimp.   *Wow.* Nobody understood what came over him, I don't think that he understood it himself, but he was vehemently committed to becoming a pimp and there wasn't much anyone could do to alter his path. One afternoon he stopped by to visit and was patting himself on the back flaunting his new occupation. At that point the man I revered became the source of tragic comedy. Despite the presence of several ornamental prostitutes his life had become nonsensical and stupid to me regardless of the rationale he used to justify ruining his life.

Zeke already had decent money and brand new cars. The man was lucky to have a wife whom nourished the good in him, gave validity to his existence. Established him as a man that provided an exemplary role model to those who witnessed his walk through life. Now he was toting the bag of self-deception and drowning the voices of his soul in alcohol, while surrounded by a bunch of shifty individuals who only soiled his presence. In the eyes of the streets he was boss pimping. In the sight of those who loved him dearly, he had lost his damn mind. He became the source of bewildering anxiety that inflamed the disappointment leaping from Moma's eyes. Once she told him, "You just don't know how silly you look and sound running here talking about you are a pimp. You need to be yourself instead of running around here trying to be like everybody else. What they do may be alright for them, but you ain't them, and that stuff ain't gonna take you nowhere, besides making you look like a fool."

Zeke responded saying, "I am not going to spend the rest of my life working for some thankless white man! I know how to get my own money."

Moma said, "You sure do, just like somebodies rabid dog and sooner or later you'll be the cause of your own downfall."

The man left his better half to play games in the streets, and didn't consider how pathetic he had become in the eyes of those he would have to return to when his need to pimp came to an end. Instead of rebelling against racism and oppression with superior values that would belittle any bigot, he wrecked several brand new Cadillac's and abused several whores. He lost his humility and his warm smiles disappeared, yet, he strangely prayed a lot as his life was losing a meaningful purpose. I don't know what he prayed about, or what demons lurked within him. But when he knelt before his deceased mother's portrait that was the only time that I sensed the presence of the person I had grown to love.

Zeke's life became filled with drama, stabbings, fights and disciplining prostitutes. Those who loved him wished that he would come home. At one time he took a lot of pride in baking fish, and would tickle you regardless if you wanted to be bothered or not. Now everything was serious, his rhetoric and hatred deepened without reasons known to our family.

He had come to believe that his wife didn't respect his manhood, and was trying to lock him into the role of a slave. Somehow misusing prostitutes empowered him. He stated, "Every time I looked up she got some boot licking Negro in my house impersonating a white man. I was tired of them hypocrites a long time ago. It just took a while before I decided to do what I wanted to do instead of what everybody else thought that I should be doing. Moma and the rest of them are more mad at me for leaving Yvonne, than they are about what I am doing. As far as that white man's job he can stick it up his ass. I am tired of being his or anybody else's slave to tell you the truth about it. If I have to get my money out of a bitch's ass, I will."

His very nature appeared to be in conflict with himself. He was allowing alcohol to be the spiritual force behind his callousness. Sleeping in strange places was depriving him of rest. He only ate when he was hungry from fast food restaurants. Personally I had no fear of him whatsoever but he was slapping men and women without notice. I became wary in anticipation of what bizarre behavior he might display. His drinking didn't make him lethargic; it energized his crazy ass into a totally different person. Moma said, "The boy done lost whatever little mind he had." I accepted her words literally and looked for signs of insanity when he was around. There was a time that I respected all that he had to say.　　Then he went from a role model to a source of bewilderment.

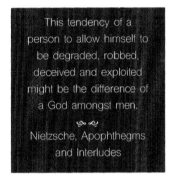

This tendency of a person to allow himself to be degraded, robbed, deceived and exploited might be the difference of a God amongst men.

ఞ ఞ

Nietzsche, Apophthegms and Interludes

Louis and *the Magnificent Seven* made pimping an empowering image. He was a good man and loyal to those he dealt with. That is why some saw him as a path to success. My uncle's best friend, Louis was a member of a renowned group of pimp dignitaries known as the *Magnifient Seven*.

In his youth, Louis had earned his respect as a *Rebel Rouser*, but his true ghetto stature was achieved through enterprising as a pimp. My uncle had enjoyed success for being good with his hands, before he transcended into the respectability of a family man. He seemed not to understand that the streets were a full time commitment and not a singular act of aggression. Foolishly, he chose to pursue the acclaim that Louis enjoyed. Louis was collecting fees from women that were willing to do whatever he wanted them to do. He possessed the looks and charisma to make it appear effortlessly, whereas Zeke was a machinist with super fly aspirations.

Being with them made ordinary errands exciting and what would normally be mundane became adventurous. Whether they were parked on the hoe stroll or visiting family, every encounter was met with high spirits and the level of their intensity easily captivated me. Broadway Street at Slauson Avenue was a daytime display of carnal insanity and a disappearing sun shined brightly on nocturnal wretches of sin. The area was inundated with prostitutes, and parked somewhere near was a pimp in a shiny toy. Females were flossed like high priced merchandise made available to the perverse and depraved sightseers of lust for a price. This was the Wall Street of flesh. Exposure of moral illusions was the essential element in the growth of vending sexual desires, which was intended to invigorate clientele participation. We often spent hours surveying potential customers as they drove slowly down the street scoping out the stable for temporary self-gratifying investments. Professional females made themselves alluring to the public under dim street lamps. Even in the daylight their purpose for being there couldn't go unnoticed. Some women only had minutes between clients and the constant demand for her services made her a prize possession that was desired by all the pimps.

Sex brokers lurked in the night seeking to shield their occupation in the recesses of storefront facades and alleyways as they conducted their business. Their illicit activity drew gamblers and other hustlers to the area because the atmosphere was charged with energy. Everybody attempted to shine in their perspective roles in a theatre that could turn deadly in a blink of the eye. Every echo that escaped from a shadow intrigued me. Every silhouette of a fallen angel danced with their own demons against the emptiness of red brick walls celebrating the dark magic of carnality. It was often perplexing to engage a female in her natural essence as caregiver, then witness the magic of witchcraft transforming her into a utensil of physical pleasure for strangers in dark places. I watched Queens sink into whoredom for the ol' mighty dollar which she then turned over to a pimp in compliance to the role she was playing of a good hoe.

Pimps engaged each other in the philosophy of pimping at every opportunity, questioning each other's fortitude and ability. They analyzed and appraised the performance of each prostitute to pass time while they observed the uncloaked business of sex. Louis and Zeke sparred with each other about the particulars of the game they were playing like adolescent boys throwing punches at one another to sharpen and refine each other's skills. Other pimps would join their conversations and they would spend a lot of time discussing the ideology and the causation of the rise and fall of other pimps. Some were determined to be naturals for the game they were playing, while others were declared fakes whose future would end in ruins. One's status in the eyesight of other pimps depended on the class of the women he employed, numbers of ladies under his control and the amount of money they were making. Some possessed special talents for perverted clients, all unconsciously displayed signs of realizing that there was an expiration date on the roles they played in the presence of other pimps. It was part of the profession to detect possible defectors, because no one wanted to be hoeless. It was an element of the job to realize that the spell that motivated women to parade up and down the street half naked selling their bodies was delusional and wouldn't last forever. They tried to stay one step in front of a prostitute fearing her disillusionment with the game would result in her defecting to the ranks of another pimp. Boasting was a right of passage amongst pimps, as well as a past time activity. No one wanted their name associated with backwards pimping or decrepit hoes.

Pimps patronized businesses that catered to their profession, which was often operated by players who had gone legit. Once we were in a tailor's shop located in the Leimert Park area of West Los Angeles and they began discussing a chocolate goddess, Tammy. She was a pimp's dream, seductively assertive and loved paying her man. The girl was raised down on 39th Street and Dalton Avenue. A good girl gone bad whom they knew from attending Foshay Jr. High School and Manual Arts High School. According to Louis she had been one of the popular girls in school, and she just didn't understand having sex for free.

Louis said, "I'm gonna knock that fine bitch, she gonna pay me. I remember when she was a little girl demanding gifts from young suckers. They said that she turned herself out to the game. Anybody that pulls her is going to have it his way. She tried to make me believe that she ain't with the pimping then out of the blue the bitch is knocking on my door knowing that I do this for real. Tell me what I am supposed to do when the baddest bitch in town shows up at my door pretending that she ain't with the business. She wasn't fooling nobody but herself. My pimping does not sleep. I seen the bitch was trying to choose and I made it real easy for her."

Louis was sprite without being flamboyant, and contemplated an exit plan from the streets as thoroughly as he pursued a daily quota from his team of prostitutes. He moved from one area to another in the tailor shop without missing the opportunity to capture the attention of listeners. He was confident that his path to financial security would work. Never once did his tales of million dollar whores or his proclamations of economic success interfere with his getting measured for an outfit that he was getting made. The tailor never paused as Louis spoke of his business related endeavors and seemed empathetic about the day-to-day challenges of a real pimp. Having pimps and other underworld figures as clientele made his particular business a huge success, he openly approved of the life they led and never complained about grandstanding customers.

The night before we sat in this tailor shop getting his clothes hand made the goddess that pimps dream of possessing knocked on his front door. He spoke about looking through her like she wasn't even there because he had no desire to be toyed with in the same fashion as she had done other men. He mentally debated letting her into the house until she boldly stepped through without saying a word to him and took a seat on his couch. His mind deliberated on what she could have to say that didn't involve getting him some money. She was truly gorgeous, petite and was wearing a black mini skirt that fanned her high setting pretty black ass accentuating creamy chocolate thighs and a cute fluffed cotton aqua blouse that caused her breasts to look like ripe melons, firm and inviting to be touched. She sat down and crossed her legs exposing black silk panties with intoxicating wavy pink lines embroidered across them. He was a pimp, but the man in him wanted to know her intimate secrets personally. Feel her warmth. Before all that could be approached he had to let her say what she had come to him to say.

They sat and talked about the old neighborhood and caught up on who was doing what. She pulled a couple of joints from her breast and he poured them a couple of glasses of wine as they talked. He knew that she would get to the point of the visit before long, so he was content on waiting her out. Finally, she relaxed saying, "Daddy, I have been knowing you since I was a little girl, and I have always admired and respected your style. I knew that you were capable of being a real pimp long before you started pimping. I ain't never gave no man my money but you have that honey tongue that causes me to get wet between the legs. I don't want to be bothered with a man that's not smart enough to out think me, and tries using all that gorilla shit that a lot of them fools be trying to do on their girls. So I was thinking about the possibility of us going into business together. You know that I can pull just as many girls as you can, plus get the money as well as any bitch out here. I need someone who can manage women and money without getting confused about why we are out here in the first place. If you are interested give me a couple of days to get my business in order, than I will show you what a real thoroughbred hoe can do. Babe, I just don't want to walk out the game broke. All that I am asking is that you be fair with me, and I'll be the best bitch you ever had."

Tammy possessed a spirit that captured the attention of most men. Every inch of her body was illuminated with sensuous possibilities. Unconsciously she employed all of her physical faculties just to walk from one room to the other. I was a child without the benefit of a sexual experience. She made me mindful of a need to grow up and discover the depths of what intrigued men. She was a hooker with the dignity of a true Queen. She could have successfully sold anything that she wanted to with her charm. She made the consumption of a banana erotically naughty and something observers could fantasize about.

When she chose Louis life changed for everybody. He already had three or four women who sold their bodies for him for various reasons. Then she delivered a squad of other prostitutes to work for him. That ensemble changed the dynamics, and intensity of his a pimping. What leisurely constituted a living out of the vagina of a woman, became a purposefully driven business free from the pettiness and degradation of local street corners. Now they were touring military bases throughout the state and jumping on planes to provide girls for an assortment of conventions across the country. All the while accumulating lists of clients with varying needs and deviant appetites of which some in the employment of a pimp satisfied. He maintained a group of prostitutes that functioned as colleagues and friends, who could opt out of their venture whenever they chose. Occasionally they celebrated someone's retirement from the game in a full partying atmosphere with dancing, drinks, cocaine and smoking weed in a jubilant setting. The success of one was encouraging to the morale of all. They all understood that the youthful physical appeal of a woman had an expiration date tacked to it. They sold pussy to capitalize on the illusion of the moment with no intent of making it a life long career.

Zeke wanted another man's power. What he found was his own destruction. Pimping seemed glamorous when the stories of the failures are not told.

Increasingly there was something wild and unnerving about Zeke. He drove a new Cadillac, had abandoned work

> He who knows other men is discerning; he who knows himself is intelligent. He who overcomes others is strong; he who overcomes himself is mighty. He who satisfied with his lot is rich; he who goes on acting with energy has a firm will.
>
> *Lao-tzu*

and casual clothing for fashionable or handmade clothing. He went from being lighthearted and humorous with an interest in simple things to intense, if not hateful. He advocated pimping but seemed to be uncomfortable with the role that he willingly sacrificed everything he had that made his life rich to play. He had become volatile and would attack without warning. It's understandable to seek a station in life that completes you as a human being. Unfortunately, he lost touch with himself in the process.

I would listen to Zeke and Louis plan their next expedition with such jubilance that I resented being denied the privilege of trekking along with them. They shielded anxiety with laughter and prepared meals and accumulated snacks like they were going on a picnic. Alcohol was becoming a major problem for Zeke. His family life was in shambles, and drinking was interfering with his business. It was obvious that things weren't right with him, he was definitely too angry to be happy. Once while they were out of town doing whatever pimps do, Louis called home asking Moma had she heard from Zeke without explaining as to why they had

> To conquer fear is the beginning of wisdom, the pursuit of truth as in the endeavor after a worthy manner of life.
>
> Bertrand Russell

parted company along the way. That phone call ignited worry, and she reacted to every sound that was generated, hoping it signaled his presence. Later we found out that he had cut a trick, unnecessarily.

Their trips out of town provided them with a lot of money in the most expedient fashion, minimizing their risk of arrest. Zeke had become frustrated dealing with unfamiliar environments and quit going out of town. His ego was taking a whipping. Three of his hoes had disappeared. He was forced to keep his pimping local with a scandalous whore who loved drama and to be beat occasionally. His other girl was from Bakersfield. She was somewhat pathetic and foolishly believed she was pleasing individuals. When that bubble burst she begrudgingly continued to be a prostitute that was passed along from one pimp to another until she found herself being pimped by a dope fiend, and walking the streets to keep him high. For a while I didn't see much of Zeke and it was understood that he wasn't doing too well with his new life. Then he moved to a back house, next door to us, with all of his newly found dysfunctions.

Zeke decided to go back to work and make a housewife out of a woman who satisfied her need for drama through prostitution. Drinking and arguing had become a major part of his life and due to being drunk he wrecked his Cadillac. He had brought a scandalous hoe home named Brenda, and expected her to stop being a hoe. My family was still in love with Yvonne, his wife. Brenda the prostitute met a whole lot of standoffishness in dealing with my family. Because of proximity she was in and out of our home frequently for a period of time which no one really appreciated. She performed all the tasks any other functional women would have done and nobody paid much attention to her profession. Even though, she and my uncle appeared to clash all the time, she was generally respectful towards everybody else.

During these times mini-skirts and hot pants were the fashion and she dressed accordingly doing great favor to the style. My uncle had tore-up his Cadillac and used another vehicle he had obtained to take care of whatever business he had. Brenda didn't mind setting out on foot to take care of whatever errands she needed to run and occasionally I would join her on walks to local businesses. The attention she received made these errands interesting. She entertained me with talk of me being her pimp and paid me with hamburgers and junk food. Then she goaded me into taking a walk with her that had to stay private. I agreed out of boredom.

The Hayes Motel sat on the corner of Western Avenue at 37th Street. By the time we reached that location, she transformed from someone who cleaned house and watched soap operas to a temptress, without visibly changing her demeanor in any way that I noticed. On Western Avenue she was an apparent attraction without exaggerating her existence. We couldn't walk fifty yards without a car pulling up trying to persuade her to get in, despite my presence.

A car driven by a pudgy white man pulled up and they talked for a couple of minutes, then she told me to come on and motioned for me to get in the car with her. I was surprised, but not threatened by what was occurring. Then she pulled the front seat up motioning me to jump in the backseat. This episode was weird but I went along without protest as they discussed whatever arrangements they were making. He pulled into a motel parking on Santa Barbara Blvd at St. Andrews Street and I stayed in the backseat of the car as they went into a motel room. I wasn't in that car long before she came back out. She gestured for me to get out of the car and we walked back to Western Avenue and went into a Better Foods Market where she bought me some junk food and gave me a couple of dollars to keep our secret along with seasoned encouragement that I should become a pimp, someday. For the rest of the day we crisscrossed West Los Angeles with her jumping in and out of cars turning tricks. Brenda entertained me with my yet to blossom pimp attributes. We played this game a few times until she disappeared.

I was repeatedly being told that my uncle didn't want to acknowledge the fact that a hoe is not promised to a pimp. Instead of finding another hoe he became angry and began combing the city for any signs of her. Louis and others were telling him to let her go, that his behavior was socking the game in the eye. He refused to listen to anything but his own demons. By the time he quit searching for her, he was a pathetic alcoholic, and didn't want to see a bitch, of any kind, anymore.

> Alienation means you don't feel at ease in any situation, any place, or with any person, not even with yourself! You are always trying to get "home," but never feel at home.
>
> ❧ ❧
>
> Eckert Tolle, "New Earth."

Zeke should have stuck to being a fun loving, talented machinist. That's where his respect resided. People came to him with appreciation of his knowledge of machinery and the aptitude paid him well. I will never know what bomb went off inside of him causing him to self-destruct. Whatever caused him to turn against him self and his family allowed me to witness someone that I loved lose his humanity and self-esteem. He played a role that draws upon evil within men to perform. Once he dwelled in the lower part of human nature he never had the strength to get back up on his feet. He literally lived several more years but in actuality he died trying to be a pimp.

I didn't have to look for death or the penitentiary as it came to me. Prostitution, drugs, and mayhem took root at my home. I didn't have to leave my house to find things that would destroy my life.

I was ten or eleven years old when my uncle's calamitous pimping career came to a degrading end. Zeke's attempt to take on the persona of others was foolish. Moving out of the back house next door to us announced the victory of the demons that reeked havoc on his soul. I don't know how it came about but as soon as he moved out of the back house he was living in, dope fiends moved in and created a shooting gallery. I never entertained a physical threat, but the realities of an area being inundated with dope fiends seeking pleasure and finding tragedy, changed my perspective.

The darkness of life was unleashed on innocence and it truly did not matter whether I indulged in the euphoria of a powerfully intoxicating white powder or not. The presence of heroin revealed the bowels of human nature. Childish fears of the boogey man became comical in relation to the hideous dark reality of a junkie's world. What grown folks did was none of my business and keeping my mouth shut about their activities was without question mandatory. There was a lot of money to be made, the only real obstacle to preventing someone from getting rich at that location was my Moma. If she had known what was transpiring outside of her window there would have been a huge problem for those

> King Heroin
>
> I came to this country without a passport, ever since then I have been hunted and sought. My little white grains are nothing but waste, soft, deadly and bitter to taste. I am a world of power, all know its true, use me once and you will know it too.
>
> ❧
>
> James Brown

trying to get some money. Strategically I was recruited and paid to maintain my silence.

Initially, the coming and going of dope fiends was exciting, like the playground had come to me. I was too big to be tossed in the air, like a child but those with ulterior motives and seeking access to poisonous treats entertained me anyway. I knew a secret that highlighted weaknesses and belittled users. Regardless of age, gender or class being addicted to heroin garners little respect. If a child is the one with the bag of dope in his hand, he's definitely not looking up to users, at best he may be looking eye to eye and in most cases he's looking down on individuals who use dope. Watching them shoot dope really didn't bother me because the act itself belonged to grown people. Once the drugs had done its job of delivering them to a state of hypnotic tranquility they were amusing. Often I would find them in need of assistance with whatever task they had committed themselves to before getting high. Normally that's where I made my money; they weren't so guarded with every dollar after they had a fix of dope.

Exposure to their world was interesting in a dark sense. Especially in light of the fact that the closer they got to death was equivalent to being a good high. Their circles were formed, and triage instructions were known to each other in hopes of a fellow drug addict having the compassion to save a consorts life when he or she overdoses. Strangely, overdosing was the objective, taking life right to the limit of expiration, and then coming back the next day to do the same. Although the vigil of determining if someone needed assistance was soul stirring, the actual craving to experience that place right next to death has never been understood by me. It doesn't take long at all to learn that a dope fiend will never win in the game that he plays. It is just not designed that way. From the first moment that a junkie enters that game he's someone's victim, and there is no sympathy awaiting him. Some are motivated by money and want an addicts every dollar. Others are motivated by pure evil and they utilized the potency of heroin to heighten their own inadequacies. Just like crack cocaine allows those with their own insecurities to belittle men and women who naturally would stand above them in the absence of their addiction. Here at Folsom State Prison a man will declare himself a dope dealer as though it's a glamorous profession trying to lift himself above the stench of his own product, 'the dope fiend', although he can't deny being a parasite and a co-conspirator in the genocide of his own community. In some countries he would be relegated to an international court to be charged with hating his own people. They pretend to love a dollar, but are not smart enough to exit the game with it.

Many players end up in these penitentiaries abandoned by family and friends. The big man on the block becomes a pitiful individual when his power is taken away. Prison is designed to degrade and humiliate him. Instead of drug treatment he swallows the philosophies of conquerors. Some choose to be subservient to whoever exudes power. The addicts that I came in contact with were all grown, and as a young child I had no responsibility for the product they were shooting into their veins. The temporary escape from life they were enjoying turned what they had when sober, into a real nightmare.

My Uncle Zeke, Louis and Lil' Joe had grown up together. All three were *Rebel Rousers*, and all three pimped hoes to together. Like Zeke, Lil Joe had retired from pimping because of a volatile temperament. He struck fear in pimps, and hoes alike. He demonstrated little to no respect for either. Then he ventured into selling heroin. He was medium build, 6'2", fair complexion, and always dressed well. His demeanor was quiet and purposeful. During this period of my life he had become my mentor. My job was to listen and learn, not talk. Even though he was older than my parents, he treated me as a younger brother. He analyzed everyone that he came in contact with and enjoyed sharing stories about the intricacies of what men did or didn't do with me. Around his peers he generated fear. When he entered a room the tenseness in the air was palpable. The man was dangerous, if you violated the rules of the game. He respected those who stuck to the codes of the streets, and would hurt those who didn't. His life lessons of survival were intriguing to me.

I was a kid who recklessly believed that being grown would ease my pain. My curiosity was not going to be denied when it came to the activities that were transpiring in a backhouse not ten feet away from my bedroom window. Excessive foliage and tall trees shielded the location from ordinary street traffic and helicopters, but the activity, especially in the dark captured my attention. My uncle had recently lived in this house and I had played in this small house on numerous occasions. But now it was littered with syringes, burnt spoons and bottle caps. At one time this was a playground for hide and seek. Now the atmosphere had changed. It became hectic as heroin started claiming its victims.

A few years before heroin claimed my home as its stomping ground. Moma had given me specific instructions to go to the mailbox on Exposition Blvd at Halldale Avenue to mail some letters for her and bring my ass directly back home. I mailed the letters but while returning I was waylaid by the sounds of a speeding car racing down a quiet residential street that caught my attention. I was after dark and alone, running a simple errand in a world that was full of suspense when the car came racing past me. I would have been satisfied returning home with only that unusual event to report. But as I approached the corner mindful of the racing car, the driver leaned over and started opening the passenger door and swerved close to the curve and tossed a female body out of the car. The car's speed increased and it was gone, leaving a dead body crashing unto the sidewalk. My attention was then paralyzed. She was probably the first casualty that I ever witnessed laying lifelessly in the streets. I had been told not to even look sideways and get my ass back into the house, But at six years old, I was captivated by the sight of this beautiful dead Black woman. Her big natural hairstyle was perfect outside of the damage done by the asphalt. Her shorts had collected rocks from rolling in the streets. Her earrings were in place, but her knees and elbows showed patches of white flesh as a consequence of losing a battle with concrete.

I was in a trance as neighbors started coming out of their homes. I didn't touch her, neither did I cry for her. She appeared to be asleep, not dead. Although the aura she admitted was nothing like the thrill of someone dying on a television show. After a few minutes of being mesmerized reality kicked in and broke my daze. But before my good intention could be actualized I saw Moma turning the corner. The hurried language of her body told me that I was in trouble. She was definitely upset and I was prepared to hear that this was the kind of situation that could have been avoided if I would of done as told. I readied myself to offer an explanation and an apology for standing in a group of spectators over a dead body. As she got closer and saw what we were looking at her anger vanished and she pulled me to her side trying to shield my eyes with her hand from the body that lay quietly on the ground before she started sharing some words with neighbors.

The crowd that had gathered on the sidewalk was solemnly speaking almost in whispers trying to understand what kind of world allowed beautiful young women to be discarded like unwanted trash. Older women reasoned that they had lived their lives and were better prepared for death than the young lady lying motionless on the sidewalk. They discussed the family's painful reaction once they received news of their lost. They concluded that whomever had killed her was less than human.

> One must subject oneself to one's own tests that one is destined for independence and command and do so at the right time. One must not avoid one's own test, although they constitute perhaps the most dangerous game one can play, and are in the end tests made only before ourselves and before no other judge.
>
> ❧ ❧
> Friedrich Nietzsche

I should have had a foreboding of things to come when heroin showed up in my yard. I had some knowledge what it was to be lifeless, lying in the streets, battered and dead of a suspected overdose. Later on when Lil' Joe was explaining to me why people were being found dead, I should have realized that life was going to involve treachery instead of happiness. Around this time two other people had been found dead close to where I had once lived with my mother on Montclair Street at 8th Avenue. Someone had mixed battery acid in their dope over being cheated out of some money by them. Lil Joe always threw a warning into our conversation about messing with poison. He ingrained the fear of God in me about chipping with heroin under the pretense of having fun. He said, "You don't fuck with this shit. The first time that you try it, you might get your ass hooked and when someone's dope or money comes up missing they will think that you did it. Then they will find you just like they did those two suckers on Montclair Street." That bit of information was a warning that has never been ignored by me.

When I shared with Lil Joe about seeing a dead body, on the corner by my house he surmised that the girl's body that had disturbed the quiet of the night had probably been greedy and used too much dope or that she had stolen someone's dope and he killed her. Either way somebody had gotten scared and got rid of her body. Obviously he didn't know where he was at because police frequented that particular block enroute to their favorite Japanese restaurant that was owned by a police.

Lil Joe was my mentor; he spent hours conversing with me about what I didn't see in the men that I knew by name or relational title. He served me a wealth of knowledge that was way beyond my years. I listened to him intently but it took years for me to actually comprehend the entire scope of his revelations. It was absolutely clear that who I was in his eyes was totally dependent upon my actions alone and independent of parental shortcomings. That viewpoint attracted me to him.   At the same time his perspective diminished any adolescent obligations to listen or accept parental role models or guidance.   He was adamant that biological connections were insignificant in determining what I chose to make out of myself.   He repeatedly said, "You're cool! You ain't responsible for what your mama and the rest of them do. You're made for this game. Your uncle and me are going to make sure that you get the rules right. You just stick to them. Motha' fuckers know that you ain't to be fucked with, and you're still a young motha' fucker."

While the man sold heroin, he shared things with me that changed my perception of a lot of people. After listening to the bedroom habits of some women, I felt empowered and capable of approaching women that he had mentioned or who demonstrated traits that he had spoke of.   One's respectability hinged on the insight that I had about their nature and activities people didn't openly speak about.   'Everything that glitters is not gold'. I learned about who was using dope, and came to understand how drugs were a weapon to empower small impotent people to gain advantage over others.   Even though he had been a pimp for a while he had little respect and almost no tolerance for pimps. Generally he was ruthless in dealing with them.

Once he told me, "These niggas ain't pimps. Getting their high school girlfriend hooked on dope ain't the way a real pimp turns a bitch out. In the penitentiary these fake pimp ass niggas would be punks."

There was a young brother who had started coming through buying heroin regularly. He was fresh with a real big natural, was a fashionable dresser, and drove a new Cadillac Coupe De Ville. Every time he showed up he had two or three sensuous ladies following his lead. He hadn't long before graduated from Manual Arts High School. He appeared to be real cool, jubilant, bounced as though he was having fun. The monster that lurked on his back hadn't begun feasting on his soul yet.

Lil Joe said, "Watch what I tell you. That nigga thinks that he's slicker than grease, copping dope for them bitches like ain't nobody supposed to know what he is doing. He ain't gonna last in this game long. He gonna fuck around and get found dead somewhere."

I absorbed his disclosures with intrigue. His accusations about women and criticisms of men were only informational because I lacked the faculties to use anything he had said to my advantage. His admissions narrowed the gap between adults that I encountered and myself. The young pimp's name was Sam, and he definitely enjoyed flashing his possessions like a badge of honor. Obviously it hadn't dawned on him yet that he was chasing the dope man too much. We would meander around the side of my house or stand in the driveway of the vacant house as Lil Joe served his customers. Pimping Sam liked racing that Cadillac to the front of my house like he owned the world. I was told to watch him. Pay close attention to what happens to him when the dope snatches the breath out of his bad ass. The streets were teaching me a lesson and my mind was actively vigilant of the deteriorating process of dope. The result could turn a promising future into a reality of squandering in shit.

As time went on Sam kept bringing his happy ass around but eventually using heroin started taking the bubbles out of his bubbly personality. He entered the game for fun and relaxation, now the community sat back and witnessed the game he tallied as spectacular rob him of his dignity. Everyday that he journeyed into darkness stole some of the Downy freshness that his clothes once possessed. His girls appeared a little worn and dirty themselves. They had become a classic case study in what not to do. Now when he came around instead of socializing like a player he was rushing off immediately or slipping into the back house to shoot his dope. In a short period of time he went from riding on top of the waves to drowning.

Pimping Sam's scenario played over many times with different faces until I became indifferent towards those who use dope. By nature I have never been disrespectful of anyone, intentionally. I grew defiant and sometimes intolerant of junkies, if provoked. Zeke was removing all doubt away from the fact that he had become an alcoholic, to the amusement of some, and the horror of others. He was performing bizarre stunts. I was being groomed in a world where everybody had a slick scheme. Justifications for doing whatever they felt would further their cause. Almost any wrong could be vindicated by the evil presence of the white man. Some people stood in their own way and allowed ignorance to anchor them into being content with nothing, becoming experts in finding excuses for a life of nothingness. Others found comfort in being stifling, jealous, and enviously counting the next man's fortune, instead of trying to achieve something of value for themselves. Some dedicated their mind, and sold their souls, just to dance in a womb absent of love. Under Lil Joe's tutelage what was hidden started coming to light, and I just didn't respect what a lot of people had to say anymore. From my vantage point there was something evil about a temporary euphoria that left you internally wounded and stripped of self-respect.

I knew nothing about life but found it confusing as to why people fell in love with other people and substances that hated them, and would most likely usher them to their own destruction. Lil Joe would comment, "They're weak." Those words were given credence by the fact that some wanted to be high all the time at the risk of losing everything, wife, finances, respect and keep right on using. Lil Joe told me, "If they don't care about themselves, I sure don't care nothing about giving it to them, they will just go somewhere else to get it."

I was playing in the streets, and finding excitement in adult matters. Lured by cash, foolishly believing that acquiring superficial things and knowing the pleasures of a girl would quiet my yet to reach puberty anxiety. I played where dangerous people played and where bodies were routinely found. Charlie Neils on Western Avenue at Jefferson Blvd. The gambling shack on 39th Street at Normandie Avenue. The shoeshine stand on 35th Street at Denker Avenue. Some literally lost their minds and soul at these locations. It might as well have been printed in neon lights upon a billboard that patrons of these domains wanted the cash, they didn't want the ass. It was unusual to see prostitutes or dope fiend females in these quarters. The game they were playing in these locations wasn't meant for them.

It doesn't take long to figure out that the faces of a dope fiend sub-culture were mostly the same. If one was spotted with a dope fiend he or she became suspect of searching for the same escape from reality. Eventually they would be pursued by predators and face the same degradation that junkies are forced to live with. Playing in the streets caused me to stumble into people from across the nation who had been told that once they made it to Los Angeles to head to the Dirty Thirty's, because that is where it was happening. Oppression created fertile soil for whatever one had to do to survive.

The mobility that a bicycle gave me drastically expanded my familiarity with the streets. I grew comfortable playing in the cubbyholes of those who played with their own demise. It was strange viewing a dope fiend with his family. Knowing that he loved them, and they probably loved him. Love has to be a painful experience when being massacred by drug abuse. There is an unspoken bond amongst children who grow up trying to cope with destructive environments and dysfunctional families. Because of whom I was introduced by, the eyes of those I was introduced to asked the question of whether or not I knew their dirty secrets. If so, did I judge them by the sins of a loved one. We would engage in small talk in front of family, while coveting a secret. The streets started providing me with a family whose foundation was conceived in pain and disillusionment due to circumstances that we had no control over.

Being exposed to the hardship of another's life, taught me that dysfunctional families were the reality for a lot of people. I was raised in a community known for playing dirty. You're taught early on not to worry about people liking you, as long as they respect you when all is said and done. People who have nothing have to assume responsibility for establishing their own sense of respect. In the streets dysfunctional families and bigotry might be the catalyst for you playing but you can't blame them for your rise to respectability. That is gained through your own actions. I delivered newspapers for the Herald Examiner distributor for a little while. Actually, I enjoyed the challenges of the job. As time passed, I grew stronger in completing the tasks associated with being a paperboy. I tend to believe that my endeavor caused my great grandmother to be proud of me. She and other neighbors use to help me assemble Sunday papers. I was growing up faster than she actually recognized.

My world was changing fast and although I appreciated innocence in others it was losing significance in my reality. Unfortunately, I had some innate drive to want to be grown, which was all right when applied to work ethics and matters of respect. I was purposefully trying to prove myself to be a man, and choosing a dollar was a path to that fulfillment. I fed on the acceptance and respect that I was receiving from what I was doing. I learned quickly not to flash bankrolls on everybody because some people's hustle was to beg and borrow.

Lil Joe liked knives and kept one close to him at all times. Throwing them was a hobby of his and we practiced for hours on a Palm tree in the front yard of one of my neighbors. We talked and practiced with balanced knives until I got the hang of it. He took pride in sharpening his own skills. As we played with these knives we talked about life, manhood and my job. I told him the routes I had and whom I was seeing at different locations. He proceeded to tell me about life and the perils of the game. Then the police pulled up and parked with a brother in the back seat. I didn't know him, but Lil Joe did. We continued to throw knives into the tree as though they weren't even there, then he calmly said, "Nigga's like that gonna let them pigs play him out of their chicken shit ass life." The tone of his words informed me that whoever that was in the backseat was going to get cut a new ass-hole if he was ever caught without a police escort.

As the police dangled the life of a pathetic creature that sat in the back seat of their car in front of the world, we discussed his fate. I was given twenty dollars to buy two fifteen cent sodas, and told to run two fingers across my neck when I passed the snitch sitting in the back of the police car. When I passed the police car I looked him in his defeated eyes and performed the task that I was paid nineteen dollars and seventy cents to perform. At eleven years old that was good money to me. Those who witnessed the message enjoyed the meaning and I felt as though I belonged.

I respected what Lil Joe represented. I paid close attention to what he had to say about everyone. His character judgments didn't exclude anyone, and he wasn't a fan of my parents. I admired hustlers and gangsters. Those who could have been a role model went unnoticed by me. Children my age were unable to extract the insight to differentiate between the egos of a man, and what he held close to his heart the way Lil Joe could. Life can be ruthlessly dehumanizing and especially humiliating when you realize that you have been played by a weakling. While looking for signs of strengths I failed to witness how compassion and tenderness in a man could make him more of a man. I didn't see the hidden motivation and sacrifices that many were making for their families to survive. I paid attention to the performance, not the reason for playing.

Being responsible for myself was satisfying and garnered some respect amongst adults. I was losing interest in children's activities, attempting to be a man. Lil Joe and I discussed my paper route and how much I was making. Lil Joe scowled, and then went on to another subject. Most of the time it wasn't hard to interpret his facial expressions, he didn't try to shield likes or dislikes to my knowledge. We discussed the details of who paid me, how much I got paid, why I was paid in cash instead of check. Finally he came to the conclusion that the dude I worked for wasn't a bad man, even though he exploited the paperboys who worked for him.

I had mixed feelings about him attacking my job. The work was hard but the money was good. If he was using me, I didn't mind being used. The size of my route determined how much money I made, and taking on additional routes was totally up to me. About five of us worked for the man, some really needed the money to supplement the family income, and I did it for pride.

Then Lil Joe offered me a deal to make some real money, saying, "You make two or three hundred dollars a month fucking with dude. I will give you a hundred dollars a day to watch my back, you hanging out everyday anyway for free." He didn't need to say anymore after offering me more money than I could have imagined making. Cash was status with me and I wasn't concerned about the way someone made it. Whether you inherited it or found it having money improved your life.

He studied my paper route collection book with genuine interest. We talked about the business end of buying wholesale to sell retail. He warned me to keep business and friendship separate. Saying that if I was going to do something for a friend, than just give it to him without expecting something back. If I was indulging in business, then keep it business, and above all keep my word solid. He was giving me a hundred dollars a day. All he wanted me to do was place balloons of heroin inside of unused newspapers and trail him to different locations. I would aimlessly ride around on my bicycle waiting for him to gesture towards someone to give a newspaper to. It worked out just fine for me, because he only sold what he came to get rid of, then we left the spot.   Both of my jobs were flexible and interchangeable in schedules. He worked a.m. and p.m., and as long as my papers were delivered that day everybody was happy, I never had a problem blending the two.

I was enterprising, and the accumulation of responsibility and wealth felt good. I stuffed newspapers, went and got money, then left. Lil Joe gave me a special gift, a balance knife, suitable to my hand size. That knife was a symbol of passage into manhood. I accepted his endorsement along with the values that went along with it.   That gift also inferred an obligation to use it if aggressed upon or if I felt disrespected. He imposed upon my psyche that fear was a personality trait that belonged to the beholder. Any man can be dangerous and is susceptible to getting what he gives. Don't worry,   about what a man might do to you, instead be concerned with what you might have to do to him. As a man that is your only real responsibility.

Like clockwork he would show up, and we would go into the abandoned back house that now had become a den for dope fiends to stuff newspapers and clean up the paraphernalia left behind by drug addicts.

Moma owned our house, so I didn't have no bills beyond going to the movies, skating and partially buying my clothes. She never quit shopping for me regardless of how much money she held on to for me. I took pride in saving money. The problem I encountered was caused by sharing news of my financial standings with family members, who took pride in borrowing with no intent on paying me back.

Occasionally, Moma would question me about the money I would have her hide for me.   I would deflect the question by saying that other paperboys were making more money than me. She would respond by saying that she should get a paper route, and we would leave it at that. Sometimes she would say, "Some of these grown people around her need to be delivering papers as much as they beg."

It didn't take long before I was embedded in a dope fiend world. By day I played where they played. At night they lingered right outside of my bedroom window and any sound coming from that area captured my attention. I had become somewhat territorial, and wasn't beyond tripping on some of them. After all, I was the one trying to erase any sign of their activities by cleaning up their discarded trash. I lived on the streets that dope fiends only visited when they needed a fix. I was aware of how lowlife they could become when they needed money to buy some dope. They were capable of doing scandalous things to one another, which evoked defensiveness in me. I was being tutored on ways to deal with anyone who bled. I was anxiously prepared to deal with having my home disrespected by a dope fiend. The streets would understand my pain.

I was still too young to have a strong voice in reprimanding adults about what they were doing to themselves. I would let my sentiments be known about shameful behavior. At eleven or twelve years old I lacked true moral fortitude and held my tongue the majority of the time with adults. At this point I was being raised by the streets and was just a voyeur when it came to family, values and all the other square shit. Instead of dealing with my issues I multiplied them by channeling my anger into self destructive paths. My empathy was being replaced with indifference and the potential to utilize violence as a problem solver. Pursuing what grown men pursued at eleven and twelve years old was a bad choice for me. I lacked true understanding of where I was headed. The void in my heart caused by circumstances beyond my control left very little room for empathy in my life.

The world I saw was ruthless and only the strong survived . My boogey man was real and flaunted himself in my world proudly. I feared being made a victim more than I did death. Unknowingly I announced to all the monsters in my pre-adolescent world that I lacked the power to take a life. But I would do all I could to arrange a meeting between them and their God to discuss the matter of life and death. Ultimately it would be God's decision to relocate them to heaven or hell. My responsibility as I saw it then was to set up an emergency meeting between the two and leave the rest up to God.

People who pursue their own destruction by using drugs often find what they are looking for, death. I was growing accustomed to stories of near death experiences or of some dying for one reason or another. The drug that made them vomit in a near death experience overjoyed dope fiends. Corpses were being found outside my bedroom window that represented a final picture of someone who pursued drowning in their own vomit. As I viewed the tragedy of someone else's mistakes, I didn't comprehend the extent to which my own life was being hijacked by those seeking to evade reality.

Outside of my window there were a few large trees that blocked sunshine and the glare of the moon. Someone could be standing in the shadows unseen at night watching all that transpired. You had to let your eyes adjust to the dark to see. Once that was achieved, I sought the glow from the tip of a cigarette to give away someone's position in the dark. Seeking the glow of the tip of a cigarette to give away someone's position in the dark became a survival skill,. There was a lot going on in the dark, sometimes it could be eerie sitting in my bedroom knowing that people were out there in the dark doing things that they would be ashamed for others to witness in the light. The wind blowing through the leaves of the numerous trees only added to the suspense of the unknown. Although the reality of the dark was that someone was going to be in need of assistance soon. The power was off back there and they were going to eventually have to knock on the front door for ice or milk in their effort to prevent someone from over dosing. Death waited outside of my window, shaking trees, and causing our old house to creak for attention. My anxiety was tied to living not dying.

One night while I lay awake in my bedroom listening to the squeaks of our house and the sounds of cars going to and fro. I heard the sounds of female voices cheerfully walking down the side of my house. That was all the justification I needed to investigate what shenanigans were taking place in the dark. I opened my window just as three attractive women passed by in short dresses jittery of what awaited them in the vacant house. They probably felt some strength in numbers, not knowing that the monster that waited on them could choose any or all of them as an offering to newly vacated positions in hell. But they proceeded down the path disturbing the peace with their girlish nervous laughter.

Avocado, lemon, sour orange, banana, plum, persimmon, tasty kumquat, cherry blossom and switch trees surrounded my house. Which gave cover to those who did not want to be seen. At night you could be watched without knowing you were the star attraction in a tragic scene. I observed these women for a couple of minutes, then lost interest and allowed my curtain to fall back in place. About fifteen minutes later the sounds of a commotion was coming from the back house. This time I went immediately out of my bedroom window to see what mayhem was unfolding.

When I got back there two of the women were good and high, practically useless crying over the unconscious body of their friend. Lil Joe squatted over the unconscious woman slapping the shit out of her saying, "Dumb bitch wake your dumb ass up," repeatedly. Then he yelled at me to go get some ice, saying, "This dumb bitch ain't gonna die on me."

I ran back to my house using the back door to gain entrance and retrieved two trays of ice quickly, running water over both, and made my way back to the vacant house. When I got back Lil Joe was working hard trying to keep her alive, still slapping her face and yelling at her. When I presented him with the ice, he told me to pull her panties down and stick as much ice as I could into her pussy. Her dress was in disarray anyway and her panties were fully exposed so I did as told sliding about six cubes into her body without a problem. He had never quit trying to keep some glimmer of life in her. He slapped and yelled at her trying to keep her conscious.

The ice caused her to moan and try to wiggle it from her body, and then she went limp again. He told me, "Man this bitch is dying. Keep putting the ice in her and you get over here and slap this stupid bitch to keep her woke, and I'll be right back." The other women were still sobbing but too high to be of any use in saving the life of their friend. Slapping some woman in the face was abnormal to me, but I tried to hit her as hard as he was slapping her. He returned with a small bag of cocaine and poured some in a burnt spoon, added water and dissolved it by burning the spoon. Then he pulled it into the syringe and shot it into her neck.

She woke up immediately complaining about a stinging face and water coming out of her ass. She said nothing about the puddle of vomit that someone was going to have to clean up once they were gone. Obviously she was too loaded for her own good and didn't grasp how close she had come to being a corpse. She wanted to know who had pulled her clothes off. Lil Joe said, "Stupid bitch, I should have let your stupid ass die, and don't bring your silly ass around me anymore."

The next day we went over the events of the night before and he explained to me that those bitches play square all week long with real good jobs and square ass husbands. When they finally get out of the house they always over do it with alcohol or red devils. They talk that square shit but always find themselves in harms way out here in the streets. They work for the city so if one of them overdoses around here pigs will be everywhere. Lil Joe told me this is my block and if I am not here and you have to bring one of these stupid motha fuckers back, just shoot cold milk into their ass, that will work just as good as cocaine.

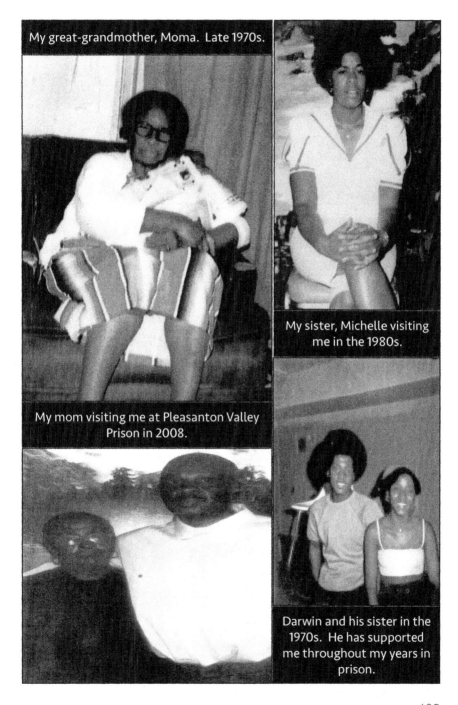

My great-grandmother, Moma. Late 1970s.

My sister, Michelle visiting me in the 1980s.

My mom visiting me at Pleasanton Valley Prison in 2008.

Darwin and his sister in the 1970s. He has supported me throughout my years in prison.

Me (front row with suspenders) as a young child with my next door neighbor, Patricia Ann and other neighborhood kids. Early 1960s.

Hucabuck, Poochie, Chris Watts. Hucabuck is deceased.

My daughter, Monique and her boyfriend, Scott in 2005.

I began contemplating what I was capable of doing to another human being. Empathy was sliding out the door. I was playing with the springs on a trigger, musing about hurting someone close to me. Around this time I was willing to stand by my judgments of

> I have more respect for a man who lets me know where he stands, even if he's wrong, than the one who comes up like an angel and is nothing but a devil.
>
> Malcolm X

whomever, and willing to take it to whatever extent necessary. My sense of being wronged was anger was spawning an outlet.

As what I couldn't see started to come to light, I started bumping into the dude that my mother said was my father. I was encountering him at locations frequented by junkies. I wasn't four years old any more and wasn't pretending to care about a fag who tried to violate me. We never questioned each other as to why we were in places that neither one of us should have been. I knew a few things about the streets at this point. I definitely didn't use drugs. Life had changed our roles, and my gun was loaded. The only real question for him and I was would I pull the trigger.

Apparently he had not actually considered that whatever relationships we once tried to form were shattered beyond repair. It was obvious that someone had shared privileged information with him. I had access to what they liked. I understood that a couple of individuals who frequented one of the places that I ran across my father at had probably mentioned my access to people that was restricted to them. I was offended that he felt at liberty to test my loyalty to the game and to the men who trusted me and had always been nothing but good to me. He didn't understand that I knew what a functional closet dope fiend was. I made sure he understood that my loyalty was to the game, not him. He was placing a large burden on my shoulders because if I were to reveal the path that he was trying to go down they would have killed him. I didn't respect or like him whatsoever and had to wrestle with justifications for not taking the opportunity to bury his worthless ass. He was no longer a true threat to me; in fact he had become pathetic.

My mother and siblings had moved back into my great grandmother's house by then which gave my father limited access to my house through whatever weird relationship he had with my mother. Now he was low-key snitching on me. He consciously experienced difficulty in adjusting to the realization that I held no respect for him whatsoever. Nor did I give much credence to the man that he impersonated. He definitely came to understand that I looked down upon him on many different levels. It was dangerous for him to tread upon the principles which I had learned. What my Moma thought meant the world to me. What this dude thought was of little importance to me. My reluctancy to shoot him was in violation of the game I chose to play. The pain caused by my parents was alive and being displayed destructively in the streets that loved me. It was important to me that he understood the fact that he was going to respect me as a man or get hurt.

When it became beneficial everybody wanted to play the parent role. Despite the pain, I loved my mother. I was going through puberty and it seemed logical to allow God to forgive my father because I was experiencing difficulty attempting to. My male role models intimidated him and I learned from them what causes people to respect you, which gave weapons a lot of meaning. I thought about hurting the man, a lot. Obviously, he was mindful about not giving me any provocation. In life I have never liked his kind and have dealt with them with open contempt. It is what it is; oil and vinegar do not mix well.

He was chipping with heroin and cocaine, faking like he is selling both. But the streets don't lie, the idiot was getting high on his own product. Nobody lasts long doing that. He didn't understand that one has to want something from you or care about you somehow to be deceived. When someone doesn't want anything from you, you can't cheat or lie successfully to them because they can see right through your deception. All of a sudden my father wanted to introduce me to unknown family members and hang out. I wasn't feeling that at all. Denker Park was my family. The men in my life fed me in more ways than one and instilled a sense of pride in me. I had no logical reason to hangout with trash, regardless of what name my mother placed on garbage. The man had a new evil master, known within my community as heroin. His new master degraded himself due to a lack of selectivity and accepted individuals without morals, a soul or principles. Yet, I was supposed to believe that I meant something to him beyond my access to his master's hypnotic influence.

My mother was watching too many soap operas and didn't see life clearly. She exercised her mouth against the streets that loved me, and the men who sustained me when no one but Moma cared. My mother defensively declared that dude was my father. I really doubt that assumption. She was adamant about that proclamation without recognizing that my relationship with my father was based on bullshit. I reluctantly appeased her fantasy for about one week, before learning that he thought it was slick to entrap those around him with the tools of his master. He was introducing heroin to people to feed his own addiction and would get highly upset if they didn't return the favor. He was narcissistic and pitiful in his thinking. He forced me to resent every breath he took; there was nothing worthwhile in him continuing to breathe.

There were some apartments right off of Denker Avenue at 35th Street and a woman named Geraldine and her two daughters lived there. Geraldine was a dope fiend and my father was a parasite that tried to keep her supplied with a monster on her back. She had allowed her apartment to become a shooting gallery, where they sold and shot dope all in the same location. She had two daughters that were my age. The youngest was named Erica and she was definitely ebony pretty. I felt sorry for her and have often wondered her fate. I can't imagine her surviving the circumstances of her existence because some form of death awaited her.

Erica was petite, soft spoken, and her dark skin glowed with beauty. Unfortunately, the place she called home was always filled with human maggots that catered to the lowest part of their nature. She wore a crown of pain majestically. Erica never mentioned what went on in that house when the crowd was gone or when her mother had nodded out on heroin, or was drawn away on a dope fiend mission. Just by the comments that were made to me during my visits, I knew what was transpiring was not right.

One time I went over to her apartment and there were five or six low life ass dope fiends sashaying around her apartment like they lived there. I was offended that they felt that comfortable in a house that kids were in. They understood my belligerence. When all was said and done this was still *Rebel Rouser* territory and Denker Park Boys may not take kindly to the wretched doings of dope fiends. Nobody cared about who they used to be while sitting in a shooting gallery. Enjoying the drugs in their veins stripped them of any obligations I may have had towards adults to respect them. That's how the game goes, I didn't write the rules.

I stood in their living room as the girls were going in and out of each bedroom. Obviously their mama was in one but I never saw her. There was an alcoholic dope fiend sitting his fat ass on their couch looking like a black bear running his junkie mouth. Erica drew his attention as she went from one room to the next and this junkie felt a need to tell me that I need to get some of that fine black tender pussy. Saying, "Ain't nobody gonna say anything." The man was speaking to me in a tone as though his words were providing him some kind of sexual gratification. Confrontationally, I told him that I had come over there to get my money and that he needs to get his fat ass out of their house before somebody fucks him up! We both understood that it wasn't going to end nicely for him if we started feuding over his desire to have sex with an eleven year old who probably hadn't experienced her first menstruation yet. I was capable of hurting him for more reasons than one.

Everybody in the house understood that my challenge wasn't empty including him. I guess he didn't want to mess up his high, and decided to let my disrespect toward him go as others advised me to be cool.

The exchange of words brought everyone into the living room to witness the clashing of viewpoints. Strangely, I was the one being told to be cool, as though I was the one disturbing the atmosphere instead of questioning the motivation of his child molesting statements. From then on Erica tacitly assumed that I understood her situation. Consciously I could only touch the surface of what life made her endure. Obviously I knew that something was grossly wrong but in fact I was still a child and lacked a real solution to the evil she would come to know. Clearly her mother knew what the disturbance was about in her living room and apparently didn't take offense about some thirty something year old dope fiend discussing her daughter's eleven year old pussy in an open forum. My sentiments were not a secret so I don't know what type of low life games were really being played. Erica and I maintained an unspoken alliance until they moved. I would see her occasionally until I came to the penitentiary.

Physical pain wasn't a real threat anymore. I played football, got punched and didn't mind socking someone else. I sit as close to hell as a man can get. The only guaranteed relief I have from my extreme misery is death, do I really fear ending a tragic life? I was tired of the absurdity of pretending to have a father. I felt a sense of humiliation by even being connected to trash. He also had to be embarrassed by the fact that I was invited to sit at the table with men who found him unworthy of entrance. I grew not to accept those with any trait of who he was either.

Dude thought that he had figured out something real slick. His conniving ass had conceived a real plan to back door real players like the snake he was. The man never in his worthless life comprehended the value of loyalty and respect and died never knowing either. He propositioned me with a deal absent of anything beneficial to me. He gave me a door key to where he kept a 357 Magnum and his stash and a couple hours later showed up with a small brown bag full of balloons expecting me to get rid of them. It was like Christmas to me, I had held dope for people that never expected me to sell anything.

The streets had introduced me to boys that shared similar aspirations. One of them was named Lil Bumpy, his daddy was a respectable bookie. I shared with him what I was expecting from the mark and we devised a plan. My father was hanging out at Geraldine's with the rest of them low lives. Right around the corner was Marvin's Liquor store on Denker Avenue at Jefferson Blvd. Directly behind the liquor store set Porter's Shoeshine Stand and all kind of things transpired there in the open, which caused the police to be frequent visitors to the area. Our plan was based on routine police harassment.

My father loved a drug that hated him. He was proud of a son who entertained firing the shot that sent him to hell. My father was real proud of me. The idiot enjoyed the story of me about to go to jail over Geraldine's daughter. He handed me that bag of dope feeling like a real player who was about to come up, get rich off my efforts. That had to be a brilliant idea. He didn't take into account that Bumpy and I had our own plan that would not afford him a dime. As soon as I left the apartment that he was in, dope in hand, I proceeded back to the corner. I meandered around for a while, Bumpy had already snuck into a backyard before I even went to the apartment to get the dope. The first time the police acted like they were about to stop I made a spectacle out of putting the brown bag behind a fence for everybody to see. When I went back to retrieve the bag it was gone. I had a block full of witnesses that some one beat me for it. What was I supposed to do? He was furious. Huffed and puffed a while and got in his car and drove up and down the street a few times, then got his punk ass on just like we planned he would do. The streets were allowing me to exact revenge. Three weeks later somebody broke into his stash spot and took his brand new 357 magnums and all his dope. The game can be cruel.

Somehow he felt that I had something to do with his financial ruin. I wasn't going to snitch on myself and in actuality it could have been anyone that he associated with, none of them were any good. He couldn't tell my mother as that would not have turned out right. She still entertained some hostility over the fact that he had never provided me with a diaper. By then I was wearing my manhood on my shoulders and wasn't comfortable accepting disrespect from him or anyone else. Life had changed, my pride was worth dying for. The streets I was walking were like Vietnam and everybody was pulling the trigger. It wouldn't have hurt my soul none to pop his ass and we understood that I possessed adequate finger strength to pull the trigger.

When I first started playing with Lil Joe he was adamant about me getting rid of everything in my possession at the first sign of danger and worried about my Moma killing him if she found out what we were doing. Instead of my father being concerned about giving me poison to play with, he was emotional about his financial loss. He should have paid attention to the big picture because I could not have cared less about what he thought.

Hanging out out with junkies is not the healthiest thing to do mentally or spiritually. After the initial thrill of the unknown, a dope fiend's life is dark and ugly. One day a few of us were in my backyard playing basketball when we heard shots being fired. I ran around to the front of the house to witness two dope fiends shooting at each other in broad daylight. One was shielding himself with the Palm tree that we used for knife throwing practice and firing his German Luger across the street at another dope fiend who was on a neighbor's porch with a punch shotgun firing back and ducking for cover.

We came running from the backyard not realizing that we were directly in the line of fire until one of them yelled at us to get out the way. They continued to argue about something important only to them, and fired a couple of more shots. Then they came and stood on my front porch and discussed their uses. All of my neighbors were watching the excitement up close and personally, then without flinching one of them shot himself in the leg with the German Luger.

Those types of events caused some parents to warn their kids to stay away from my home and me. Tragedy provided compelling jargon for me to share with others as street validation. At the same time the streets were stealing my humanity. Little things were thought of in the extreme and indifference was becoming normal. The experiences of this vast resource of junkies minimized the dullness of my world, while pushing a carefree existence even further away.

I don't believe that anyone was born to be a dope fiend although circumstances lead some down that path. The world admits to poisoning the path of innocence with obstacles that if you stumble over will kill you or have you locked up for the rest of your natural life. Some play their part well but from the first injection until they gasp for their last breath accepting they were the prey in life's drama. A supposed good time may lead to hell and can strip a person of their honor. Rejecting our reality can lead to embracing the values of another world where if you lack malice, you become fair game.

This was an era that pride was derived from being soulful. We enjoyed soul music, tried to display a soulful rhythm in dance, some even tried to add soulful cadence to our speak. Civil rights dominated the times and defiance was totally expected and displayed by all age groups and gender. What person was not aware of Rosa Parks, Martin Luther King, Malcolm and a large list of others who exercised their spirit to uplift a whole race of people. I saw what was in front of me not what lie in the bushes. The awakening of a soul caravan is exhilarating but veiled the tentacles of destruction.

The timing of death, like the ending of a story, gives a changed meaning to what preceded it.

Mary Catherine Bateson

Life was foreboding, and alternatives were beyond my knowledge. Tragedy was playing on every corner whether it was death in the living room or murder outside. Run and hide or fight. I chose to change games.

Everybody that played with poison wasn't necessarily a bad person. Some walked into the cage of addiction not understanding the nature of the evil they played with. Wanting a momentary escape from hardship introduced them to a monster that took more than it gave. Three young men lived on my block named Charles, Carter and Pep. They were all addicted to heroin but didn't exhibit the scandalous conduct associated with being a junkie. Two of them had fallen within the grasp of addiction while actively serving in the U.S. Marines in Vietnam. Charles lived two houses from me with his father and his flat-footed girlfriend that made comedy out of being a prostitute. Her efforts to walk in high heel shoes was half pitied and half laughed at.

Carter and Pep were also veterans of the Vietnam War and liked talking about places they had visited while in the service. They planned on using their veteran benefits for a good life. They wanted to return to an Asian country where they felt they were treated better than they were here in America. Carter wasn't much bigger than me and was always pleasant to everyone. His day seemed to be consumed with filing for loans for school and looking for work. From his vantage point my life was sad. He thought that I should have been afforded the opportunity to be a kid. I wasn't in any position to feel sorry for myself and ignored what he was talking about when it came to my plight. I enjoyed his stories about foreign countries that he had visited. I was particularly interested in his plans to return to Taiwan on a shopping spree.

Carter had some handmade clothes that we had discussed him selling to me. He had plans of returning to Taiwan to get some more made, I wanted the ones he had. I just had to catch him in need of some money to complete the deal. He rented a room down the street from my house and one evening told me that he was ready to make the sale. I went and got the money and proceeded once again back to his room. Carter, Pep and Charles had just got through fixing some dope. Now the urgency for my money had been satisfied. I wasn't deterred, sooner or later when his money got low that monkey that he carried on his back was going to need to be fed . They were busy enjoying themselves, while I was being persistent without becoming annoying so they invited me to their next destination to a neighbor that I really didn't know.

When we reached the neighbor's house it was obvious that he was in the process of preparing to go fishing. That's all he was talking about, the joys of fishing. They appreciated his love for the sport but were drawn there by the pot that was simmering on the stove. Their focus was on the potency of alcohol, which I knew little to nothing about. He had been cooking 'White Lightening', for a few days and it was now Friday and time to unwind. He was boastful about his creation daring everyone to taste it, swearing that it would kill you. We all laughed in expectation of his clear brew. I took one sip and felt like the breath had been snatched from my body. That was good enough for me.

The drink caused me to remember why I was there in the first place. So I turned my attention back to Carter and the clothes he had in his room next door that I wanted. We had already discussed how cheap it was to have them made somewhere in Asia where I had no fantasy of traveling to. Going back to Asia was his fantasy, not mine. He explained to me the value of double stitches along the seam, along with why you go to tailor shops with your own pattern. He was high so he went through his repertoire of likes and dislikes. He shared the feeling that Asians treated him well while Americans tried to degrade him. He was about 23 years old and no bigger than I was at twelve.

We danced around the subject of me giving him my money in return for some clothes he didn't want anymore. As we talked and they continued to drink, Curtis Mayfield played in the background, "Two bags please, for a generous fee, make your world what you want it to be, got a women that I love desperately, want to give her something better than me. Been told I can be nothing else, just a hustler in spite of myself, I know I can make it, this life just don't make it, lord, lord."

I was feeling that song, and the culture that went along with it. All of them images from minstrel shows didn't play well in my community. Sambo, Step-and-Fetch-It and the rest of them caricatures would have got their ass whipped on my block by people embracing Black pride. Those clothes were instrumental in trying to solidify the image that I pursued. He was a dope fiend, but well dressed. I not only wanted to mimic his attire, but I was prepared to buy it in its entirety. I enjoyed the accolades of having nice clothes, a lot of money for my age and attraction of girls. I was persistent knowing that I had messed up in allowing him to get loaded before we finalized our business.

Once the alcohol was consumed and they were ready to depart the neighbor's house, he told me that he had to go to some apartment down the street, and as soon as he got back we would take care of our business. I showed him a stack of money again as motivation, as I rolled my bike along side of them as they crossed the train tracks on Exposition Blvd. and Hallsdale Avenue, and stepped into the grass foyer of the apartments. I rolled into the grass foyer with them letting Carter know not to be in there all night circling away as they knocked on the front door of an apartment. When the front door opened the living room was lit by only a dim red light, then Carter stretched out his hands in front of him shouting, "Man, stop, what's the matter with you. Please don't do this." His cries only brought attention to himself because dude let him have the first blast from his shotgun right in the stomach, which caused him to fold in half as he was being propelled backwards. Too high to react Charles got hit next in the chest and lay quietly in a puddle of his own blood. Pep attempted to flee but the gauge caught him at least three times.

They laid there for a few minutes, moaning and speaking incoherently in the voice of death. People were coming out of their apartments, but there wasn't anything they could do as the damage was done. It all happened real fast. I froze. Not feeling threatened but dismayed by the suddenness of the events. Two minutes earlier they were on top of the world and as high as they could be without a concern. Now their bodies were like fountains, squirting their own red blood that stained the pavement, and the gross area was being watered by the same blood they rested in until it became gummy.

In the streets anything can happen to anybody at anytime. Some folks embrace the fear within them and ambivalently nurture the coward that they are. Others face whatever confronts them. I had issues already, the street was my home, where was I gonna run to without being equipped with the knowledge of where I was at. I was just reacting to life, there was no intelligent direction to where I was going. The presence of danger was insurmountable until met with dehumanizing tenets of indifference. Everyday down in them Dirty Thirty's someone is presented with a choice between self-respect or death. Either way who you truly are is determined by the decisions you make.

My mother and her boyfriend, Big Yard lived with us, which was all right with me. The time apart had allowed my mother and I to grow apart. Big Yard was the only man in my life I can honestly say ever resembled a Daddy and I

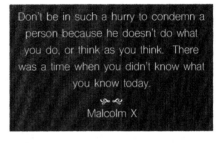

Don't be in such a hurry to condemn a person because he doesn't do what you do, or think as you think. There was a time when you didn't know what you know today.

Malcolm X

accepted him as such. His presence was comforting and he would handle whatever I couldn't with anybody. He was a man that didn't care much for the flashy slick shit. He protected and did what he could to provide for us but stayed in his own lane and wasn't impressed by what others did.

The murders were somewhat surreal to everyone because none of the men who got gunned down were a threat to anyone. Yeah, they used heroin paid for by benefits afforded to them from the U.S. military but I never heard about them doing anything scandalous or breaking a law. Charles momentarily had a hoe but he wasn't no pimp. Big Yard didn't like the company I was keeping and was especially concerned over what I had witnessed.

He worked at a company that made tires from hot sticky rubber, which clung to everything that it touched. The father-son scenario was cool, but I didn't particularly like going to work with him. He made it an issue and I didn't really have a choice in the matter. The streets talk and he was sincerely concerned about my welfare and that was felt in spite of his limited interpersonal communication skills. I knew that I was close to his heart and he trusted me with his secrets, which caused us to bond even more.

He smoked weed occasionally, didn't drink too often and was staunchly against hard drugs. I don't know what he thought I was doing but whatever it was he preferred that I do it at home.

He didn't try to slow up the ambitions of me becoming a man at all, he did try to provide some parameters in that pursuit.

I didn't make the world or the turmoil that surrounded me. I was just trying to survive, without being cognizant of the cause. In trying to put a foundation under myself that was absent of chaos I made a deadly mistake of drawing from the same pool of self-destructiveness. Players play in several different variations of the same game. Some command their respect through their actions, while others have acquired techniques to demand their respect even when its questionable whether or not they truly respect themselves. Winning doesn't necessitate a respect for how you play the game. Playing passive leaves you at the mercy of others. Life in the Dirty Thirty's is dangerous, and one must decide to fight or live as a coward. It's often offensive to the conscious of men when cowards drape themselves in the apparel of intelligence and pretend to be men. Cowards playing with the wrong people might get them killed. The nature of a coward is deceptive and he will play with anybody against those he fears while smiling in their face, he's a true bitch indeed.

Lil Joe was a trusted mentor that understood when it was time to back up. I was naïve and failed to comprehend the time to retreat and return to a location of safety. With the varmints coming in and around my house safety became a lost concept and in large part was predicated upon the threat that I posed. My mentor was judgmental without restrictions, loved my Moma and chopped everyone else up. My uncle had become a dedicated alcoholic. Lil Joe's warning to me about getting high scared me away from alcohol and drugs for the rest of my life. I would rather die with a chili cheeseburger in my mouth, than a needle in my arm. His warning became part of my personal constitution.

One evening Lil Joe came through and we socialized as he waited on someone to bring his money. The frustration of being disrespected by a junkie delinquent in his payments was readable on his face. Then the man drove up in his nice sixty-four Lincoln dressed like a player. I anticipated the shit hitting the fan and zeroed in on misfortune. The man should have stayed at home in Long Beach because he wasn't gonna leave my neighborhood looking cute.

Lil Joe said, "Who does the motha fuckin' nigga think he is? This punk owes me money and he won't even get his bitch ass out the car to talk like man!" Then we proceeded in the direction of the car. The man exited his vehicle on the driver's side and proceeded to the back of his car. Ironically the man was parked in the same identical location that the coroner normally eats his lunch in. He should have known that he wasn't gonna get to the trunk of his car in my neighborhood, they don't play that there. He should have had his pistol in his lap if there was a problem.

He allowed Lil Joe to walk right up on him with wildness in his eyes that alerted me to the possibility of drama unfolding within the serenity of a peaceful night. Once Lil Joe was within arms reach he cordially asked, "Nigga, do you think I am a bitch or something?" The man had to be crazy and was mumbling something incoherently. Lil Joe asked, "Where is my money punk?" The man spat some more words out that added up to mumbo jumbo. Then nervously uttered, "I'll try to get it, I will try to get it for you when I go back to Long Beach." In a flash barely visible to the eye Lil Joe cut the man under his cheekbone down to the corner of his mouth. He grabbed him by the neck and choked him over the trunk of his car saying, "Nigga I want my money! I ought to kill your bitch ass!" Then he let him go. The silence of the night was never disturbed as the man's teeth were visible through the side of his face.

A few days later we talked about what had transpired. I was told the cut signified that the bearer of such a wound wasn't no good, was probably a snitch or unethical in his business dealings. The coroner had begun to park regularly on my block, Lil Joe recognized the signs of the times and only played occasionally. I began spending time with my cousin, Junior. He was about ten years older than me, drove a green sixty-two Chevy that had been lowered and he added customized chrome rims for effect. I was pushing for my own car but until I achieved that, driving his car around satisfied that craving. He rode around all day long pursuing a good time. When he got too high to drive, I became the designated driver. I enjoyed getting behind the wheel, so it was all fun for me. At twelve I felt like a man behind the wheel and didn't give a damn about driving licenses. Junior chased girls in an innocent way, content with a good time only, so we frequented the beach and parks for the joy of it.

Junior liked taking barbiturates, 'Red Devils', and drinking 'Silver Satin', wine. He worked at Pizza Man on 84th and Western Avenue, and we spent time racing around delivering pizzas. I drove better than he did, sober or not. Hitting corners had become my playtime and increasingly getting high was becoming his.

Junior lived in Inglewood and his parents were still happily married. His father owned his own barbershop and his mother was a Registered Nurse. His parents seemed to give him whatever he wanted and I often wished that I had parents like that. He was grown so it wasn't my place to check him about his affairs. I was satisfied being the designated driver.

This night I was concerned about going to school in the morning, so I went home and laid down on a love sofa in the living room watching television until I went to sleep. About one or two in the morning Junior knocked on the front door and he had some woman with him that I didn't know. He was good and loaded again, wanting to use a spare bedroom we had in our house. Everybody was asleep in the house and I looked at the girl with him and told him to go ahead.

They went into the bedroom and I fell back to a slumber momentarily imagining what they were doing. I was asleep when he came out the bedroom to go use the bathroom. When he returned he sat on the floor next to me bragging about his sexual conquest and on how good he felt right then. I didn't want to hear about either, I was trying to sleep and rolled over turning my back to him.

About five fifteen in the morning the phone wouldn't stop ringing and everyone ignored it, which irritated me. Finally, I answered it. It was Aunt Mae, Junior's mother. She was telling me that she had a dream that Junior was with me and that he was dead. I told her that Junior was right there with me and that he was all right. I wanted desperately to go back to sleep but she was adamant about speaking to him. So to calm her down I called out to Junior telling him that his mother was on the phone. He was making me mad because he wouldn't acknowledge me, causing me to have to get up and carry the phone over to him, which I assumed he wanted me to do.

I got up and walked over to Junior and kicked him in the back and told him that his mama was on the phone. Junior snored profusely and could begin to snore while still awake. I noticed that he wasn't snoring at all and when I looked to the front of his body his face was laying in a puddle of green vomit. That's when I panicked and tried to wake him up. I turned him over and slapped his face hard as I could but there was no sign of life that I could detect. I could hear Aunt Mae yelling into the phone. I picked the phone back up and told her that I could not wake him up. Her wail hurt the core of me and I went directly to my mother's bedroom door to wake Big Yard up and tell him that Junior was in on the living room floor dead and Aunt Mae was still on the phone crying. He jumped up and went to check on Junior. There was nothing anyone could do for Junior. He was dead.

Big Yard wanted to know how Junior had even got into our house, I told him that I had let him and some girl in last night. At this point I was feeling guilty for having done so. Junior was a lost cause. Big Yard did all he could to try to revive him. Then he told me to go check on the girl that entered the house with him. I immediately went into the bedroom that she was in and found her still in her red bra with her panties resting around her left ankle. The soles of her feet were planted on the bed, in the exact missionary position that they had had sex in. She looked very comfortable to me. I shook her a couple times to make sure that she was all right. She moaned and flexed her legs like she didn't want to be bothered. I pulled a blanket over her and went back into the living room to inform Big Yard that she was all right.

He went to the bathroom and found some heroin, a syringe and some barbiturates Junior had dropped when he went to the bathroom. Aunt Mae was hysterical on the phone and my mother was trying to calm her so she could call for an ambulance. When the police showed up they put my siblings and I in my mother's bedroom as they did their investigation. When they checked on the girl Junior had brought with him, she was also dead. Big Yard lied and said that he had let Junior in the house and the police accused him of selling dope.

There was a little bit of a stigma associated with your classmates witnessing dead bodies being dragged out of my house. While they had us quarantined in my mother's bedroom I remember watching the kids on their way to Foshay Jr High School react with astonishment to the presence of witnessing dead bodies along their routine path to school. The realization the others had witnessed my darkness was perplexing. I knew that they would inform the teacher that I wouldn't be at school that day. Death's shadow has always been close to my life.

I had never seen Junior mad, he could find a smile even in dangerous situations. Now he was dead. Why he danced with the dangers of being a junkie I will never know. Sadly, I remember being indifferent and without tears. I felt for Junior but was too weak to experience grieving. Somehow Curtis Mayfield's lyrics capsulated that tragedy by singing, "In the back of his mind he said, didn't have to be here, you didn't have to love for me. When I was just a nothing child, why couldn't they just let me be, let me be."

With that hanging out with heroin addicts lost its luster and offered very little to smile about. Their world was a little bit too much for me. I wanted to get away from something, badly. Where I was headed became the problem.

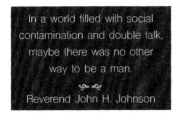

In a world filled with social contamination and double talk, maybe there was no other way to be a man.

Reverend John H. Johnson

We were focused on family and Black pride and reasoned that the end of adolescence would deliver us into a realm of manly endeavors. No one foresaw the dog biting his own tail.

My astrological sign is the bull. Most of my life I have suffered from a hard head, and that personality trait created a lot of discomfort. I must admit that there is truth in that observation that a hard head can create a soft ass. I am capable of staying the course and holding on to thoughts and sentiments for dear life. My truth is mine, and I resent any attempt by someone else to define that truth. I believe that Osiris as he sits on the perch of judgment will know my reality in its entirety, and I will accept that verdict. I am grateful that life allowed me to live long enough to find some clarity and enjoy inner peace in an otherwise tragic journey.

Sophisticated demons distance themselves from repulsive agenda's by giving the responsibility of subjugation in the form of crime, substance abuse, dysfunctional families to those purposely targeted for destruction with power plays and empty utterances. They give immunity to the perpetrators of inhumane ambitions and craft simple clichés that admit placing obstacles in the path of human development. They make it sound Freudian to poison the well that many are led to by a lack of opportunity or total disenfranchisement. This is justified by the mere fact that a group of individuals may have the audacity to seek meaning in their lives from a non-subservient reservoir. The inclination to be free is all that's necessary for someone's child to become unworthy of another breath.

My life has been spent in the penitentiary not from any sort of pathological neurosis or inherent deviancy. I played adult games with the insight of a child viewing danger as a right of passage. I had no true way to gauge the depth of hatred and jealousy. My personal fears and disappointments blurred the presence of truly despicable demons in my world. I should have pissed on some and wrecked the career of others that assisted evil in stealing meaning from my life. Life itself has given testament to that fact. The problem was that I truly loved my community, its strengths and weaknesses. I was determined to step into manhood enjoying the respect and benefits of being a man. That should have been a natural course for healthy and honorable minds. The hand that resides in the shadows understood that mindset and laced my path with multiple detours that led to graveyards and Folsom State Prison . I have no doubt that in every grouping, whether it is due to geographical locations or race that there are a few cowards in the crowd pretending to be a man, while shielded by illusive disguises.

I wish I had the ability as a child to recognize the purity of a man's heart and ignore deceptive appearances and tough talk. Maybe then I could have seen through the forest and focused on a path to achieving meaning to my life by establishing heaven here on earth. I was so baffled by the drama of others I failed to see the warning signs of catastrophe awaiting. In the penitentiary you learn real quick not to disrespect people because by doing so I have placed the burden of responsibility on them to decide how to respond to foolishness. Behind these walls friendship is rare, and true love is practically obsolete. While isolated from friends and family is a true blessing for a man to be at peace with himself. If he's fortunate self-respect will also accompany him. Unfortunately most spend their times and energy hiding the truth about who they are. Barking out proclamations demanding respect but little do they know that the solace that comes with owning inner-peace commands the respect that will always be denied to a fake. He will die an expert in creating excuses to mask his coward inability to embrace the principles of love and loyalty. He thinks everybody is luckier than him and chooses to empower himself through studying the many facets of deception. He should have applied himself more in school and learned a vocation because he is nothing more than a field hand elegantly masquerading as honorable. There is a strong possibility that if he would use his back and the energy that he spent deceiving himself of grandness that he may have find some meaning in his worthless life.

I am the fourth generation of my family to have played in Denker Park. My uncles, great uncles, and great grandfather all had coveted memories of feeling at home there. They all have personal grand memories and experiences at Denker Park. The pinnacle of my uncle's existence was actualized through hand-to-hand combat in defense of the honor of Denker Park. He spent his adolescence and young adult years being praised for his fighting ability. His transition into adulthood pivoted on the adolescent accolades he had become accustomed to. He enjoyed the sense of comradery that was rooted in being a Denker Park boy. He threw everything away to feed his ego and to become the big man once again. He crashed and sadly lacked the inner-fortitude to ever get back up.

I was the child of *Rebel Rousers* and considered those who patronized Denker Park as family. The negative connotations of gangs went beyond my scope. They embraced me as family, picked me up when I fell, taught me to play different sports and included me in activities that still rank as some of my best experiences in life.

Without question at one time Denker Park instilled pride in the whole community. They were highly ethical, loyal to each other, saw themselves as the protectors and warriors of the community. They would defend anyone who was considered part of the community, whether they are storeowners or individuals that found themselves the victims of thieves or being bullied by someone of unequal size. They would definitely accept the responsibility of defending one another without expecting a reward. Some toted infamous reputations obtained from displaying fluent physical power and a proclivity to utilize those talents. Some have alluded to the possibility of a clannish culture existing within the community. I will leave that determination to those who contently sit in the stands as life goes by to determine whether a clannish culture existed in the community or not. I will admit that a culture of principles existed that prompted mothers and fathers to defend children that were not theirs. These were ideals that protected one another. This was a neighborhood that everybody is somebodies cousin. And yes, outsiders regardless of race, creed, or color did not have the authority or moral platform to disrespect one's family. It was clearly understood that anyone who witnessed a family being aggressed upon unfairly without intervention was labeled as a coward, who might have to explain their traitorous behavior. Anybody can find one's self unwelcome anytime behind displaying conduct unworthy of someone viewed as family. Many people have been given the boot, kicked in the ass, and told not to bring their punk ass back around there. It happens like that sometime, especially so for those who lack a spine and have no love or consideration for the concept of family and chosen associations. Life in the neighborhood I was raised in is not like what is portrayed in a Hollywood movie. You have to earn your position or accept a role that truthfully fits your character.

People are simply who they are and each family has strong and weak members based upon genetics. Most people have some kind of talent and when I am hungry or in need of getting my car fixed, those with abilities shine brightly. Its always better for a good mechanic to demonstrate his skills instead of making an ass out of himself pretending to be something he's not. It has to be a fearful experience to partake in bamboozling those outside of the ones who love you when your heart is not truly into the image you attempt to portray. Them boys down the street may be struggling with their own issues, which caused them to be indifferent, and sincerely offended about being made an unwilling partner in your charade. Trying to be from Denker Park doesn't always work out for some people. Like any military deployment, there comes a time when tour of duty is over. Then you focus on supporting your immediate family with the honors befitting a veteran. Being accepted by Denker Park is a discernible path to garnering one's respect. Loyalty and courage are two personality traits that activate mental faculties that lead to awareness of oneself. The ability of an individual to place himself in jeopardy out of love for others, also allows him to love those he is responsible for and grasp a better appreciation for life. The acknowledgements of danger naturally provides some wisdom.

It was clearly understood that running with the homies was only a phase that transcends one into the responsibilities of manhood. The possibility existed to satisfy whatever feat necessary in earning the respect bestowed upon men of accomplishment before reaching your legal adult age. I accepted the challenge and avoided skipping over knowing the respect of my peers. Standing for something is equivalent to standing against something, which naturally aroused those who cloaked in their deceptive claim of being man to resent me. Today my understanding of the inner-structure of a man prevents me from being mad at anyone.

I played Little League baseball at Denker Park on a team called the *Braves*. I had no illusion about playing professional sports. Professional athleticism just wasn't in the cards for me. During that era I found myself being invited to participate in functions with those who were the vanguards of Denker Park boys like Lil Wag, Poochie, Donnie, Blue, Ricky Crayon, Sin, Easy, Rudy, Pee-Wee, Jonathan, and Ronnie Byars. Wherever these dudes went that meant that Denker Park had arrived. They maintained an active social calendar with their association with different females. A heads up fight might occasionally transpire, but admittance in that group signified that you were cool. They didn't allow those who might get beat up to travel outside of the neighborhood with them. I enjoyed picnics, movies, attending parties and going skating as a community. The values they shared were honorable and comparable to any ideals of a healthy family.

There was a lot going on in the world and I knew very little about any of it. I was having difficulty in dealing with what was right in front of me.

There were a few families that lived in the neighborhood that I was raised in that had migrated from Harlem New York to California. They shared the story of a Black underworld legend that equaled any celebrated mob boss of any race. It's a sign of ignorance when I encounter Black men named after white racists, like Al Capone, Gotti or Dutch. They definitely need to read a book about whom they are honoring. As a community we were fortunate to have story tellers narrate examples of Black Pride as exhibited through the battles fought and won by Bumpy Johnson against mobsters that employed the local authorities to assist them in achieving their objectives.

We were adopting the concept of being thy brother's keeper and protectors of the community against anyone regardless of who you were and especially because of racism. One account told of a massacre of Blacks in New York City in 1863 after the government enacted the draft. An Irish mob angry over being forced to fight in the Civil War, rioted and killed hundreds of Black men while city officials did nothing. Even after the Civil War riots there were numerous incidents of white brutality against Blacks, many of these assaults involved the police.

White gangs in Southern California benefitted from not being the focus of corporate media attention. There were several predatorily motorcycle gangs, the KKK had migrated from southern states to the beauty and sunshine of California and the American Nazi headquarters was located in Southern California with chapters spread out across America.

The then Chief of the Los Angeles Police Department, Darryl Gates was never a man to conceal his prejudices. Italian mafia boys enjoyed the lucrative nature of getting money out of the Black community.

Most men in my area did what they did to survive without destroying the sense of community. *Black is beautiful. I am Black and I am Proud. Black Unity.* Black power colored the consciousness of those times and the life of Bumpy Johnson easily blended with the make up and vibe of my community, generating a sense of pride. The negative aspects may dominate public opinion. But people who live or socialized in that area were empowered by knowing that successful lawyers like Johnny Cochran, doctors, real estate investors and performers like Marvin Gaye, James, Brown, Red Foxx, Ray Charles, Natalie Cole, Smokey Robinson, Chaka Khan, Janet Jackson and Bobby Brown, have played in those same streets. Those who never actually became rich or famous enjoyed the fame of claiming that area as home.

I was transitioning from being concerned with adult affairs and losing any consideration for the opinions of hypocrites who advocated a higher moral platform with their asses tooted to the moon. Plus my stepfather was adamant about me refraining from a path that was learnt outside of my bedroom window. Even though I saw the same people everyday my focus changed.

I was about twelve years old when I found myself drawn to individuals who knew my pain in their own individual way. Sentiments were openly relayed without words ever being attached to singular thoughts. It signified a sign of friendship to be accepted without judgment over conditions beyond my control. This group of neighborhood boys provided comradery based on your own merits. At the time Denker Park wasn't committed to any allegiance with Crips or Bloods. We were focused on getting a dollar and chasing pretty girls around. Denker Park's philosophy was our moral compass and there was a belief in the physical ability of the men and boys from our community to fend off any possible aggression from outsiders.

Within the different clicks at the park there was a crew who were not old enough to be real *Rebel Rousers*, but were Denker Park boys. I have known a lot of bad men in my life but Ronnie 'Lightbulb' Fuse was one of the most dangerous in his role as the enforcer of principles. He didn't like white people or cowards much at all. He surrounded himself with a variety of strong character types and, they were all in agreement during these tumultuous times, which gave birth to the Harlem Crips.

The name Harlem was a tribute to the legend of Bumpy Johnson and his exploits inn Harlem, New York. We were rich in the mythology of his story and soon there was a collective representation of a consciousness that encompassed Malcolm X's death before dishonorment attitude towards life in the spirits of Ronnie Ruse, Jede Rodale, Sad Sack, Pistol Pete, Little Bumpy, Doc, Blue, Cowboy, Yogi, Den Den, Dominoes, Kevin Gill, Micahel Johnson, Dead Eye Hurk, James Miller, Cadillac Jim, Skip, and Baby D. There is a roll call of others that could be honorably mentioned but these individuals placed honor before death.

Beyond what we were focused on there was a lot going on in the city of Los Angeles and in large Black communities across America. The killing of Bunchy Carter and John Huggins at a U.C.L.A. Afro-American Studies meeting by supporters of Ron Karenga on June 18, 1969 gave birth to the Crips and Bloods.

For the next year or so after the murders we enjoyed some neutrality because we were neither Black Panthers or in anyway associated with the US Organization. The Nation of Islam was more of a prominent fixture in our community than either revolutionary group. Their strict adherence to discipline and moral fortitude was a little bit for us although the Nation of Islam wasn't deterred by our lack of interest. Tension was rising all over the city, we started to have brushes with other teens basically over girls and the jealousy they generated from others. The killing of Bunchy Carter allowed the charisma of Raymond Washington to obtain our allegiance. Between him and Black Johnny and a host of others Denker Park was convinced to side with the Crips against all else. Until that point I enjoyed the freedom to go where ever I felt like going without having any thought of another Black person being some kind of enemy. Neighborhood lines started being drawn in terms of a group territory.

August 1967, the F.B.I. initiated COINTELPRO to disrupt and neutralize organizations which the Bureau characterized as Black Nationalist's Hate Group.

ల్ల

Senate Committee to study Government Operation.
With Respect
Intelligence Activities United States Senate
April 23, 1976

I was a child trying to find my way out of darkness. I knew nothing about COINTEL, agent provocateurs, or the corporate media dehumanization programs. I enjoyed Black exploitation films until I bled from disjointed illusions of what constituted a man. Now the same powers provide me with cellmates with devastated souls and confused identifications.

Embedded in the essence of being Black was a fear of subjugation, humiliation or an outright assault on your physical being. The whole concept of unity and Black pride wasn't designed to gain advantage over another brother but to achieve some equity from those who coveted power. Clearly a Black man possessed no official power. Agents of the F.B.I., with the assistance of local police and the media had launched covert operations to destroy those who sought civil rights. Once Black men started demanding equal rights and demonstrated a willingness to protect himself against whomever aggress upon them, he was then demonized in the media. His portrait was grayed before the public. Societal problems and injustices became the result of his presence eluding the fact that he was going to be the first to suffer from any societal shortcoming.

A man can only die once, and dead men make no excuses.

ల్ల

Bumpy Johnson

I have no way of knowing to what extent that the Federal Government utilized agent provocateurs to nurture and exasperate hostilities between those fighting for freedom to live as human beings equal to other beings. History speaks unfondly of Ron Karenga and the federally funded US organization. According to Senate Committee hearing evidence he was working with the F.B.I. as an agent provocateur to create genocidal conditions within the Black community. They state that on May 2, 1970, "The Los Angeles Division is aware of the mutually hostile feeling harbored between the organizations and the first opportunity to capitalize on the situation will be maximized. It is intended the US Inc, will be appropriately and discretely advised of the time and location of Black Panther Party activities that the two organizations might be brought together and thus grant nature the opportunity to take her due course." When the police provide intelligence and logistics on your enemy then you are working with or for the police.

There were a lot of strange occurrences taking place. Two punk kids could have a one on one fight and become the source of breaking news alerts that claimed they were gang members from ironically none existent gangs. Songs were aired on the radio that voiced lyrics to a generic beat claiming to be Crip Dogs. No one within the Crips knew who was responsible for recording this song. Most people were still torn between seeing each other being divided by gang rivalry. Mysteriously military intended flamethrowers, cases of 30-30 Winchester, M-1 carbines and cases of 38 special handguns were being stumbled across in places frequented by teens or being made accessible to thievery. It didn't take long before the honor of hand-to-hand combat was lost to gunplay.

I was enjoying the comradery, partying and was really beginning to appreciate the beauty in the smile of a young girl. I was attending

> We will make them rip each other's hearts apart and kill their own children. We will accomplish this by using hate as our ally, anger as our friend. The hate will blind them totally and never shall they see that from their conflicts we emerge as their rulers. They will be busy killing each other. They will bathe in their own blood and kill their neighbors for as long as we see fit.
>
> ⌘ ⌘
>
> The Secret Covenant, Book of Shadows

158

Foshay Jr. High School as a 7th grader. I had no meticulous plan for my future navigating the moment was my sole priority. I was never the subject of bullying because I was willing to fight. Calling me out by my name would suffice, if you wanted a squabble. I wasn't going to allow someone to wear himself out by running his mouth. I had been trained to get off first, and that's probably why some preferred me on their team.

Like generations before me safeguarding my community was apart of what was expected by men and I had accepted that challenge. A crime against my neighbor became a crime against me. A group of us hanging out meant absolutely nothing to neighbors whether they be young or old because we posed no threat to them. In the beginning Ronnie Fuse, Jede and Big James warned us about parasites and many were rejected from membership because they just didn't have the heart to be from Harlem. Ironically, once we were decimated by law enforcement, their parasites took center stage claiming to be OG's opening the door to a tragic comedy.

If summoned by a pretty smile I took liberty to travel across Los Angeles with no real fear or animosity towards people from other geographical locations. Occasionally I would cross paths with dope fiends that I knew, but I had lost interest in their activities. It was often bewildering to receive news of someone my age using heroin or having been found dead somewhere from an apparent overdose. Using hard dope was forbidden by the homies. Even drinking in public was frowned upon because you had to be ready to defend yourself at all times.

> The search for dignity is understood instinctively by those who hold the clubs and who recognize that apart from violence the best way to undermine dignity is by humiliation. That is second nature in prisons.
>
> ～～
> Noam Chomsky

I bought my first raggedy car when I was thirteen years old. My life was good because a car could get me to where ever it was happening. Attending school became difficult on more than one level but Big Yard made sure I got there regardless of what time I went to sleep. As my hormones raged out of control and a 1954 Chevy sped my world up, I crossed the city from Watts to Venice and from Carson to Altadena. I might show up full of desire and ready to cash in on the promise of sex.

Gangs were becoming part of the fixture in Los Angeles with the help of the media and police. Strange things were happening and idiots could become famous overnight. Hustlers earned their status by what resided in their own pocket. A man doesn't boast of another man's fortune where as some gang members gain notoriety through association and not own their own merit, which brought the credibility of some aspiring tough guys into question. We groomed each other with ass whippings. By the time we came out in public there wasn't that many people of comparable size that were capable of winning a fair fight with any of us.

We didn't openly advocate it, but most of us thought we were players. The cash over ass kept us chasing a dollar and we relaxed with the beauty of a female. Beauty wasn't isolated to our neighborhood and pursing the obsession while being bewitched by charm could lead to confrontation. As a rule we didn't fight over girls. If someone had been mesmerized by a female to the point of being willing to engage in violence over her, then he was informed to do so on a personal level as it wasn't Harlem business. That kept our disputes isolated.

Things changed when one of the homies was invited to a party by a girl. He put on his best clothes to go on a date. As he was enjoying the company of a lady friend he was accosted by members of a street gang called the Brims. Physically they didn't really hurt him. What they bruised the most was his ego and they took his leather coat. Instead of facing reprimand and gathering the troops he returned to the area of being disrespected and killed the man who robbed him for his leather coat. I don't know what was running through their mind when they took his coat. After all he was running with Harlems, they should have known that it was bound to get ugly. When Lil Country got killed they immediately did a whole lot of huffing and puffing like they were mad until the homie showed up at the funeral wounding some mourners and placing a couple more bullets in the corpse. The game had changed.

There were grown men with full beards who were out of school coming up to Foshay Jr. High School bullying kids and chasing middle school girls as they picked up their baby's mama. That stopped once we introduced their child molesting country asses to an Harlem ass whipping. Their girlfriends were impressed by boys their own age kicking the asses of men who had led them to believe they were tough. That moment of awe shook their panties clean off their ass, and standing for something was then rewarded.

At this point in life I still wasn't threatened by community activities. Foshay Jr. High School was having dances at lunch and on Friday nights. Denker Park threw dances regularly. Each week there had to have been at least six parties being thrown by someone going to my school. At school I had hooked up with this boy named David. He didn't gang bang at all. He was riding high on the fact that the most popular girls at the school had a crush on him and had invited him to go to a party. So he and I joined forces for the night hoping for it to end in a pleasurable experience.

We walked to these girls house on 37th Drive and Western Ave plotting on how to best position ourselves to be blessed with sex that night. The party was three long blocks away. We had to pass directly by my house to get to the party. We had decided that I would steal some weed from my stepfather to enhance our chances of actually achieving our goal. So when we passed my house I ran in to get a couple of joints. It didn't take anytime at all to acquire what I was after. The party was only two blocks away by then on Budlong Ave and 36th Street. By the time I retrieved the joints and got a block away from the party people were warning me to stay away because as soon as thirteen year old David got to the party they had beat him to death. Things would never be the same.

Even though David wasn't a Harlem Crip his murderers boasted about killing a Harlem. That turned out to be a big mistake. Because then the Harlem Crips took it personal, and set aside hustling to wage war that none of our enemies were ready for. The L.A. Brims were the largest gang in the city of Los Angeles. We decimated them. Whipped them into extinction. Now their territory is divided amongst Hoovers, East Coasts, Neighborhoods 40's, 60's, 55's, 58's and 8 Tray gangsters. Most of their leaders left town and the majority of what remained turned Crip of one kind or another. They should have left us alone in our pursuit of a dollar.

Then we turned our attention to our western nuisance, the Black P. Stones and whipped them into submission. By the time we were through with them they had one block in the jungles, August Street. We gave birth to School Yards, Marvin's and Gear St. and West Blvd. Without us they would all still be Bloods. We did allow a select few to defect to our ranks.

The Twenties were a joke and often confusing. One minute they were professing to be Harlem Crips and the next minute they were Hoover family. Their main enemy was or should have been 18th Street. They shared their neighborhood with a Mexican gang called the Harpy's who were a punching bag for the stronger 18th Street Mexican gang. I have yet to figure out why they chose an unwinnable war with Harlem. It didn't make sense. They had a house here and there, they didn't really have a neighborhood because they shared a community with Mexicans. Some things aren't supposed to make sense to me.

At one time the Van Ness Boys were deep with a lot of older members. Their leadership was treacherous and manipulative. They would declare a truce anytime they were in a no win situation Then they killed a pregnant female because she was having a baby by someone that lived in my community but didn't associate with anyone from Harlem. The majority of their neighborhood is now divided amongst the 40's and 60's neighborhoods. They should have stuck to their word and honored the truce instead of tasting defeat.

At David's funeral I was introduced to the spirit of My N.O.T. and we sat quietly observing the tears of angry frustration being revealed by those attending the service. Even though David wasn't actually from Harlem he was the first casualty that could be attributed to our death count. My N.O.T. took the murder personal and pursued exacting revenge on those he believed responsible. We got tight playing in death's throes. My N.O.T. had watched too much television and fancied himself as some kind of gunslinger. I was drawn to him because he didn't identify with wearing masks at all. His world was dark, pained and he didn't fear death, at all. Many people assumed due to my relationship with him that I wouldn't make it to see my sixteenth birthday. My N.O.T. and I accepted that revelation as a possible truth that served to validate a need to be respected while we still had breath in our bodies.

Enemies were speeding past my house discharging firearms, cruising the neighborhood pretending to be looking for me, but in my presence would recoil in fear. Some declared themselves my enemies that I had no knowledge of who they actually were, threatening my life without cause. I guess talking tough made some people feel tough. I am still breathing, so they weren't the killers they professed to be. There were a few foes that My N.O.T., myself and the rest of the Crips wanted to hurt like Terry Cadeaux, from the L.A. Brims. Ironically, I ran across him in the penitentiary and respected the feel of his spirit. The only true difference between him and I was geographical. The mental characteristics were striking, and I had to decline an invitation by his beautiful younger sister GiGi to join their family. I had once entertained animus thoughts about him. Once we had the time to sit and talk I respected him as a man. This was during a time when I had lost respect for some who professed to be my homies. They were traitorously joining any group available in search of a power that they lacked internally, unabashedly bargaining off the principles of loyalty and integrity to stand with strangers against the family.

It's natural for us to allow loved ones to get away with doing things that we would never allow enemies or strangers to get away with. You can have homies that stand by your side out of love. Then you have homies that stand by your side with jealousy and envy, which nurtures a real bitch-nigga in their heart. My N.O.T. and I played a lot of tough street games with a host of dangerous dudes. I never would have fathomed that some who stood for what I represented could be so unlike what they chose to profess to be about. Just because a nigga claims to be Harlem, don't mean that his heart is into it. My homies had become my exended family, I was loving them. I was prepared to step into the darkness for them and my community on a moment's notice. What I failed to fathom was the tenets of fear and jealousy. As I played by the rules and enjoyed the rewards of keeping it real, some homies looked in envy. Gangbanging was an unnecessary distraction for me. I associated getting a dollar with being a man, believing that economic success would elevate me to matters and issues that men dealt with. Thus leaving adolescent activities to teenagers. Beyond dealing with the drama, my focus was on getting a dollar. I found great satisfaction in reaping the benefits of being fancied by a young girl. I knew what a trick was and I had an idea of what a sucker was. It was unimaginable that those I looked eye to eye with would patiently wait for me to pull my penis out of a loving girl to enjoy a moment of desirous condoling. They found pleasure in putting their lips on the lips of a girl whose mouth still carried the odor of my membrane. What was really dismaying about some homies was the absence of loyalty. He played the role of informant

> Death is not the greatest loss in life.
> The greatest loss is what dies inside while we are still alive.
>
> ∽
> Tupac Shakur

to taste my seed, while he rode with me pretending to represent the same principles that I did. When the back door games had run their course and what had transpired in the dark came to light then I realized what a mistake I had made by assuming that every one that claimed Harlem did so out of the same love that I had for the homies.

Over some unpossessable pussy, a homie wanted me dead, or vanquished off to a penitentiary.

We went from Denker Park Boys to being known as the Harlem Crips. Under that banner we engaged enemies for the next couple of years. By 1973 we were enjoying the spoils of war and was mercifully allowing enemies along with cliques outside of our territory to join our ranks under our new name, Harlem Godfathers. Death definitely began to track our egos. In the summer of 1973 we foolishly flexed our muscles by amassing several hundred Harlem Godfathers at a Black Celebration called Wattstax. Our numbers defied the police as we maintained the order in one of the most festive and without real incident events ever attended by thousands of African Americans in the city of Los Angeles without assistance from the police. We partied for hours in a real sense of community and pride.

Unwisely, I still held on to the dream of transcending the moment of finding love and establishing myself as a man with my own family. By the time I was fifteen years old I was trying to veer my life back onto the track of being concerned with getting a dollar. The O'Jays said it best, "They smile in your face, all the time wanting to take your place, the Backstabbers." Between the parasites who awaited their opportunity to suck blood from the living and the Chief of Police, Darryl Gates whom had declared war on local gangs as though he bared no responsibility for their creation I was in trouble. The parasites that had implanted their fangs within my flesh were directing all the drama my way. Like real bitches they made sure the police knew who I was.

With the help of the media

> *Wattstax brilliantly captures how the urban rebellions nurtured a strong sense of community pride that reached its zenith in the Black power and Black Arts movement of the late 1960s and early 1972. Conversely, the vicious backlash by the state, law enforcement and National Guards anticipated the rise of mass incarceration and the expansion of the modern "carcereal" state in the decades to come.*
>
> ❧ ❧
>
> *Donna Murch*

the word gang member, became a code word in the conscious of most people that justified killing. L.A.P.D. was openly taking things personal and would threaten to kill you like rival gang members. If you ran too often, you might spend the rest of your life in a wheelchair from a bullet in the spine. Some people mysteriously came up dead after being threatened by them. Obviously they recruited from amongst your own ranks for intelligence and logistics, which they freely shared with antagonistic overtones with rival gangs.

Ronnie Fuse, Big James Miller, Jede, Dead Eye, Michael Johnson, all found themselves incarcerated on various charges. With the real leadership in jail the mindless were required to think. I disbanded the Harlem Godfathers and retained all gang-conquered territories. The police and the courts concocted a clean streets policy with an arbitrary law called malicious mischief. The streets were being cleaned by that statute of law, along with curfew violations. They could detain you at 9:30 pm, question you until 9:45 pm, have you at the police station at 10:00pm, then charge you with a curfew violation despite the fact you were in their custody for the last thirty minutes. After being instrumental in the fostering of Black on Black crime Darryl Gates and his boys from the L.A.P.D. became the captors of those they dehumanized, demonized and desensitized to oppression.

These were truly glorious times within the lodges of the Klu Klux Klan. They could take off their ceremonial hoods and become patriots, advocates of law and order. Under the guise of right wing conservatives they could attack any social program they deemed beneficial to Blacks. With the media in their pockets deception was only limited by one's creative juices and the ills of America became Black issues.

They even employed the theories of Willie Lynch who taught slaveholders how to divide Africans by trivial characteristics like the tone of one's color. Racists recruited prostitutes of color to push their agenda across America. Now days house Negroes stand against anything beneficial to Blacks, while draped in African garb.

They have been employed by the Heritage Foundation and other right wing groups to advocate their cause. Hollywood has made whores out of fake gangsters that disparage themselves for a small bounty. Anytime you degrade and disrespect yourself you are a hoe. To make songs that have no value outside of disrespecting your own moma is whorish. Who would pay someone to say Nigga, Nigga, Nigga repeatedly but someone who don't like you. Sex with an enemies women is exciting when the bitch is shouting terms of submission and calling you Daddy at the top of her voice.

I listen to these rappers qualifying their tough talk by claiming to be gangbangers. I don't know how you can do that without gangbanging. The tough talk that they advocate would have my kids locked up within twenty-four hours for the rest of their lives. I don't believe them. I do wonder about who is paying idiots to advocate foolishness. They wouldn't walk the yard at Folsom State Prison safely with nigga, nigga, nigga coming out of their filthy mouths for long at all. They will be shown the light to hardship or protective custody for sure with their fake tough asses. I don't respect anyone who encourages my children to an early grave or the horrors of life in the penitentiary.

Everybody wants street credibility, saying that they are from here or there. They need to quit playing and acknowledge that they are what men step on along their path to fulfillment. The Harlem 30's have their share of parasites. Those whose career was built upon authentic street values like Ice-T. Then he is quoted in Don Diva magazine talking about how he played the hood and how he always thought that he was smarter than everybody in the community. Somehow he has forgotten about the broken spirits that littered the community. He ignores the dead and those rotting in America's prisons that he sought credibility from. As Shakespeare and Tupac state, "A coward dies a thousand deaths, but a soldier dies but once."

We have experienced parasites who proudly classify themselves as dope dealers while claiming to be a warrior of the community. The punk ain't never done nothing in service to the community besides feed his neighbor dope. The living and the dead know what a catastrophe drugs have reeked upon our community. Yet they proudly use that title as glorification of their existence. Well, a hoe with money is still a hoe, and they can't drive a Maybach in Folsom and don't nobody care about them having money. Big talk don't make a big man. Some like Ricky Freeway Ross should be tried by the community on charges of genocide. He worked with the federal government to sell drugs and weapons in his own community, and like a good hoe turned most if not all the money in to fund a war in Nicaragua. The San Jose Mercury News along with Rosalind Muhammad of the Final Call reported his genocidal acts. Instead of hiding in shame he pursues movies and books to depict him as a celebrity. He is more suitable as fertilizer. The man worked with L.A.P.D. and the Feds separately as he snitched on everybody he did business with. The acts of him and his kind have done more damage to my community than Aids and gang violence combined. He helped destroy the moral fiber of a people and wrecked many individuals with his cowardice ass.

Life can often be complex, especially when you have in your mists those who profess loyalty to an ideal of honor but hate the concept of integrity. I come from a community that was full of women and children and we were sworn to protect them against whomever. I don't know when it became alright to be a rapist and still claim to be part of a community. There is nothing honorable or tough about taking pussy and those who partake in those activities should practice on their own mother. Harlems don't do things like that. We came together as players, not tree jumpers. For all them tough guys who have never engaged an enemy and have lived a life fighting your neighbors you do not count amongst men. Save that fraudulent war story for someone who loves you, I don't believe it. I don't know what to say about the man who disparages his own when in the company of enemies and outsiders but professes to be from Harlem. They should go and live amongst those they love and respect and stop muddying the image of the community with their spineless ass.

By the time I was fifteen or sixteen I was cool on gangbanging. Had actually enough of it. My money was sufficient for my needs, and I was enjoying young love. What I didn't understand was that the streets weren't through with me. People I didn't even know attempted to make themselves look tough amongst their peers by threatening me over issues that weren't my concern. Some of those around me wanted to wear my shoes and embarked on playing bitch games where I would become the sacrifice. Boys got a new gun and sought me out for target practice, then testified against me when I shot their punk ass. I knew then that there had to be a better life somewhere.

I needed an extraction plan from my community to circumvent learned responses to aggression and the environment. In my heart I sincerely wanted a good life but my mind was programmed to the behavior that I knew. I stumbled between other people's problems on a daily basis, which pushed my personal issues to the back of my thought process. I had become the big homie regardless of my commitment to that role or not. I wasn't smart enough to depart from everything I knew.

I could sense disaster approaching but was too dumb to do much about it. I continued to stand my ground and make feeble attempts at changing the course of doom. I had people coming around me that pretended to like me even though they had true cause to feel differently. I also coexisted with people that I couldn't have cared less about. Finally they introduced me to my undoing.

A spineless boy of little worth whom had his car taken a couple of years earlier which was found stripped by my house came by seeking a minor favor. The boy he had with him was the victim of repeated robberies by other member of the community. I agreed to call the wolves off and allow him to coexist in peace. We weren't friends at all and he wasn't from Harlem. Like an idiot I bit on a story that he relayed to me about himself. The boy told me about where he lived and before his family had moved to the

Dirty Thirties. The height of my feeble plan was to get away from the chaos of the life I was living by finding some pretty female to fulfill a dream of being happy that lived a safe distant away from circumstances that were ugly. Harlem was on the verge of civil war due to bitch-niggas. The 30's had accumulated the muscle to win a war against Harlem's. I kicked it with both sides and it was uncomfortable knowing that mayhem was justified. When you wrong another person, you place the responsibility of righting that wrong in his hands. At that point nobody gives a damn about who you know if they are committed to right a perceived wrong.

Thinking that I might find a way out of the bullshit I was in, I allowed this boy to lure me away from my community with the objective of finding love. Instead of pulling up at a female's house he runs into a store and attempts to rob it. It all went bad. Two of us were shot and one of the owners of the store was murdered without cause.

Thirty-eight years later I still can't justify being involved in the death of someone who wasn't playing the game I was playing. In hindsight I should have never gotten into a car with a previous victim. There was no love or loyalty between us. As soon as we made it to the penitentiary he joined the first prison gang that stuck their hand out to him and was stabbed to death soon afterwards by another prison based rival gang. He robbed me of the last 37 years of my life wanting to be a gang member and as soon as he found acceptance he was murdered anyway.

There are not a lot of happy stories attached to gangbanging. Pushing that line for respect creates a candidate for the graveyard or the penitentiary. A few were lucky enough to make it through the wrath. Many are forced to admit what they are not, which gives birth to self-deception and they will never be much more than the lies they tell to perfect the mask of being a warrior. Death, and the mirror in which they look, knows differently.

Fighting over nothing is stupid. Murdering your own brother is unnatural. There is something twisted that allows a man to hate himself more than the enemy who taught him to fear. Some bring their own personal issues to that game, and act out accordingly. That game was designed for us as a knee jerk action over fleeing civil rights victories of the 1960's by people who hate us and promulgated by their flunkies. After the blood was shed it became easy to forget love and what trivialness ignited the feud.

Everybody has their own reason for playing a game that tithers on self-destruction. Many a family has drowned in the sorrow of their tears due to a lack of understanding of the vastness of evil minds. My strength isn't of this world. I am propelled by the spirits of those who have passed before me sacrificially as a Harlem Crip to warn our children away from the pitfalls of hate. Nothing is begot from hate outside of a theft from one's own sense of humanity. It creates a void within one's soul, and subjects one to subjugation and incarceration by those who profit from our despair.

I am disheartened by the descent of what was an honorable rite of passage into manhood. At the end of the day you came of gang follies a man. These days what they are doing has no meaning. When they are not protecting and serving they lose the shield of street warriors and become the opposite of what was intended, 'parasites.' Feeding off the life and blood of their community. Amazingly, soon as they hit the county jail they espouse conviction ripping was based on seek the protection and camaraderie that they should of been providing for their community. They detest raping and robbing each other. Although those same acts were acceptable when pillaging their neighbors. Instead of trying to substantiate a sense of decency for their neighbors, gang members have allowed the commercialization of their culture to cause them to lose focus of the meaning of a man. The evolutionary process entails that someday we shed the buffoonery and self-denigrating images provided to us and institute family values that not only benefit our immediate loved-ones, but also your neighbors. Unless you are a professional dancer, grown men shouldn't be worried about crip walking, or what colors to wear. Some have failed to transcend from adolescence games, and find themselves infantile in thinking like men of a world stage. They play dangerous, but in the meaning of what it is to be a man the act is embracing. 'Superficial.' They should quit playing something lesser than what they are capable of being.

My best teacher revealed himself during an internal preparation for death. Who I wanted to be on judgment day became more important than the perspective of men. Knowledge dispelled false pride as a human defect. Struggling and suffering may be what makes a man.

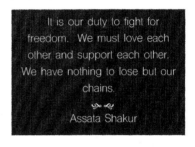

It is our duty to fight for freedom. We must love each other and support each other. We have nothing to lose but our chains.

Assata Shakur

With a good heart and happy thereafter intentions, I played myself right out of pocket. There was no peace in my life. I was armed with a litany of genuine excuses that spawned more upheaval. While blinded by chaos I was deficient in foresight. I relied on faith to navigate me through the darkness when in fact I needed a logical plan to guide me thorough turmoil. Death was ever present, and my future was cloudy. My biggest impediment came from not understanding past conditioning, or where I stood at that moment, personally and socially. I had changed my style but unknowingly the game was the same. Despite my lack of interest in the bullshit part of gang banging I still found myself involved in matters that were irrelevant to me. I was trying to muscle my way through disappointment and pains with a gun in my pocket. It took a long time before I realized my thinking was the problem. Trying to navigate life with a kaleidoscope of half-truths and rhetoric invited failure. Indifference became a dependable defense mechanism that often overshadowed my intense love for some people in my life. Outside of the homies no support system existed and I was being driven from one accident to the next due to a lack of thoughtful calculation of future plans.

My ideals of man, family, and community were intact. Although, I still had to deal with those who paraded around me as homies but lacked the morals, love and honor of being part of that community. A collective mindset was festering in the mud that okayed pillaging amongst neighbors. Everybody that smiled in my face didn't like me, and friendship based upon fear is meaningless. Painful circumstances and stupidity was leading me straight to the graveyard. Instead of resting in peace, I found myself sitting in a dimly lit room with several other convicted murderers trying to figure out how I got there in the first place. Surely being in prison wasn't by design. These once a week meetings were being held by Dr. Isaac Slaughter, an African American Psychologist who in time I garnered a great deal of respect for.

Initially all this was just some jailhouse activity that meant very little to my life. These folks were foreigners to the world I knew so I didn't expect them to understand my inner void, confusion and apparent mental rigor mortis of the brain. Even though their lifestyles didn't appeal to me, I participated cautiously. Some of these men's stories were bullshit and others were a little bit crazy. After a while my true desires, resolve and intellect came into question. It's one thing to deceive others about who I really am with clichés, platitudes and boast about a mindset of self-destruction, human failures and unrealistic portrayals of a future I couldn't really see. I was full of mottos that sounded good but I lacked the insight to what they actually meant in terms of being human. Clearly there was a divide between slogans that occupied my brain and what resided in my soul. My voice was muted by an internal death that had occurred way before I found myself convicted of murder. Physical death was assumed preferable to a life in the penitentiary. Privately, my purpose for existing was a burning question within me. I needed some clarification in trying to obtain some inner peace and justify continuing to breathe.

When I first arrived on this blossoming plantation an old convict whom had spent twenty-four years of his life on three separate terms of touring hell took me into his tutelage. He counseled and tried to cram as much of his life experiences in me as possible before I was transferred to another institution. There were only so many places in this man made hell to occupy while you serve your time. You can momentarily empower yourself by joining a prison gang or find your salvation in religion. Many chose the role of a coward and submitted to every power that stands before them without compunction. Some are capable of being another man's girlfriend, others associate love with a man's buttock. Education and rehabilitation have been all but outlawed and severely diminished by the state in an effort to build the self-esteem of uneducated staff. Family ties have come under attack. Rehabilitation is a joke within a culture that's wedded philosophically to punitive ideations. Seeking a cause for one's transgressions against societal norms become a pariah the scope of prison as a profitable industry.

From the peephole that allows me a glimpse of life, it's not often that I find absolute truth coming from the mouths of those who are most adamant about reality. Truth is subjective to one's perspective and many easily adopt the words of hypocrites and shortsighted traitors as their own. Rhetoric doesn't prevail against the winds of time, nor does it prove fruitful in providing meaning to one's life. That old convict uttered something that mattered. A truth that could be revisited everyday for the rest of my life. Knowing that his opportunity to engage me beyond the superficial was escaping he posed the question of what purpose did I have in life? Honestly I could have rattled off some logical excuses for continuing to breathe but outside of being free my mind was numb to the concept of true meaning in one's life. He continued to push the analogy of why would a man continue to suck up fresh air when the right thing to do would be to take that one drop of honorable blood in your veins and act upon it, which would allow someone with any potential to occupy my worthless space. He stressed that a man without a purpose had no real reason for living. His perspective was that sleepwalkers were just props in some else's life.

We sat on prison bleachers enclosed by rolls of razor wire on three sides. Other prisoners milled around on a short leash playing baseball and lifting weights discussing the proposition of committing suicide. This impound provided one view of freedom and it was guarded by two gun towers that stood between us and institutional sheep that graze freely on a huge pasture. I was just starting a life sentence and what lie before me was less deadening than the freedom I had just left. Although his perspective posed a question that I had no immediate answer for, I don't think that he really understood that death was the least of my worries, everyone dies at some point. Being alive in the process of living was my problem. I had stumbled through life with indifference and void of true happiness looking for life, strangely the proposition of death may provide a cause for living.

The game I played you had to be ready to die for insignificant reasons at any time. His argument that I should commit suicide left me with the dilemma of finding a purpose that I could stand on in death, and thereafter. Knowing myself became more important than just transitioning to some other role life was prepared to offer. This lecture was meant more to motivate me into educating myself and nourishing whatever sense of decency that existed within me, above the dogma that I was better suited to be a corpse.

I found myself receptive to this indoctrination because I had moved through life accepting who played the role of being a homie even though their performance lacked authenticity. I went along and juggled bullshit with indifference until I was shot in the head in a robbery gone bad that was initiated by an idiot that I didn't even know. The issue I had with the circumstances was the fact that I thought so little of myself to risk my life for people and issues that meant nothing personally to me at all.

Due to a lack of concrete direction and meaning in my life I had entertained things and individuals that would prove to be worthless. The community had become under attack when someone gave pitiness the voice of a homie. The spirits of men were being muted by immorality and an unnatural collective mindset of evil was somehow substantiating the essence of a man.

Unbeknownst to me death and the penitentiary are close compatriots.

I had managed to escape the scene of a murder robbery leaving an unconscious crime partner and a dead innocent victim behind with a bullet in my head. That tragic evening was an accumulation of a life spent pursuing the wrong path. I lay in the backseat of the car physically dying from a gunshot wound and I was awakened to the potential of spiritually failing as a human being. I slipped out of consciousness and for the first time in my life sensed what tranquility truly was.

What began as an effort to maintain my freedom became a juggling act between life and death. I lay in the back of that car dying and bleeding from the neck, ear, nose and mouth, viewing my cohort's reaction to my death. I viewed them from above, in an out of body experience, scramble to relieve my pockets of all valuables. I listened to their frantic discussion on where to dump my body. It was interesting that there was no shortage of alibis to elude prosecution and explain to the homies how my murder was unrelated to that evening's crime because several people wanted me dead anyway.

Pandemonium dominated the vehicle for several different reasons. There was a presumed dead man in the backseat. They needed a cover story and gas was running low. Strangely while all this was taking place I was without fear, pain or insecurities. My life seemed to have left the chaos of the automobile and I found myself feeling the warmth of Moma as I travelled down a brilliantly illuminated cylinder where there was no fear or confusion. Within the death experience I was sensing a coveted peace. A peace that was undoubtedly forgotten at birth. Without a word being said, I sat in judgment paralyzed in amazement of the

Many have told that they felt that their Lives were broadened and deepened by their experience, That because of it they became more reflective And more concerned with ultimate philosophical issues.

Raymond Moody, M.D.

magnificent array of colors that seem to leap off glittering diamonds the size of cantaloupes. An omnipresence voice was discussing me without seeking my opinion in an all knowing realm of understanding. Excuses were useless. Standing on the actuality of my existence is what appeared to be under consideration. Two significant things came from that experience, my great grandmother would be hurt by my death and that I never had a chance.

I awoke to find my homies pulling on my legs. We were parked in an unlit alley and they had already relieved my body of anything valuable and were struggling to get rid of my body when I startled them. They had been driving around aimlessly convinced that I was dead. Opening my eyes threw in one more complication.

Somehow that old convict knew that peace for me dwelled in death, not in the life I had lived. He also made a strong suggestion that the peace I knew from a near death experience also existed in life but I would have to search my own soul for it.

I sat amongst this group of men reflecting on my recent experiences of death's tranquility but still too immature to trust the voices in my heart unless angered. Death before dishonor makes sense. The questions I needed answered most would eventually have to come from my own soul. I had to be honest with myself about the past and present to enable me to see a purpose for breathing.

I found very little value in attending therapy. The psychologist, Dr. Slaughter was cool and had achieved more in his life through education and determination than any other man that I personally knew. In our weekly meeting he would nod like a dope fiend. Sometimes saying nothing as we discussed whatever we chose to talk about. It didn't take long before I realized that he was a long way from being asleep. Our sessions were held during the evening in a barely lit room. We sat in a circle of lounge chairs and he allowed us to divulge pieces of ourselves as a ploy to get to relevant issues. Once you boxed yourself into an indefensible corner, he would come out of his nod and prove you wrong by your own standards. I had a hard head and most people couldn't have told me about my life without having worn my shoes. He knew racism up close and the pitfalls of the uneducated, so I had nowhere to hide with the excuses that fueled my ignorance.

I was so narrow minded that I believed the world was doing what I had been doing. He attacked the cornerstone of my beliefs. Because of my respect for his knowledge and sincerity, I accepted that I could be wrong about a lot of things. As my viewpoint loosened he pushed me further into education. The more I learned taught me how little I actually knew. It had been ingrained in me that white folks were not going to let me succeed in their society so why try. Dr. Slaughter arranged for some older convicts to engage me in book studies of my culture. Also, he persuaded staff that viewed young African American with contempt to not be an obstacle to my academic pursuits. The rest was up to me and I received a high school diploma.

My view of the world was formed by microscopic circumstances. The things that transpired in my small circle didn't occur across the street. Even though my life was in a shambles I held on to what I had been taught as desirable. Then Dr. Slaughter pointed out to me that out of 35 million people in California only 17 thousand found themselves in the penitentiary so in no way could that small group signify representation of the world. That bit of factual information shattered the cornerstone of my beliefs. I learned the definition of options and variables and realized that everyone's reality wasn't based upon my truth.

I knew the streets, my only real achievement rested in that narrow perspective on life. It became blatantly apparent that what I missed in my teaching was how a responsible man conducted himself around those he loved. Very few people knew that I was capable of compassion and love. What they witnessed was an assortment of images I had collected during my upbringing. I knew

to anyone who wanted to fuck with me overtly.   The
of empathy had been numbed, lost or stolen within me.

to get that ass, what somebody's mother felt as a result
of her son messing with the wrong boys wasn't a consideration of
mine.

Upon reflection the instructions that programmed my mind
pained my heart.   I feared my own inhumanity more than I feared
death,   The possibility of reaching the other side without any
valuable human traits is frightening. I tend to believe that's what
turns the heat up in hell.   Following my own heart became more
important than not being liked by anyone who had a role they
wanted me to play. Prison gangs meant nothing to me, I didn't
necessarily like or respect that game anymore.   There was a
similarity between jailhouse religious conversions and gangs.   I
didn't need anyone's protection nor was I willing to submit to a
leader of any domination or affiliation. I appreciated the wisdom of
all philosophies, but my heart was starting to speak for itself, and it
didn't need a mask to be understood in search of my authentic
self.   I had no desire to die in service of another man's cleverly
constructed attempt to shield his own insecurities with theories and
philosophies that lacked historical and scientific credibility.   Having
faith and being played are one and the same.

Life had stolen my voice, providing me with the ability to
listen.   Your soul can be a dangerous place to play, especially
when the core of who you are is worthless. Small people have big
mouths and smaller actions to substantiate their worth.   The mirror
and smoke performance of being superior is a comforting effort to
assimilate and prostrate to another man's definition of who you are
supposed to be. I wasn't sure about who I was but there was no
desire to be the pawn of a possible idiot.

Education dispels the foundation of excuses and gradually
opens the mind up to the presence of pretense especially when
you are in search of truth.   It was unbelievable that simply reading
a book could take a young African American male from the true
beginning of mankind with Isis and Osirus to the genius of Imhotep,

down to the spiritual courage of Nefertiti, Sojourney Truth, Harriet Tubman, Dickwood Dick, Marcus Garvey, Malcolm X, Muhammad Ali, Nelson Mandela and Congresswoman Barbara Jordan. The real horror from the detachment of histories knowledge is the neglect of a God given potential. Charlatans would like you to think that pride is a sin. Knowing your potential leads to a worthwhile prideful existence.

A lot of people know horror beyond my imagination and in search for inner peace it becomes easy to connect with humble people who were enslaved not by personal wrongdoing, but by evil. It doesn't take very much research to come across a history that speaks of beautiful, petite women feeding themselves and their children to sharks to preserve some dignity. Prison may bind you physically but you have to give away your mind and your heart. Circumstances dictated that I had to lose my freedom. Nothing within man's power can strip me of my soul and force me to parrot the rhetoric of deception.

Considering what I didn't want to be the next time I was summoned by death, led to personal inventories and acceptance of who I genuinely am. But it didn't provide a blueprint on what I was capable of achieving. I realized that was a matter for life, and death would be the judge of my personal choices. Some men chose to play in little worlds, doing little things, pretending to be large in the shadows, constructing traps for those who have absolutely nothing beyond the semblance of principles. Like fleas embedded around a dog's ass they fill their bellies with the last vestiges of morals a neighbor may cling to. Parasites don't

> *Death, by implication is an awakening and remembering.*
> *Plato remarks that the soul that has been separated from*
> *The body upon death can think and reason even more clearly than before, and that it can recognize things in their true*
> *nature far more readily. Furthermore, soon after death it*
> *faces a 'judgment' in which a divine being displays before*
> *the soul all the things — both good and bad- which it has done in its life and makes the soul face them.*
>
> ೞ ೞ
> *Plato's Phaedo*

venture far from the camouflage of the block. They know that without the psychic attachment to the title of being one's brother, homie or neighbor they may get slapped in the mouth by a man who is not deceived by their performance. Cowards are aware that they are cowards and are just too cowardly to reveal the lack of individual substance. They embrace the collective verbiage of being tough, and partake in the games of children with authority and shiver in the presence of men. Tragedy and misfortune are often the best of teachers for those who experience sacrifice in its totality. The coward glorifies the story, leaving out that he was hiding in the brushes when warriors performed like warriors. In a community where any resemblance of a male role model is craved by the inhabitants, the lesson of bloodshed and strife is lost when recounted by those who lack courage. A coward's view of reality differs from that of a man. In the same sphere a man can't adequately describe pain of child birthing, that's within the domain of women.

I noticed what made men shine in life and I also took into account what frightened other men about men. That left me ill equipped to cope with the total picture of life. It took awhile before it came crashing down upon me that life wasn't as simple as what was portrayed on the television show, *Have Gun Will Travel*. Neither is it realistic that a fifteen-minute brawl amongst neighbors leaves no hard feelings. Actions good or bad have consequences that are known and unknown. Everybody that hates you is not going to tell you about how they feel and fear is the foundation of hate.

There was a time when a simple trip to *Fat Burgers* could end in criminal acts to defend one's honor, unless you had no honor. While opportunity seemed a million miles away I played with what was the reality of a war zone. Guerrilla tactics were being displayed opportunistically daily until my identity got trapped within defining self-destruction. The streets, clergy or government officials didn't give a damn about what my heart sought, and weren't above being complicit in placing obstacles of foreboding and treachery in my path. Men of power proudly admit mining to lives of innocence with tragedy. Declaring that navigating minefields of self-destruction is a personal responsibility. Whether it is parental or as a result of this society, the death of a child is someone's fault.

Graveyards are filled with men and women who demonstrated courage before death, becoming someone's personal hero. Immaturity allowed me to become a magnet to defy death. Like a child I failed to construe the finality of death along with other actions that once committed could not be undone. Later in life I learned the wisdom of picking your battles wisely. But as a child I was an open invitation for whatever someone wanted to do. My people did not trust police at all for a litany of reasons and didn't much care for politicians who fought to preserve the status quo, Black or white. When your face is in the dirt you don't give a damn about whose foot is on your neck, you just want to breathe. A Black family that was foolish enough to approach the justice system for help was sacrificing their child to vultures.

Realizing that I had been methodically guided back into slavery connected me with the spirits of all those who suffered that atrocity against mankind. Fake drug wars, jail instead of treatment, removal of safety nets leads to chattel slavery and a boom in the prison industry.

> The United States world champion in incarceration is at once a delayed reaction to the civil rights movement and the ghetto riots of the mid-1960's.
>
> ∞ ∞
>
> Loic Wacquant,
> Class, Race and
> Hyperincarceration in
> Revanchist America

What makes the snake deadly is he doesn't make noise. The snake can smell your existence while you are oblivious to his presence. As you excitedly stick your hand into a barrel of fruit he strikes, stealing whatever dreams you may have had. We had no idea of governmental strategies to incarcerate specific demographics in a social structuring scheme that identified us as potential chattel for an industry that was declining statistically. Instead of elevating innovation the mindset of evil chose hyperincarceration. My community was bombarded with media seasoning that eroded love and fabricated a false sense of individual pride. It didn't take a lot of effort for agent provocateurs to recruit and put poison in the hands of insincere serpents that slithered amongst the brave for protection. Soon their job of establishing an acceptance of immorality and crime to the benefit of those who wish for the good ol' days of the Klu Klux Klan and Jim Crow was done.

Camaraderie is empowering, even in the absence of intellect. Despair can be mutually felt while the circumstances of the cause of that emotional condition remains hidden. The bond of two souls connecting can be stronger than those of biological ties. Accepting the responsibility of true friendship is a key ingredient in the development of a man. Only the mentally ill and those who are denied entry into manhood rest comfortably with only loving themselves. It is in a man's nature to shoulder more than his own weight. In a country where one might sense that he is not being treated as one's brother, symptoms of that human cruelty are not viewed within the scope of man's inhumanity to man, but sadistically criminalized. California has a three-strike law and some in the populace wish it was only one strike and your ass is out. Who in their right mind would embrace ideals that only evil would impose upon its brother. Apparently the pretense of the brotherhood of mankind has been abandoned. Hate is acceptable when resides in the house of strangers. When your babies get a taste of hate, it's not gratifying.

We tend to fend for ourselves when nobody else will. Unfortunately, a pursuit of honor can be waylaid into immorality and unintentional misfortune by parasites within your ranks, giving the noble and courageous a bad name. Just like a baby opens it eyes to the world, so does man have the ability to witness reality. If fortunate the baby will view the world with some clarity. Identifying the character of pretenders who are incapable of loving anything or anyone beyond themselves. Those who unconsciously feed impotent, consciously belittle love and honor. To mask their feelings of smallness they promote games of self-destruction.

For a long time I pursued a peace of mind in things that was outside of myself. I was hoodwinked into believing that my peace existed with external things. I viewed life with blinders on in search of a glimpse of myself. I had hoped that it would be all right someday. Turmoil is never far away from a lack of education and insight about one's environment. Especially when love is replaced with unnatural aims and naturally evil agendas. Many lost and shattered souls quiet their pain with drugs and alcohol in an effort to deaden themselves.

Sitting in the penitentiary is a definite sign that something was wrong in the life I was living. There are some people behind these walls that found themselves confronted with predesigned circumstances that required them to come to prison. Others are an accident waiting to happen. One morning I realized that I had become cynical of God, government and the homies. I neither existed in the revels of the past, nor was I delusional about the future. Grief has dredged out lines of pain upon my forehead while uncorking realization of a tragic path I had taken. A path that knows the glory of a warrior, and has cuddled with the tears of misfortune. Increasingly I have become more reliant on the dead for comfort and enlighten than I do the living.

Realizing the values of a civilized country and accepting what's inside of myself clued me on what it is to be human. Opening the consciousness to wrongs, socially and personally. Life can be unfair beyond one's comprehension and justice might not be on your side, leaving you conflicted over values that may only serve the designer of such thoughts. Some opt to cower into being defined by the powers possessed by the rich. Becoming someone's puppet, not realizing that the puppet master is smart enough to offer a variety of paths that will lead to a humiliating submission to his needs. I doubt that a man is capable of finding himself while wearing the face of someone else.

In these penitentiaries you have to be able to stand on your own patiently. This is hell, with all kinds of demons willing to claim you with their own ignorance. Fortunately I crave my own authentic dream and wanted to approach death genuinely secure on my own feet as a human being in spite of being uninformed on how treacherous the world can be when you can't see for yourself. I would rather fall short at realizing my full potential than failing to impersonate someone else.

It would have been nice to live the American dream. But life wasn't going to allow me to know that peace. If good was going to be achieved it would have to be obtained from some source close to my own heart. I had lost trust in what might be lurking in another man's heart. I came to prison believing in the absoluteness of God and country thinking that what was written, as law was concrete in meaning. I didn't look for that low-bottom craftiness in the verbiage of the honorable. I had been sentenced to a 7 to 13 years and that was supposed to be based upon my conduct in prison which was clearly defined by a matrix that categorized crimes. Thousands of authoritative words were written as law on the subject and thousands had been dealt with fairly by these sentencing statutes. After fifteen or twenty years of being in prison I had to accept that what I had been told about the absoluteness of law was bullshit.

I was reminded by imps of the 13th amendment of the U.S. Constitution that allowed slavery for those guilty of a crime. With the same tactics of real pimps, politicians were spitting elegant rants filled with half-truths and innuendos about the prize stock on a plantation. I then realized what it was to be a slave. The human in me was not being considered at all in those words. I had become an economic commodity in the portfolio of those who benefitted from societal ills. Seeing a beneficiary awaken the idea of root causes, toiling the soil, seeding the dirt and who ultimately profits from a social product.

I started playing in the dark at a young age weary but not fearful of death's presence. In my most exhilarating moments death was with me. Sitting upon my right shoulder, keeping a watchful eye and noting my every action. In my youth I misinterpreted voices from my own soul, wrote them off as confusion. I didn't heed to the signs of death thinking that a man is not suppose to fear anything. In fact, the more life challenging a situation became, the more I was drawn to it. Prison has never been a home to me. The smell of nauseating food and unwashed inmates has never made me feel welcome. I have meandered in prisons throughout the state of California as payment for my wrongs against society. Not acknowledging the fresh ocean scent or a gentle breeze in a room void of circulation. I didn't give significance to things that I didn't understand. Then visions of dead loved ones and martyrs that I have no way of knowing began to play a large role in my subconscious providing some peace in my dreams.

Either we spend a lot of energy deceiving ourselves about who we are or we accept our truths and build upon that. There is no hiding from oneself behind these walls. Spirits stripped of camouflage speak more profoundly, their meaning is better understood regardless of who they truly are. Everything alluring is not necessarily good and valuable time is lost on navigating deception. There is a truth moving amongst us that only death can substantiate. I find strength in relying on the definitiveness of mortality. Dying is not the question when death beckons me to join it's ranks. It's important that I give credence to my existence, validating universal mysteries beyond of the fleeing nightmarish righteousness of man.

The prison experience will teach you how little life can offer. Rolls Royce dreams can be replaced by wishes for a simple hot shower. In time you will suffer from the reality of loss. Being handcuffed in a cage while those I love succumb to vices and parasites is a disheartening recognition of one's own failures. You can't love someone and not be pained by their troubles, especially when your presence would have altered events. Sitting in here watching the feeding frenzy of parasites unfold can generate a hate that allows you to stand either for or against someone. Taking no position at all is the stance of a coward.

I mistakenly entertained foolishness from a lack of knowledge when it came to my freedom. I believe that those holding the key to my freedom could see when I was ready to be released in some kind of empirical knowledge of mind and spirit. Instead fine chicanery was employed to deny me a human existence. The world was being desensitized in levels equal to the levels of inhumanity I was being subjected to. Faith in things outside of myself waned as my spirit relied on African American history for an explanation about the transition from rehabilitation to the hyperincarceration of inmates to better protect society. Which resulted in the communization of inmates to the benefit of profiteers of human bondage.

The tactics of divide and conquer strips a community of pride and unity. To be ravaged by principles based upon evil, immortality and drugs guarantees the creation of walking cadavers.

It's a curious phenomenon to witness a mindset of someone who will fight his own brother at the bequest of strangers. Anything that destroys my own house can't be good for me. The power of drugs can make little men appear large and quiet the voice of large men by glamourizing superficial guises. Power doesn't always work for the good of the people and more often is sought by the weak to quiet their insecurities. The destitute can be lifted to nobility, as royalty is disgraced.

When evil prevails ignorance is allowed to repeat itself and we find ourselves muddling through one fabrication of the truth after another. Twenty first century slavery is doing well in a society that only holds five percent of the world population but 25 percent of all the people incarcerated on this planet. Crime and punishment has been made a Black male problem through all the resources made available to this powerful nation. Instead of vagrancy laws entrapping us, gangs, drugs, and mental health issues have been fostered and exasperated to eradicate those who emerge differently.

According to the United States Justice Department the nation spends approximately 80 billion dollars a year on crime. My existence no longer depends upon who I am or my ability to function without the use of violence or thievery. I am getting pimped. I am worth $47,201 to somebody and they want their money. The shattered family I left behind don't matter to criminal justice profiteers. They could care less about what makes me human, livestock is perceived as not having a heart and mind.

The mindset of the good ol' boys really showed itself in the philosophies of establishing a penal system based upon Draconian theories of punishment. Naturally little people want to see me as they see themselves, effeminate and subservient. This state has stripped inmates of everything of value starting with family ties. Visiting went from seven days a week to two days and the process of visiting is meant to deter strong family bonds. Anyone who endures the humiliating process of visiting really loves the inmate. Educational programs that offered quality marketable skills to inmates were abandoned to increase employment opportunity for correctional staff. According to United States Attorney General Eric Holder, "Incarceration should be used to punish, deter, and rehabilitate. Not merely to convict, warehouse and forget." The diabolical systematic dehumanization of a man who consciously watches himself be devalued as a human to the point of becoming livestock is shattering to one's existence. Any form of murder is wrong by any standard of being a decent human being until it got to me. Now psychological, spiritual, and physical death is all right for financial profit and political gain.

Programs that were designed to enhance me, as a person were subject to be discontinued because I was no longer worthy of specialized training or self-help. Funding for those programs went directly into increasing the pay of staff who were especially happy to take high school equivalency education achievements and received the same pay as those who sacrificed to obtain doctoral degrees. God was definitely good to followers of bigotry and draconian mindsets. Evil spewed from the hearts of those that modeled themselves as exemplary models of what I should be, while sounding like hateful criminals.

It shook my belief in the moral foundation of justice when its representatives starting spouting the rhetoric of hate from their position of power over me. I am doing a life term for murder which I accept all responsibility for. The length of my incarceration and all factors of my case were well substantiated in written law well before I was born. So I was dismayed by the nonsense and whimsical thoughts of my keeper. I felt like they wanted me to grovel in my own vomit while they urinated on me. Any signs of integrity meant you were unsuitable for parole. They gave me a parole date just to take it back for fictional reasons. I was stunned, confused and the only thing I could absolutely rely on was the promise of death. Reaching for its doors the man I wanted to be became more important than the ideals of men I personally no longer believed in.

Naturally there was the possibility that I was wrong and the system was right about what I felt. Then I read a declaration from a

Parole Board member who granted and rescinded my parole date. Albert M. Leddy a representative on the Board of Prison Terms states, "Governor Wilson, substantially intervened to reduce parole grants, in actual affect his policy practically eliminated paroles. He accomplished this, first by appointing and re-appointing BPT commissioners known to disfavor parole or to favor a 'no-parole' policy. These appointees were all crime victims, former law enforcement personnel or Republican legislators who had been defeated in elections and who needed a job. I am aware that he wanted previously set parole dates rescinded." They snatched my life away from me due to their personal failings. Twenty-five years later they still refuse to apologize for violating their own laws and policies to enslave me.

My nightmare includes inmates who sleepwalk through life. These idiots often parrot the ideology of their masters without real thought of their role on the plantation. Drugs have produced a rare inmate who is as firm in his addiction, as he is submissive to the agents of his demise. Many are willing to exist in these decadent dungeons as skeletons of what was human, for the purpose of feeding an eighty billion dollar corporation in which they are the commodities. A lie is still a lie regardless of how it is spun.

It is logical that as President of the United States of America during the heights of the civil rights movement that then President Richard "Tricky Dick" Nixon needed to quiet Black unrest. Thus, COINTEL was allowed to set into motion Black on Black violent crime. Then we were slapped with a bunch of federal funded Black exploitation movies that portrayed a false image of the Black experience here in America, eroding the concept of what it is to be a man with individualism theories. Those who lacked foundation became a caricature in someone else's minstrel show. Laughed at by men who cleverly designed the buffoonery that Black males were being defined by. The superficial composition of a mask bears no fruit; meaningful love will never be realized by a fake. Those who love you love your potential and are confused and saddened by the forfeiture or arrest of natural human development.

Unfortunately, many of us never connect to a truth that lies within all of us in full awareness and clarity. We tend to sleep walk through our days conflicted over our reality. We fail victims to the intellectual partaking of President Ronald Reagan who oversaw the agenda of cultural annihilation and declared a real war on a part of the American population that was too distracted with the reality of feeding themselves to even know they are supposed to be fighting. Simultaneously three fronts were attacked on Reagan's watch, Iran, Nicaragua and Black males here in this country. Agent provocateurs and puppets of the rich brilliantly fertilize the soil to eradicate love between brothers and to justify murder and enslavement of the few who sought equality. Old hatreds and beliefs are hard to extinguish especially so when they question the foundation upon which we stand. The 13th Amendment of the United States Constitution affords us the right to volunteer for slavery. It doesn't discern coercion or manipulation. Being mindful of responsibility to one's family and self is a personal obligation. Deception and evil doesn't rest while we sleep. It's the responsibility of those who love to prepare for a world that don't give a damn about you.

Presidents Herbert W. Bush and George W. Bush both acknowledge a war on drugs that was isolated to a particular group. Vice President Dick Cheney invested his cash in legalized slavery by constructing private prisons for profit. I have learned that politicians do what they do and crave power, like any prostitute they cater to the needs of the powerful by doing their bidding. Obviously there is a strong voice against this country providing a safety net for the misfortunate. The concept of educating the poor is constantly under attack and has been diminished in the last couple of decades. Somehow welfare got blackened and became an urban plight. In reality, whites in rural areas and corporations receive the lion's share of the welfare budget. According to Loic Wacquant, professor of Sociology during the presidency of a soulful Bill Clinton, welfare dollars were taken from the needy and redistributed to incarcerating groups unfairly targeted by this country pretentious war on drugs. With no safety net available in society the prison yard became cluttered with the mentally ill, drug addicts, and those who lack marketable skills.

California's protective custody population equals or surpasses the general population inmates because most of them woke up in circumstances they just were not built for. Many were tricked by the media into believing they were gangsters. Others were led down this road by individuals they trusted. They should have listened to the people who cared something about them instead of allowing themselves to be influenced by purveyors of self-destruction. There are no real miracles behind these walls. Jesus and Allah would most likely find themselves in administrative segregation indefinitely here at Folsom State Prison.

> I never thought of losing but now that it's happened, the only thing is to do it right. That's my obligation to all the people who believe in me. We all have to take defeats in life.
>
> ৯৯ ৵৵
> Muhammad Ali

Evil sought the treasures that I plan to spend peace in eternity with. Couldn't see me with love or self-respect and demons wanted me to bow and suffer in subservience. Efforts to dehumanize me kindled my spirit.

Strangely within the confines of chaos, solace can be found. I have existed in stoops considered as one of the most dangerous places on the face of the earth. Countries were at war but San Quentin was considered more dangerous per square foot than any other place on earth according to Ted Koppel of Nightline. When everything outside of me was in turmoil I found myself seeking peace in what was irrelevant before all that I valued was lost. Nature became important when peeped at through dirty windows. Clouds and flowers grew personalities and the ocean came to life. My peace of mind was far removed from the cesspool of my confines. It has been said that war and prison allows a man to find himself. The last days of my freedom ended chaotically, prison was a natural consequence of the way I was living. While in prison, surviving with some self-respect became my goal, even if it meant dying prematurely. I had no desire to follow any man and questioned a God that allowed my hell to exist on earth. Understandably it's easier to stand with the majority for strength. Standing by myself blessed me with the solitude to listen to my own soul, birthing genuine values. I accepted dying within these prison walls. In prison life was cheap and you always died alone. I became determined to meet my fate as who I wanted to be, and not a caricature of someone else's definition of me.

Standing for something means that you stand against something. Whose truth is it that robs your spirit of its authentic voice causing you to be a servant of another's agenda? Too many have died and have been destroyed within that isolated barrier of my community for it to be a natural occurrence. Tears are shed, hearts are hardened, allowing ruthlessness to become the norm. The world is not going to claim culpability for the deaths of its children. They point fingers either in justification or deniability of hell designed by man.

All kinds of men come in and out of these prisons. Drugs gave a lot of inept men artificial powers that they would have never known naturally. Instinctively the impotent will turn on those closest to him to exploit artificial power thinking that thrill of dominance makes him a man. He enjoyed making his neighbors have sex with animals until he comes to prison and meets their fathers and brothers. He has murdered not for power or money, but out of jealousy and insecurities. Many profess to being built by the game but in fact are double agents, loyal to no one and capable of betraying all.

When the money is gone, the artificial power vanishes. In prison they are nobodies amongst their victims. Their eyes dance around like frightened children. They worry about who seeks their manhood as retribution for their deeds. They come to these penitentiaries wanting to redeem their soul and hiding behind the chaplain. Reciting the Bible won't save them. The Muslim's can't protect those who collaborated with Colonel Oliver North and his squad of drug traffickers. Death will recognize the absence of a soul in those who have empowered themselves with evil.

It's not the length or the comfort of a man's journey that matter, the true test is how he deals with adversity. Some of us need respect as though it is an essential part of our nature and death becomes an acceptable cost for that respect. Driven for acceptance at judgment day, but blindfolded by life I sought the comfort of awakening to a plateau of inner peace. Foolishly, I accepted challenge after challenge as though my manhood relied upon it. It was extremely naïve of me to run the gauntlet of self-destructive behavior expecting to capture a peace that doesn't exist in that arena. I put off battles to the next day that weren't physically threatening but would eventually challenge the core of me. Some men usurp the valor over another man's fight. In time I learned that everything that I was fighting for wasn't necessarily fighting for me.

> If you leave here a tormented soul, you will be a tormented soul over there, too.
>
> ❧❧
>
> Raymond Moody, M.D.

Just because you have the ability to love others doesn't mean that they love you back. Weakness can reside in those closest to you. We can be ready to die for people who want to see me dead. Smile in my face but envy me. Although it was confusing, I came to realize that I couldn't be mad at the cowardly or evil for being true to one's self. In actuality they taught me that who I was didn't depend on what cowardly and evil men thought of me. The very essence of their nature is weak and prone to lies and deception to cover their weakness. Some of us realize that the fires of hell will be inflamed by our truth.

I am loved by some and equally hated by others and was a grown man sitting in the penitentiary before I understood the tentacles of jealousy. I have witnessed men become victims of violence and shamed before their peers not because of wrong doing or breaking some prison code of ethics but because he was endowed with the love of his family in the form of regular visits and enough money to sustain himself while in prison. Little men empowered by the crowd will go after those he feels threatened by for reasons related to his personal insecurities.

This life can be a vicious game when you have nothing outside of your personal power to draw from. At birth I wasn't included in the American dream. I didn't fit the profile for success. There are many obstacles designed to corral a free spirit. The presence of liquor stores on every corner is guaranteed to capture some souls. The vices of man were readily available in my world.

How many areas in rich communities are allocated for the mongering of prostitutes. I sit wondering what I could have done to avoid this fate. Maybe I should have thrown my hands up and prayed for deliverance from a world that didn't bring me inner peace. Maybe I could have paid a pimping preacher to show me the way. Instead my path led to what I could do for myself. I like the biblical wisdom of Daniel:12-2, and in any of them that sleep in the dirt of the earth shall awake, some to everlasting life, and some to shame and everlasting contempt.

I sit here trying to champion patience, while my keepers are laughing at my efforts. Year after year I cling to dissipating hopes of freedom. One day I looked up and freedom became a carrot presented just to keep the inmates in line, something they may never obtain. Injustice causes me to lose belief in the justice system. When those who pretend to be righteous do wrong, then they are wrong. As I grew tired of prostrating myself, my vision became clearer. My life could be restricted to a prison cell, I don't need permission to approach death on my own terms.

Death brought about a moment of clarity. Personal issues that I thought I would someday correct were going to be left undone. The less I am concerned with the garbage that spurts from the mouths of men, the more my soul is allowed to speak. At times I am tormented by what it knows. My existence is a double punishment. Not only do I have to exist in the belly of this bitch, I have people who love me for whatever reason when it was questionable if I even loved myself. I sacrificed my greatest blessings out of stupidity. Thinking that things and the opinion of others would somehow validate my existence. I was blinded to the treasures I already had as a result of a night's passion. When death grabs your shoulder he has a way of making you put your life into perspective. It's funny how unimportant some quarrels become when you know that you'll never have a chance to say again what you really feel. Death has a way of making you realign your values. Material things become less meaningful and the games I was tied to became the follies of fools.

I have supported people with my life that I no longer even like. I have defended my community wherever I ventured and have stood back to back with other Blacks just because they are Black. When death approaches I won't even know their names. I left a baby girl behind thinking that tomorrow I could straighten up chaotic circumstances and be the father I never knew. I was busy being a Harlem Crip when life gave me a daughter named Monique. I couldn't see how important she would become in correlation to my own existence at every phase. It's a peculiar feeling to enjoy the respect of your peers for staying strong while personally acknowledging a failure to be a father. I can do a thousand years in prison without breaking in the sight of men. My hurt doesn't come from being strong. My pain comes from the life I failed to be strong for. I will have to carry that scar across my soul for eternity. Other things I have done in life pale to being caged in these penitentiaries while my child fends for herself in a world that is uncaring.

I came to prison for the purpose of rehabilitation, when money entered the game I was then expected to accept that I am not human but that my real purpose in life was to fatten someone else's coffer. My keeper's gang mentality belittles my family and friends for their belief in me. Often it's dumfounding to witness dysfunctional prison staff who can barely read and write, recite the rhetoric of a crowd that promulgates killing for a three percent pay raise. The mental delineation between inmates and guards blurred and merged. Right is only right when one lacked the power to make the victimization of others right. Empowered by soul less politicians, the media and cash, prison went about the business, of revenge and dehumanizing those they were entrusted with warehousing.

What a man thinks who doesn't know me is irrelevant especially when his ego causes him to feel he is more important to me than my own child. He is an idiot and God is not in him because he can't see or denies the truth. I travelled this path for the wrong reasons and have witnessed many personal failures.

Dying is guaranteed so I am not worried about that. When my time comes I want to die with the love of my family resonating inside of me and not some egoistical pursuit designed for me by people who don't even like me. Ignorance allowed me to volunteer for modern day slavery and nobody gives a damn about the tears of my child, but me. If she was to die today my keepers won't even possess the human decency to allow me to attend her funeral. There is no humanity in the rabbit when he has the gun. Only hate and sadism establishes him as a conscientious employee.

Despair brought about a conscious inkling that illuminated the deficiencies of deception, while I remained a commodity to be bartered and sold. I accept that spiritual peace and integrity are determined internally and are fueled by me, alone.

Some things I can't do anything about, the shot was fired and it's a done deal. Things that I am responsible for tear at me daily.

> They found, much to their amazement, that even when their most apparent awful and sinful deeds were made manifest before the being of light, the being responded not with anger and rage, but rather only with understanding and even with humor.
>
> ও ও
>
> Raymond Moody, M.D.

I don't miss the parties, I miss the man I was capable of being if I would have been conscious of what it was to be a father. I have supported hundreds of men who could careless about my sacrifices. I would turn each and every accolade in to have the memories of one father – daughter dance. The flames of my hell burn brightest over my failures to my own seed. Enduring thirty-eight years of incarceration I am tortured most, not by once in a lifetime occurrences or the coldness of the bars, but by my failure to be a parent. Maybe one of these days my keeper will figure out that my pain comes not from deeds that can't be undone, but from those living that I would give my life to improve their existence. Maybe then they will drop the hyperbole about who they would like me to be in justifying their own inhumaneness and see things as they are.

I am already in the penitentiary so I derive no joy from glamorizing criminality. There is nothing pleasant about relishing in the behavior that got me here in the first place. I dream of picnics at the park, barbecues at the beach, rated R movies in the quiet of my home and playfully tormenting my grandkids. I would like to mow my own lawn and keep up my garden. There is nothing exciting about having to carry a gun everywhere I go because I am living wrong. I would prefer reading and having unlimited access to information that would cause me to believe that I know something about what it is to be human with virtuous values. Some poets and philosophers have awakened parts of my soul, giving life to parts of me that were asleep or dead. I am more interested in spending time figuring out the complexity and purity in the work of a genius to strengthen some inner need of mine, than to listen to the utterings of a man who doesn't know what he is talking about. But my keeper never considers that his conjecture of my heart and my mind belongs to the past as he reads the highlights of a file that represents a part of me that has been dead for a long time. I wish I could re-live yesterday with the knowledge of now.

My physical entity can definitely be enslaved with concrete and razor wire but I have to surrender at the foot of my oppressors my mind and soul. My conscious refuses to be arrested. It's linked to those who preferred to be a meal for sharks rather than endure the degradation of slavery here in America. Uncontrolled notions pop into my mind daily of me participating in a more humane experience here on earth. I stand on my own principles, but that doesn't mean that I can't tolerate the values of others. While death beckons me I'm expected to deny a personal truth to indicate conformity that openly loathes me. In the absence of faith it is hard to deceive myself into believing in those who hate me.

Most mornings I hate opening my eyes to the hellish reality of another day. My dreams very seldom entertain the nightmares of my day. There is peace in closing my eyes, and there is solace in being who I am. What someone else perceives is their issue, not mine. I am somewhat suspicious of what comes out of the mouth of a man anyway. Things unseen have started to play a greater importance in bringing peace to my soul. There is an inner freedom in the lack of concern for what another might think. Confusion is a tentacle of deception and when I don't need your theories, money or friendship that rhetoric becomes meaningless. I can trust who I am and have found my true nature to be a reliable friend of integrity when I am forced to stand-alone. I don't need an honorless coward to guide me anywhere, I'm going to die by myself and I am content with allowing Osirus to be the judge of this walk through life. I may not be able to free myself but knowing that death is coming provides me the opportunity to die the man that I am content with being. What I feel is just as important as the next man. What would be the purpose of a premonition lying to me about myself? What dangers could dwell in harmless musing over personal truths? Unlike the rattlings of the tongues of men, my conscious has nothing to lose in revealing itself to me. Being prepared to listen to your own heart takes courage.

Another man has no true way of knowing what constitutes the foundation of who I am. It's questionable whether or not he truly knows himself. As the world was condemning me for a dollar, I was experiencing love in an unconditional, unselfish way. I was understanding how blessed I was to have a baby sister who never turned her back on me regardless of the circumstance and a daughter who despite my atrocious adolescent wrong doings sees the good in me. I have a wife through whom the full faculty of love reveals itself as the childish wonderment of drifting clouds, deep as the ocean and tranquilizing as the scent of fresh morning flowers. My life was being carried out vicariously through her eyesight. Reading books offered me a variety of possible futures to pick from based on my love for another. I was no longer bound to another man's chaos and heaven was of my choosing.

There is no easy walk to freedom anywhere, and many of us will have to pass through the valley of the shadow of death again and again before we reach the mountaintop of our desires.

৵ ৶

Nelson Mandela

On a special day my love and I met in the visiting room with a preacher for hire to unite our union legally as husband and wife. The punk representing the institution of God pimped at us with a rehearsed and velvet tongue. Wanting my wife to join his flock he looked at her with sincerity in his devilish eyes and told fables of deception. Gave her cause to question our love and created an opportunity for her to choose a real pimp. Preacher boy, was so confident with the lies while perceiving my circumstances to be so helpless that he pimped at my woman right in front of me, either feeling that I was so credulous not to understand the belittling of my entire race or so helplessly shackled not to pose a threat. The pimp charged me $150 to share a nonsensical lie that served no other purpose but to enslave and subjugate my ancestors. I was offended that any non-comatose individual could rely on the pettiness of the Biblical story of Hamm revealing his fathers drunken nakedness as a reason for centuries of genocide against his descendants. Empowered by the word of God the Bible totally disrespected me for a fee. There was a time I would have likely spit on him for disrespecting me but the look in my wife's eyes told me to be nice and we were married.

Love is capable of providing tranquility and dissipating hatred and I came to perceive chaos as a pursuit of fools. In embracing the miracles of life, one comes to be in accordance with death. Understanding the short time in which one has to come in alignment with his true being. Rhetoric espoused by the powers of this world means little to me, as it is understood that they have a history of lying to achieve their goals. I needed to pick a vessel to deliver my soul to the other side that was of my choosing, and of which I would assume full responsibility for the person that was delivered to death's door.

Politicians needing some cash instructed the Board of Prison Terms to snatch my parole date for reasons that still make no sense at all. "Violating a position of trust," is a joke that has cost me 25 years and counting. I made a photocopy at the request of my supervising lieutenant. They said that I showed poor judgment in following his instructions that were contrary to state policy. That ridiculous grouping of words eroded my faith in their authority. They took family visits from me at the bequest of prison staff that couldn't maintain their own healthy marriages. My whole family structure was under attack and being discouraged by correctional staff. They couldn't see me with a wife and loving family, education opportunities, decent food, and adequate medical or dental care. Visiting became an ordeal of tolerance of intrusion by guards. Even inmate garb found itself under attack, they were willing to spend millions just to degrade the psyche of inmates. Sadism was thriving in all its glory.

Life was pouring buckets of mud on me, everywhere I turned it was ugly. Friends were being murdered on the streets and my correctional masters wanted me to moo like cattle to empower their own impotency. My days were ugly and the only thing that kept me sane was the presence of love. It too found itself under attack on a lot of different levels.

I may have a problem with the world but my dreams are peaceful and full of all that I would like to experience in life. My conscious is alive and aware that what I have for a life is landscaped with demons and out of sync with whom I really am. I am not concerned with anything or anybody in prison. There's no benefit in going outside of myself to find myself. During moments of crisis the knowledge of who I really am speaks volumes about my nature when I am capable of listening. That voice has teamed with death and is empowering. They read books around here trying to learn the techniques of being manipulative and deceptive as though the way of Satan is the way of man. I am content listening to my own soul, my strength derives from a voice that clearly knows my truth. I am responsible for my truth and when my mind is clear and without expectations it's easy to detect the truth in things around me. I am human and can be wrong but that usually occurs because I wasn't paying attention to what lies in the recesses of somebody else's thoughts.

> My fear was not of death itself, but a death without meaning.
>
> ᔑᕀ ᕀᔑ
>
> Huey Newton

Most of my life I have cautiously caressed the peripheral of love. I've kissed what I thought was the core of love, but in actuality my insecurities only allowed me to taste the surface of what love could be. In a childish way I have played and have been flanked by death all of my life. Turmoil is nothing new to my life but as maturity set in, it has dawned on me that several people have meant more to me unconsciously than I meant to myself. Accepting the truth invalidates my insecurities. The love for my wife and child became greater than any other consideration here on earth and something I wanted to have in my possession when I am claimed by death. Acceptance of that personal truth made sacrificing for others honorable. I found something in myself that I would gladly die for, believing it would constitute me as a man on the other side of this earthly existence.

Instead of being bitterly defeated by life, love empowered me with a sense of dignity in this world and readied me for the judgments of the next. Another man can't touch what I feel in my heart. What I authentically feel is what constitutes my existence. I am content with allowing death to be the judge of what actually constitutes who I am. I have grown skeptical of what foolishness another man made entertain in his heart, it is questionable whether or not he has an authentic thought. Many just parrot what they believe they are suppose to say and others adorn themselves with badges of honor, but don't measure up to be much of a man. I am convinced that as long as I keep in the forefront of my thoughts what's important to me as a human being, than I will never sway from values generated by love and honor, even after death.

I accept as a tenet of truth, that what we are at the moment of death will be what we are judged by. I don't want to get caught out of pocket kissing someone's ass for something unimportant, faking or playing small before little people. My love dictates that I stay true to my own truth, I am not from Saudi Arabia or Beverly Hills and do not want to get caught by death pretending to be from either. It is what it is, and I am not concerned with what another person thinks.

There is nothing pretty about wasting your life in the penitentiary. I wouldn't recommend this experience to anyone. Those who see something of value here are crazy, outright liars and don't know the truth on any level. There are a lot of failures in these stoops – men who were drawn to crime but lost their souls in the process. Their eyes dance with uncertainty and they hide behind the crowd for safety. Men, who stand for nothing, are nothing to themselves or anybody else. Some men submit to their lower selves and evil, in the end they are as they have lived, evil. Hypocrites with their velvet tongues and fools are exactly that, hypocritical fools. If the result of your actions don't make sense, you don't make sense. Many express to their families the euphoria of being reborn and apologize for the mistakes. Knowing that the man standing next to him see's nothing glorious in their walk across the yard without the benefit of money, drugs, or the crowd to support them. The blessing behind these walls comes not in the possession of outwardly things but rather in taking responsibility for yourself for the first time.

Men are given mouths and are prone to use them even though what tends to come out is meaningless. One has to be careful not to allow the perspective of a fool to enter his mindset unchecked. Shattered souls, lost dreams, and evil men also have a voice to justify continuing to breathe and they also seek comradery as they squalor in buffoonery. I have played in the trenches of deceit without being committed to its ranks. It strengthens my resolve in understanding what characters dwell in the abyss of chaos. I have witnessed the smile of deceit and felt the embrace of wickedness. This journey has come to know many slimy individuals who think that treachery is the order of the day. It is hard to imagine evil being soothing to the soul.

Weak men play with perfidious methods as a pathway to their selfish objectives. It's one thing to tolerate loathsome behavior when I didn't have the full understanding of its consequences. It's another thing when I know the full vileness that is being perpetrated around me. I tend to dislike the man who repels from a worthy challenge but preys on his neighbor. The judgment I bestow on a big fish that devours guppies in a small bowl wouldn't substantiate his next breath. Some confuse fear with respect but fear is a fleeing emotion. Respect based upon fear will evaporate.

Many have abandoned meaningful values to justify their existence. Fill their life with decadence and asinine pursuits delusionally thinking trivia will alter their circumstances. A lot of prisoners are serving sentences they can't possibly physically do but they maintain faith in finagling people. They are missing the importance of the fact that none of us have a lot of time left on this earth. Any minute this journey could be over and instead of telling a loved one how we really feel, we squander the opportunity on nothing of significance. Failing to accept the relevance of an eventual last minute.

I am being thrashed by every moment lost to my own foolishness. Ignorance no longer yields me a hiding place from myself. My fears fled from my truth and no longer provide needed excuses for continuing to crawl and not stand upright like a human being. Those who govern these penal plantations stumble over each other with dehumanizing ideas of additional methods of controlling the daily activities of inmates. Life is being prostituted into modules of spirit deadening, honor stripping brainwashing. Menial roles are accepted as pride is abolished. What exists when the heart has nothing left to sing for?

The conduct of some of these inmates is shameful, they perform like real modern day slaves, shuffling and their presence is disgracefully comical. They misuse their talent in buffoonery, prostrating intellect and spirituality for no apparent reason beyond eating out of someone else's trash. Personally I don't need to live that long. I refused to sacrifice my soul for a few jailhouse privileges and I don't need anyone's friendship that requires that I abandon things that I value. I wonder how a man can give his soul away for crumbs and still pretend to have anything of value to offer those he says he loves. The State of California gives inmates $200 at the gate when the parole. They do not have the moral capacity to re-issue self-respect, so many return to the community destroyed, worthless as human beings, self-centered, content with physical freedom and a crushed soul. Death doesn't seem a bad option when placed up against a life with no meaning.

Pain is not foreign to me. Neither is hardship and struggling maybe necessary in establishing myself as a human being. I have already soiled my physical existence and can never retrieve all the special moments that I have lost due to my own stupidity. Love governs my essence and keeps me somewhat sane. I don't expect frills and joy to saturate my next breath, this life is hard and unyielding in the greedy need to dominate. Luckily, I am empowered with the vitality of my ancestors.

Discovering that I had volunteered for slavery hurt. Seeking the release of death, I found an inner freedom. I would have preferred that my keeper momentarily chain me to the wall while he whips my ass to demonstrate his

> Death is such a release, like an escapee from prison.
>
> ॐ ॐ
>
> Raymond Moody, M.D.

sadistic fetishes. Rather than to pompously strip me of everything I have of value and dare me to move while my eyes are wide open to the ruthless and diabolical nature of my oppressor is a worst fate. I have valid reasons for not trusting my keeper and the only hope I can rely on is the fact that I won't be here for eternity. They can't pimp me forever. I have no desire to strive to out do demons. While I have found contentment within myself. My keeper needs an enemy, a fall guy, and an excuse to exact a devilish thirst upon someone.

When you are being bullied the costumes of bullies doesn't make much difference. These folks were poking at me like they want me dead. Willfully articulating a denial of my humanity. Whatever they witness me enjoying or benefitting from they want to take away. If I wiggle in the process of being raped or come off as resentful they will punish me for having the audacity to look them in the eye before I die. My flesh is being preserved for profit. It's imperative that I hide my mind and spirit before they develop a market for that also.

I went to another parole hearing in front of strangers. We discussed again the poor choices of a teenager whom had been dead for twenty years. The man who sat before them possessed none of the characteristics of the boy who entered prison, outside of name and prison number. I had all the T's crossed and all the I's dotted in my parole plans. Didn't need or want state or federal assistance in my life plan. I attempted with great insight to demonstrate my readiness for parole. Foolishly, I didn't consider that those responsible for determining my parole suitability were desperately trying to keep a roof over their own head. These holders of my fate were unemployed politically appointed pundits who couldn't have cared less about my readiness for parole. They needed to make sure that their families had food on the table and were capable of murdering everyone I know to fulfill a campaign pledge. While I was respecting the nobility of their authority, they were counting dollars. Nothing I said or presented to them as fact made sense. They weren't concerned with the truth at all. The only thing that made sense was their social sense and finances.

I desperately wanted to be free and that need clouded my perception of reality. I sat before them not understanding that an $80 billion budget was being divided and that everybody holding the keys to my future wanted a piece of that pie. Being mindful of that reality has motivated me to preserve some dignity and refuse to participate in the bureaucratic tasks of pimps. They talked to me like I was a mannequin, without the human quality of experiencing pain or having a need for hope. They made it clear that in the name of justice they were getting their money, fuck me, my dreams, and those that I loved. Just because a nigga read a book, he still a nigga, and they were determined for me to know that. They made me understand that Due Process laws and the United States Constitution is what they say it is.

I came to prison with a sentence of 7 years to life, which meant I had to do about 11 years behind these walls. They even provide you with a matrix of categories and expected terms for specific ways in which crimes were performed. They provide you with that official description of crimes for the purpose of uniformity. It was absurd for me to expect to be treated like the next man. I was sitting in a parole hearing frustrated that somehow they were missing the truth of who I was. With a level of contempt I would expect to hear in the tone of predators they informed me that by their calculations I could expect to do from 85 to 95 years. The tone of the deliverance clearly accentuated something they wanted me to know and that was 'fuck me, and my interpretation of justice, Nigga. Bring 95 years the best way you can. There was no real attempt to be tactful, they got at me like pimps checking a whore. Justice had evaded me once again. What hope existed in my heart was reduced to simmering chips of crushed expectations of good and bad. On that day they took off the masks of righteousness and demons spoke loud and clear.

They stripped my future of meaning and my soul was not going to be bargained off for a radio or a couple pieces of candy. I can't stop men from hating me. But when they murder me they are going to clearly know they murdered a man. I don't do crying and kissing ass well. I leave those infirmities to the weak and subservient. When all was apparently lost maintaining some peace of mind became vitally important. I drew closer to death and love comforted me. Sorrow was unavoidably a part of my day, pride made death attractive.

I entertained things learned of this world. My spirit has probably seen many lifetimes in different forms. My spirit was cradled and strengthened by the hands of death, allowing my mind to roam sandy Caribbean beaches experiencing the heights of love. I don't fret my darkest hour, I am in hell, it is already dark in here. When all else fails I have a spirit that does not fear man, and keeps me on my feet when succumbing to worldly powers maybe advantageous. Man has introduced bullshit to my stay on this earth on more than one occasion. Instead permitting him to smash what remains pure in the core of me. I dawned anew with understanding, fuck him, and I will see him in hell. I can stand on the steps I have taken in this life. It's debatable if the people and their principles that I oppose are as confident about deaths verdict.

If liberty is worth having, it must be worth dying for. I have a tendency to feel like a man standing on his own two feet. Men can allow any sound to come out of their mouth. That doesn't mean that I am gong to believe their rhetoric. Especially when their definition of who I am requires that I willingly disparage myself. I was capable of feeling about others the same way they felt about me as I sat in a penitentiary complex entrapped by barbed wire and gun towers that no longer appeared inescapable. Being in prison was a choice, it wasn't mandatory. I could run away from the plantation whenever I felt like it. I had sat in prison for over twenty years being challenged about believing in the system from those who distrusted the white man. Once that system dispelled my beliefs with its whimsical actions, I was no longer bound lawfully or spiritually to its authority. I can't stop a man from wanting to steal my dreams for the industrializing of a company. Which makes me prize cattle in his coffer. Asking me to respect what despises me is a farfetched proposition, and it will be a cold day in hell before that is actualized.

I was being detained at California's Rehabilitation Center in Norco, California. The use of the word rehabilitation was an obvious joke but my imprisonment was real. As most flopped around looking for hope in despair, I dreamt of freedom. As each day passed my need became stronger. I am more knowledgeable about mistakes I have made in my life than anyone. Despite those mistakes I still deserve to be treated like a man or I had the option to die like one. My punishment had become arbitrary and capricious and not based on any civilized principle of law. It wasn't funny to me.

One April 11, 1997 I awoke blessed and in love with who I was. Overcome with the notion that death awaited my transition from one world to another with a sense of pride. My heart was in the right place and I was proudly and desiring to maintain the essence of who I was for eternity. My fear existed in accepting the ways of docility as the State of California was in the process of turning convicted criminals into chattel for profit. I held no desire to become someone else's livestock, especially while death offered peace and white sandy beaches. Begging for forgiveness ceased to make a lot of sense to me. Dying with a sense of self-respect appeared honorable. I wasn't the first slave who chose death over incarceration, and thoughts of all the young mothers who journeyed across the Atlantic Ocean preferring to feed their babies to sharks rather than have them suffer the ****humiliation that I was enduring empowered me to escape the confines of my man made hell. Whatever awaited me in death couldn't equal the agony that I knew in life.

The Board of Prison Terms mockingly told me that I would never get out of prison regardless of my readiness. That bit of information birthed an awareness that death would be my only outlet. Once I accepted the words of those who held the keys to my freedom, acquiring wire cutters and researching the easiest routes off the plantation was quite easy. People sometimes master the use of the English language and can articulate it with absolute authority. Nothing is absolute in this world but the right to die. A man defines himself, he is not to be defined by another man, even if it costs him his life. Ultimately I am solely responsible for who I am. What someone else thinks really doesn't matter when I sit before Osirus being judged for the essence of my character. What a master thinks about a slave becomes meaningless when personal virtues are being judged in death. The roles might get reversed when the truth is known and evil is exposed. The human spirit rests on it's own accord even death can't arrest that.

The only thing that lay between me and freedom was desire. My mind was aware of the philosophy of slaves that relied on a great savior to rid them of their burdens, but my soul wasn't buying that rationale. In fact, it seems kind of stupid to get stabbed by someone for no known logical reason and then expect that same person to be your savior. There is no logic in that for me. I totally expected to get killed. The only anxiety over that result rested in the question of whether or not I would be reunited with loved ones during the transition to the other side. That unknown was paramount to my concerns. On the day of my escape death stuck her sweet tongue in my mouth and my concerns vanished.

Once I accepted death, as a possible outcome of my quest for freedom the rest was easy. A win-win situation either I navigate a path to freedom or died the man I wanted to be. That night another inmate and myself left through a dormitory window. We made our way under an adjacent building to avoid being spotted by gun towers. Then we scrambled our way to an area closest to the perimeter fence. At that point we were clearly visible to three gun towers and still had three perimeter fences to cut through as institutional patrol vehicles circled the grounds. It wouldn't have surprised us to feel the lead of any one of the three mini 14 rifles during that part of our escape. It seemed as though we were making excessive noise and taking forever to slide under the wires of the fence. Our arms became numb from dull wire cutters as we drew the attention of wild cats who looked on with great curiosity. Once we got between gates, we rested and took turns cutting through the outside gate and then we were free.

Stepping into the darkness of freedom was an adrenaline rush and removing those psychological shackles I had been wearing for the last twenty years was invigorating. I had managed to escape without getting killed or even rustling anyone from their sleep. We followed an old horse trail all the way to glowing lights that represented civilization. The air was different on the outside of that compound, didn't stink as much as it did within the perimeter of prison despite the rich smell of horse manure. The neon lights of a gas station caught my attention and we headed in that direction. Enroute to the gas station we ran across a pay phone and that is where the first twist of fate stepped in. I hadn't used a pay phone that wasn't monitored by prison staff in over twenty years and the last one I had used only required that I place a dime in it to make a call. The pay telephone that I was attempting to use was asking for PIN numbers and ID numbers. I didn't have the slightest idea of what the hell it was talking about and neither did my traveling companion. So we decided on putting some ground between us and the vicinity we were in.

We ran until daybreak searching for a cooperative pay telephone to use. Around the time the sun came out we heard the shrill from the prison alarms fill the air. Then we decided to hide alongside the 91 freeway while getting our bearings on what path to take from its signs. Obtaining freedom at that juncture had personally been a small challenge to who I was. Retaining the freedom I took back from my plantation bosses brought into question who I truly was. The first thing that I had to do was separate myself from my cohort. I was glad to be experiencing freedom in whatever form.

As we waited for the curtain of nightfall to shield the whereabouts of our escape strange things started occurring. While we hid behind bushes, relying on traffic to be moving so fast along the highway that no one could really detect our presence, a mini van pulled about 8 feet in front of us and stopped. We were at a juncture where three different freeways merged. With this vast highway space they chose to pull right in front of us. A little girl beamed right in on us as soon as they parked. She was trying to point out our presence to her parents but they ignored her probably because they were more concerned with the malfunction of their vehicle. Then the father got out and walked about 75 to 100 yards away from his car to a highway call box. The child waved, stuck her tongue out and played with us in silence from the backseat of her car. At that point I knew that remaining free was definitely going to be a problem. I wasn't capable of introducing my drama into someone else's life to satisfy my need to be free. My keepers have made it blatantly obvious that they don't give a damn about my family or me when it comes to getting a dollar and plantation policies. But as we sat there on the verge of being exposed by a beautiful child I realized that I lacked the monstrous traits of my oppressors. Drinking another man's blood is not going to make me a better man. I am content allowing another man to show up at judgment day with all his pompously righteous theories with the blood of the innocent dripping from his hands. I am only responsible for my own actions and right now I will stand on that. Deception doesn't transcend death because we know the truth. Weak men with power will be powerless in that transition. Eventually whatever malfunction the family experienced corrected itself and the vehicle pulled away. A little later we changed locations.

As we roamed looking for a place to hide we encountered several different groups of people who paid little attention to our presence as we soaked in the natural sounds and functions of life. By the time the sun fell from the sky, street signs provided us directions. Trying to avoid people we encountered became more of a distraction than getting away. We went to a McDonalds for Big Macs, French fries and something to drink and became puzzled over how easy I was propositioned and offered a ride. It seemed to me that I had escaped prisoner written all over my face but obviously other people didn't sense that.

Eventually my efforts to avoid ordinary people led to my capture, life wasn't through with me yet for whatever reason. If death takes me today, I will go willingly to end this nightmare with some honor. There may not be any benefit from saying who I am but escaping showed me who I am not. My actions demonstrate that I would never victimize someone else's mother and child to further my cause, as freely as agents of the prison industry so nonchalantly does to mine.

Freedom may have been a tentative allocation but what I learned about myself will last for eternity.

> There are also celestial bodies, and bodies terrestrial: but the glory of the celestial is one and the glory of the terrestrial is another. So also is the resurrection of the dead. It is sown in corruption, it is raised in corruption: It is sown in dishonor: it is raised in glory: It is sown in weakness: it is raised in power: It is sown a natural body, and there is a spiritual body. Beyond I show you a mystery: We shall not all sleep, but we shall all be changed. In a moment, in the twinkling of an eye, at the last trumpet: for the trumpet shall sound, and the dead shall be raised incorruptible.
>
> ೲ ೲ
> 1 Corinthians 15:35-52

How did I do this to myself? Continuing to breathe is a painful choice. Awareness is empowering.

Life, it is what it is, and I have probably enjoyed the best of what it's going to be. In spite of experiences, love had shown me it's smile and disarmed me with touches of tenderness in ways that were especially designed for me. I hope that death finds me still clinging to that

> Jails and prisons are designed to break human beings, to convert the population into specimens in a zoo – obedient to keepers, but dangerous to each other.
>
> ঔ ৵
>
> Angela Davis

sensibility. Life empowered me with the resolve to define myself without being influenced by things not of me. As hate thrives on hate, love fuels on itself, and with great effort I tried to ignore the fiendish scoundrels pretending to be moral and upright.

I have suffered and hardship is my experience on earth. The journey of others causes me not to want to show up at judgment day whining about what the devils on this earth have done to me, begging for another chance, appearing feeble, in acceptance of having spent my life sleepwalking. Whether it's heaven or hell, I don't want to be outfitted in the buffoonery of hate toting a worthless doctorate degree in excuses for not being much of a man in life. I have been battling demons since birth and I am content with riding out of this world with my truth. It has proven to be affective armament to this man made hell.

I have existed for 38 years in a prison within a country that was founded on the belief that I was three-fifths human. Obviously in the crevices of some minds they still believe that. How else can a society justify allowing a human being to rot away. The same word games they played in justifying the inhumanities of slavery, they also exercise in qualifying a need for incarceration almost in verbatim. And just like slavery, greed is the underlying motivation for human warehousing. They control the environment that leads many into being shackled. They place obstacles in the paths of children to stumble over, then place blame on the child for not being intelligent or responsible enough to avoid being entrapped by clever psychological snares meant to destroy, retard or limit ones growth.

We have a tendency to allow the methodology of Willie Lynch and his predecessors to divide us geographically, economically and for trivial nonsensical differences. The sister Courtney Mann wanted to join the Klu Klux Klan but was rejected because she was Black. I bet they didn't mind violating and degrading her sexually. Senator Isaiah Montgomery argued vehemently against freeing the slaves. They should have thrown his ignorant ass in here with me. The powers to be invited the brother, Ward Connerly to dinner, gave him a University of California Regents position and a Mercedes Benz to spend his life energy against affirmative action. After benefitting from affirmative action programs he felt real special and wanted to disable the latter that allowed the disadvantaged to pull themselves up from lower economic stations to his level of success. The Honorable houseboy and judge, Clarence Thomas sits on the United States Supreme Court like a lawn fixture, shiny black with white lips parroting the ideologies of his masters.

Suffering not only became my catalyst to personal truths, but forged a conscious commitment to awareness. If the origin and results of your actions are evil, than you are evil. I don't care about who you know when the results of your actions speak loudly about who you are. Secrets are not secrets to those who know how slime operates. Smiles and accolades don't mean that they like me, all that signifies is not desiring a personal problem between us. Deception is rooted in a need to protect a truth. When the smile is no longer believable than what's the truth?

At this point in life I have embraced the worse of what I would allow this world to do to me. I'm not giving up my mind, spirit or ass while I breathe in this world like the imposters who pretend to be human beings. I know what it is to be a slave without rights and portrayed in a minstrel show without dignity, thought or consciousness. For a dollar the United States Constitution, due process laws and equality have been prostituted with deceptive imagery. I no longer believe the hype.

Man can make his mouth say whatever he wants it to say. He will justify genocide, slavery, rape and can eloquently rationalize whatever atrocity that advances his agenda. I have become shackled, lumbering, supposedly mindlessly behind barbed wire enriching my owners, in the same fashion that cattle enhances the lifestyles of cattlemen. This generation of inmates has allowed themselves to become amusement for overpaid lazy guards. They joke, sing and humiliate themselves like happy slaves without conscious thought waiting on Jesus. They dislike whom their master's dislike and have become spiritless while performing as talking mannequins to the delights of overseers. Some of these inmates want out of prison so bad that they give away everything they had of value including family and friends, snubbing their truth to appear conforming to the wishes of their masters. These bastards make me sick, they have no integrity. Some have been sentenced to terms that are humanly impossible to do by a court of law. Then they sheepishly give away any valid claim to personal pride and self-respect to a system that despises them. They say that they don't want to mess theirs off, forgetting the fact, that that occurred when they committed the crime.

The reality of life in prison is definitely depressing. One comes to understand the origin of mad cow disease. Death becomes a trusted savior from the horrors of what I viewed as my life. When my eyes sprung open this morning, once again I had to experience hell. You have to deliberately pursue being an idiot to believe that life in prison is some kind of acceptable existence in any form. The food is beyond horrible, and what you are consuming is always a mystery. The boy who at one time wanted to be tough is now ridiculed. He lacks the knowledge of how to clean his bowels out and eliminate the toxic odors that reeks from his filthy ass that nauseates all those in the vicinity. It says a lot about your character when you march to the chow hall voluntarily to consume something that looks like vomit with the stench of dirty water. There is nothing about Folsom State Prison that in anyway reminds one of a country club or resort, and anyone who says differently is lying.

This is a waste of my life for another man's profit. The justice system is punishing me in the same fashion that pimps punish hoes. They don't want any trace of life in me when they are through with me. They want me dependent on a master in the same way that hoes are dependent on pimps, degraded and humiliated. It is my conscious choice to experience the totality of being bartered by politicians. My survival depends on being conscious of the sadist nature of guards who will torture, terrorize and if need be murder my whole family for a paycheck. There is absolutely nothing in prison of meaning, or that can be considered joyful. The prisons in which I have existed are comprised of suffering. Anyone that sees it differently is delusional, and needs to be here.

After returning from my escape attempt suffering was my world. Darkness clouded my vision, and there wasn't a damn thing funny. I had reached my hand out to death in hopes of removing myself from the jaws of savages, and to be reunited with peace. For whatever reason my overture was declined. I was left with no purpose for breathing. My mind and spirit was actively alive with thoughts of someone's audacity to define me as livestock. Life doesn't mean that much to me. I don't moo or give milk. Certainly I am not scared to die. I have been playing real close to death all of my life. Everything I loved was lost, abandoned or sat comfortably in the world not knowing of my pain.

The influx of actors pretending to be Al Pacino's Scarface need to accept the reality of nothingness. Combining the mentally ill and drug addicts made manipulation of inmates easy for those consigned to manage human warehouses. What kind of man instigates melees between groups as a means of control while raping the entire population of any sense of human decency? Instead of assisting incarcerated individuals to become better people in preparation for their eventual return to society, warehouse managers chose conformity to humiliation as a rehabilitation tool. They have passed laws to put grown men in pink panties and denied us less space than dogs in kennels are entitled to. The concept of rehabilitation was massacred. If you were fortunate enough to have people who still loved you warehouse policy makers blatantly display a disdain for their existence.

My days were hard because I had to live and co-exist amongst worthless individuals who chose to rob their own life of meaning. Even though death would definitely be a relief, I don't have it in me to kill myself regardless of the pain of existing in hell. I have no desire to show up at death's door draped in illusions motivated by frailty. These bastards can only kill me one time, but every time I elect to prostitute my mind or soul for whatever reason is a death to the spirit of who I am. What constitutes a man can be chipped away a little bit at a time until there is nothing left but a breathing cadaver. His thoughts are not authentic to who he is, for he only parrots what he thinks others want to hear. He's sad and worthless having found no meaning in the life he lives. He fears truth and the finality of death. Hell won't be kind to him because what honor he projects is only a façade, to protect his feelings of inadequacy. Because of fear he accepts the viewpoint of evil and regurgitates the lowest of human nature in the belief that it makes him appear strong. His heart is filled with waste. When his physical body refuses to be a vessel for his soul, nothing of value will remain. His existence was meaningless. There was nothing of value left for those who knew him to praise. He was here, now he's gone, good riddance.

NOT WORRIED ABOUT YOUR FEELINGS
Chapter 26

> A coward dies a
> thousand times, but a
> soldier dies but once.
>
> ∽ ∾
> Tupac Shakur

When I go out to the yard tomorrow there is a boy that I need to speak with about his anger issues. I have to remain mindful of the fact that his mother's idea of self-worth and love comes from corralling a penis. His father breeds to eat, "no dick, no food, or shelter." His children are no more than a cover to hide his insecurities. The problem is their kids end up with a perspective that is detrimental to the self.

It is embarrassing that I allowed this world to play me out of a comfortable existence into one that only knows hardship. Frustration and despair have given me moments that I wished for death to ease my pain. In response to a soul wounded by emptiness my body has sent false signals warning me of doom. There have been moments when I assumed that cancer was the answer to a prayer. It took these idiots that are responsible for my health care years to diagnose that nothing seriously was wrong with me. Despair and the sense of a meaningless existence has been so great that I assumed mental illness was taking hold of my mind. I was told by mental health staff to drink three gallons of water daily as a cure.

Self-pity has never looked good on me, I don't wear it well. In my lowest moments all the world sees is defiance. I am a proud man and showing weakness is deflating to the soul. I will never show them my weakness. I had to learn the hard way that pain is transitory, but can be utilized as a source of strength. It can bring about awareness. I began to understand why my pain was so intense. Why living had become meaningless and forbid me from crying. Simply what had been taken from me equaled my pain. I was supposed to hurt over a daughter I left in the wilderness at the mercy of wolves. I should be killed a thousand times for that lack of responsibility. I knew love and made mistakes in assessing the preciousness of that gift. Sex doesn't equal love. I came to understand the difference and my mistake in treating them the same. Blood should have oozed from every crevice in my body over that misconception. Those were my mistakes and not attributable to any outside source, my ignorance created the void and indifference within me and my pain matched that realization.

My mind is capable of voicing and replaying irrelevant thoughts. I wish that I was disciplined enough to constructively apply all of my intelligent notions, but that is not the case. There is a lot of time spent on what led me to prison, and on what I would rather be doing. It's debatable whether it's circumstances beyond my control that led to feelings of isolation, or just mere personality traits that's content with solitude. Either way, I have grown comfortable with engaging myself in dialogue. My ego has at times been in conflict with my true self, leaving my soul in despair. Sometimes my mind has dictated my actions, while other times my soul was responsible for the position I took.

They lack the awareness of a meaning worth living for. They are haunted by the experience of inner emptiness, a void within themselves; they are caught in the situation which I called the Existential Vacuum.

ৎ৯ ৎ৯

Viktor E. Frankl

When all is said and done it's regrettable that I allowed my ego to muzzle caring. Now, hunger evokes thoughts of how blessed the memory of a home cooked meal was. Bad news travels fast and the deaths of the young with much promise is saddening. Definitely my belief in karma has been dulled by the reality I know. Bigots and hypocrites are doing fine in this world. The treacherous are still conniving, and the worthless are still seeking favor from what they perceive as powerful, willing to sell their kind out to savages. At birth insecure minds designed my demise, and ignorantly I assisted them.

While attempting to soothe blisters upon my spirit caused by acceptable social norms, one has to question the why of practices proven to be unhealthy for any community. It is not hard to fathom that human dysfunction is a product produced by evil. Targeted at those disowned by impotent soul-less creatures, and promulgated by those willing to push their brother in the grave, so that they may live as servants for devils.

A community gets stripped of vital jobs. The jobs get sent to foreign countries. Workers are encouraged to come to America to replace people who need work as a component of establishing their identity, while engineers of this country's social structure have eliminated empathy and love for one another. A family's main protective shield against the world is their love for one another. When honor is stripped from our daily lives, the love we should have for each other is severely damaged. Someone pure at heart would be making a mistake to accept the knowledge of a fool. A fool won't accept the wisdom of a pure heart.

Approaching the trials of life in reverse always necessitates a rough journey. This particular group of words came to me while I am in isolation anticipating my release back to a general population. General population is filled with young men who just don't know how many tears they were going to shed due to their lack of understanding of the logical consequences of their actions. Everything that glitters is not gold and the price of fun can cripple us for the rest of our lives. I have been in solitary confinement this time for six months conversing with a bunch of dead people. Accepting the finality of their existence and admonition against arriving at death's door fool heartedly armed with excuses. Every living voice back here is suspect of being rotten to the core.

I have one foot in the grave already. Merely, destiny or things destined to be fulfilled keeps me in this world. Only a couple of my childhood friends still exist in this world. Most have been murdered. Others limp through this world maimed by our own foolishness. I don't know anyone that exists without scars. When they allow me to see the sun again, 99% of what I have to share with those hungry for understanding has been revealed to me through spirits of lost loved ones. What is human in me feels obligated to share with the young. If they don't pay close attention to their lives they will also come to know more about the dead than they do the living. It's a lifestyle phenomenon. If they are lucky, eventually they will also become nauseated by the glee of tyrants.

The majority of these young brothers have been led astray by hands that try to remain unseen in the shadows or by the misfortune of having parents that weren't prepared to guide their child through this quicksand-laden world. These parents shouldn't have had kids while they possessed the mentality of a child themselves. Now their child is in the penitentiary, and has probably grown comfortable escaping death. If he is lucky Folsom State Prison may introduce him to the truth. The truth doesn't reside in Folsom, its in his own heart. Hopefully he will catch a glimpse of it.

In this game we understand that words are cheap. The results of our actions are what matters. If I choose to put something in one of these men's ear that is demoralizing, instigates rape or murder, or causes someone to become suicidal with hate for himself or the mother who had him, that was my intent. I wanted to attack his self-esteem. To see him numb, void of empathy.

It is always a weak argument when someone bases his disposition upon that of his parents. The reality might be that neither of them may have amounted to much in their lifetime, and are not really worth mentioning. In fact the relationship may be belittling or warranting my sympathy. Conversation with some necessitates that I consider the extremely negative influence of the parents. Or the lyrics that come from some rappers' mouth who are just talking, they ain't living what they are talking about. If they were I would know them personally. They would have been here along time ago feeling foolish about naming themself after a white racist. Or even come to understand what it is to demoralize an entire generation. Sadly, his words are taken literally by these youngsters on the yard and they may never get out of prison again.

I tend to hold as a truth that life might have been different for me if I hadn't been the product of a thirteen-year-old mother and a sissy. The lack of parental responsibility created a nightmare for me. I can speak on a multitude of obstacles that existed within my community. The fact remains that I should not have been allowed out of my house until I was prepared to deal with the streets. Home itself should have been a refuge, safe, and loving. But it wasn't like that and sometimes that's how it is. At this point what is learned from it is more important than what it was.

My mother was a good-looking woman and I like to think that I inherited her looks. Unfortunately in her youth she fell into the cycle of befriending men with her womb instead of principles and values. They never saw the potential of the beautiful woman in her. They copulated and existed. Out of all those she has befriended only one man showed up. The rest were worthless varmint undeserving of life. None of her associates enjoyed the value of loyalty, love, and commitment and surely none took parenthood seriously. Parenthood was a burden that interfered with partying. My father died never knowing what it is to be a man. Looking up to his child frightened of being added to my list of victims.

Adversity has introduced me to the man in me. I no longer fear the gauntlet because I have walked it. My nightmare will come to an end sooner or later because I can't live forever. How do I tell a boy that his parents failed him and that is why we exist in the same space. I don't need to know him to understand that there is nothing enriching about the path that lies in front of him. Odds are that he won't make it intact despite his best efforts. Failures exist in every corner of a prison population. What is going to be his undoing is yet to unfold. Families may receive your boy back home convinced that he was intended to be a girl, not a gangster.

You who bare these kids are also failures. The degree of your blame may vary but you share responsibility for the tragedy known as his life. There are simply too many sources of information for the lack of knowledge to be your excuse. You just didn't care, that's why he is a statistic. You can count on the fact that he was never going to win a fight blindfolded to reality. You worried about making yourself feel good, instead of priding yourself on the sacrifices you made for your seed.

It's not cute to allow your child to come to prison as a boy. He's in for a rude awakening and bluntness is a sharp weapon. Nobody here cares about his irresponsible promiscuous momma's feelings around here.   Or his irresponsible punk ass daddy who never amounted to much amongst his own peers anyway.   The truth is not concerned about whether your baby boy likes it or not. This is Folsom State Prison, and there are a lot of convicted murderers around here, he won't be the first bad man to lose his life on these very grounds.   At best he can guard some secrets about himself and those he loves. Not dealing with his issues does very little to assist his rehabilitation efforts, and the desire to straighten out the mess he calls his life.

In this viciously manipulative society there is a need for both parents in some fashion or form. 'If not the whole village.' Those who survive this era of cultural annihilation and pinpointed assassination of many African American males are lucky. We can be killed or caged up with and without justification because the power of the media has made us the villains. Powers have been utilized to paint us as scapegoats to deflect attention away from greed, while many of our women shunned the struggles of parenthood but embraced the lure if a party.   Finding personal value in sharing dicks with their counterparts as though the key to heaven resides in the tip of a penis, then counting conquests until memories are blurred and become irrelevant. Some are adamant about living their lives to equal the lowest of male conduct.   I recently heard from a friend of mine. She's good people, but her youth is gone, and the streets have discarded her like yesterday's trash.   With that realization she is ashamed, depressed and has nothing of value to stand on. She can't say honestly that she was a great mother or friend. Her loyalty was momentarily to the dick in her life. The beauty of age is not treating her well.

Trying to find love within a culture that disparages their own mothers and glamourizes male imposters has to be a difficult task for anyone trying to establish a foundation for an eventual family. Yesterday she was a pretty young woman who made the mistake of having babies with mannequins and cadavers. She never saw a man in those she bedded because all he brought was a hard dick, combined with some empty words to guarantee him sexual gratification. Having a penis is no legit determinate of a male being a man. Sadly a lot of males have the mindset of feminine girls and want to be pampered and taken care of. If you can keep a secret he may disclose that he has a little sugar in his drawers. But now he is somebodies baby's daddy. Playing the bitch and needing to be pampered and taken care of himself.

More importantly any love felt for those content with only pleasuring themselves through their primal sexual desires is innate and not actually earned. A child's love for a parent is often blinded by biological connection, not actions. Some of you treated your babies like a plaything. When the commitment to raise him got hard you abandoned him allowing the streets to raise him, until he was eaten up by the judicial system. Then you blame his shortcomings on him. Don't fool yourself, you should have kept your panties on and protected him against the demons that reside in the streets. Any love felt for you will be a result of that child's big heartedness and sympathy over your failures as a mother.

It's gonna take a lot of convincing to make me believe that a man is much of anything when he consciously chooses to neglect his own child. I have no reason to trust or respect someone who sees no value in protecting and providing for his own seed. I don't have a lot of faith in what he might do under pressure. When the bullets get to flying or when we are outnumbered I can't expect him to defend what we represent with honor. The punk is probably hanging out for protection his self and could give a damn about being a man when circumstances call for sacrifice. Baby daddy might have some hidden desires to be a baby himself if the price is right.

There are not a lot of niceties in the life I live, no good meals, no opportunities for long walks and priceless conversations with my seed or significant other.   Once I recognize someone's agenda to treat me like an animal then I had to make a conscious decision to be the animal that my keepers pressed upon me or not.   My mind may say just play the role for your freedom.   My soul demands respect regardless of the cost.   Then my losses came to the forefront of who I am.   I have no fear of men whatsoever.   I am extremely concerned about death touching me for the final time and finding that I don't measure up to the man I was capable of being.   The first deficiency in that equation upon my character would be the inability to blossom as a father.   Being cool and tough are matters for my ego, not elements generated from the core of my being.

Some of these boys were raised by strong women and embrace the narcissism of infancy.   Allowing her to provide and protect the family, instead of exemplifying strength and leadership, he becomes an additional child within the household.   He is just a prostitute who will mind somebody for a place to stay until the female encounters a real man and forces him to get her nipple out of his mouth.   Now he is mad at all women in the same realm that a child hates the cessation of breast-feeding and the responsibility of feeding itself.   Unlike the child he doesn't know loyalty.   He simply seeks another set of breasts to suckle from to sustain his life.   He proudly wears a tattoo saying 'Fuck All Bitches,' on his chest, to reflect what he feels in his heart.

It's a difficult task for individuals to align themselves with a healthy productive existence while haunted by a soul screaming from insecurities. Too much introspection is a threat that requires drugs and alcohol to silence.   Being of 'mind & spirit' is a connection that is a foreign concept that's above the pay grade of those masked by deception.   Manhood is an evolutionary process that's not substantiated by the presence of testicles.   Manhood necessitates that clarity and self-awareness are consolidated with principles.   Between primal instincts, demons, and personal insecurities becoming who we want to be is a project.   Of course we can mimic the ideals, beliefs and morals of others.   But until we truly make an absolute stand on one concept or the other we linger in an inner wilderness subject to grasp at any light that shines upon the caves of our existence. When the voices are not generated from within, evil is often the most boastful and illuminate deliverer of messages from outside of ourselves. It's imperative that a man establishes values worth dying for, without that we don't amount to much of nothing. Honor is achieved when we stand next to what's right regardless of the consequences. Throwing your babies to wolves to save your own ass establishes how filthy men can be.

Everybody is not fortunate enough to cast the demons out of their character. They deceive themselves with age and tough talk. Dressing like a warrior doesn't make them warriors, nor does any other façade substantiate who they are. They live in fear of being exposed as imposters, especially around those they advocate allegiance to. When you are the son of a cum freak your interpretation of love wears a mattress on her back which distorts your view of the world, stunting your growth as a human being.

One's parents can do what they want to-do reasoning that they are grown even when simple logic defies respecting their behavior. I am a staunch advocate of sexual gratification. But many parents should have been responsible and wore a condom. That simple gesture would have avoided a life of suffering for the boy standing on a prison yard in this country, tormented by the callous ignorance of his parents. It would have been more merciful to cross your legs on him at birth because this life ain't forgiving. Lil' Mama thought she had laid down with a man but all she got was a dick. And ol' lover boy that laid with Lil' Mama would better serve humanity by shaking his worthless ass breeding sheep. He knows that won't be counted in any serious tabulation of men.

I reside with predators, and you learn to detect the sounds of weakness in those paraded around you. One of the first odors admitted by the presence of a coward is the distasteful stench of bemoaning his own child. Masking abandonment with excuses. He was capable of tricking his child's mother out of her panties, but swears to be powerless against her when it comes to owning his own manhood through fathering his own child.   Obviously she knows a weakness that is only being sniffed at by men here at Folsom.   The act of intercourse itself is supposed to be empowering to the man as a representation of female submission to his prowess. Behind these walls its always interesting analyzing at what point and under what conditions did those roles get reversed or become confusing. Most men in prison didn't have a functional father and would have walked to the end of the earth to know one. In the minds of many, baby momma drama could have been conquered if you knew that your manhood depended on it.

As infants we are expected to whine when we were wet or want attention.   As men we should be capable of nurturing and providing guidance to what we claim as our own. I get mail from female friends informing me there are no men on the streets. I don't think they mean that literally. What I believe they are saying is that there is no one they feel protected by that would fight for them in the face of danger or would make sure the children are fed before he eats. When we settle for a low station in life we need to accept the responsibility of not having children.   That's an expensive game in which we lose when we allow our child to be raised dependent on welfare and emotionally impoverished.   The world is going to notify the child that daddy doesn't measure up to be much of a man when the child depends on hand outs, welfare and food stamps to survive. There is no respect in begging, his hands should be blistered from hard work when he doesn't possess the mental aptitude to earn a living comfortably. When he knows that he can't think himself out of a wet paper sack he should wear a condom saving his seed from the vices of hell.

You can't expect other people to love your child more than you love them.   When you give them to others to raise don't expect to be respected as he travels through the criminal justice system.   After all it was you who turned a blind eye on him as savages were devouring him. You should be bathed in hot grits for placing him at the mercy of wolves because his troubles were frustrating to your lifestyle.

I grew up in a community that most families struggled to keep a roof over their heads and food on the table. We struggled to raise ourselves but there was love for your neighbor which lessened the absence of fathers. In a lot of cases we were still suffering from Jim Crow politics that would provide for the woman as long as there wasn't a man in the home. Couple that with decreased employment opportunities and what was left wasn't much. Everybody can't be slick at winning in a losing game. Unfortunately, winning in a losing game is still a loss. The wise men around stayed out of sight and ran a strict program based on known threats and warned us about enemies that we couldn't see. We were too busy being grown children and couldn't decipher fiction from fact. We had no knowledge of agent provocateurs, or paid informants. We couldn't see beyond a friendly Black face to the heart of someone working tirelessly to enslave us with self-destructive behavior examples.

These days I really don't who the prostitute is. A pimp can act like he is sending the bitch out but the psychology of that profession necessitates that he know how to suck a dick himself. How does he survive without a hoe? Behind these walls he is the best qualified in satisfying the libido of men. With his pretty fingernails and effeminate body gestures reminding everybody of Alicia Keys.

Unfortunately when he's in full costume pretending to be a man, women will drag him into their homes. That has to be confusing for the child because cowards like that don't possess a soul. What spirit that actually resides within him is hatred towards women. I understand the female life model of a home, white picket fence, husband and two kids. Some of you need to thoroughly be kicked in your ass for bringing home a homeless dick. Any man that doesn't have a place to stay speaks volumes about who he is. If he's not man enough to provide for himself, how is he going to secure a family? He's worthless and together they are failures.

Taking responsibility for anything that doesn't satisfy him is not his strong point. He is playing mind games with himself to keep his dick hard. He doesn't see the female beyond a sexual conquest, he is performing for a place to stay until that act becomes too burdensome. If you are dumb enough to allow him to play daddy then he will do that also with a smirk. It shouldn't be a big surprise to find out that he entertains sexual thoughts of your children being receptacles of his dick. He exists in a primal state and all you mean to him is a place to ejaculate for room and board. As soon as you start talking about sacrifice and providing a good example for your children, he's gone because that is a dick softener.

> Age eliminates concern over death. There is nothing you can do to someone who doesn't fear death.
>
> ❧ ❧
>
> John Henrik Clarke

I am not that concerned with what people think about me. My obligation is to monitor my own thoughts. Killing me doesn't erase the truth, it only transcends me from this hellish existence. Ultimately I am responsible for my thoughts and actions and I refuse to be imprisoned by allowing someone else to steal my peace of mind. The chore of deceiving others and myself is exhausting. I refuse to spend my life energy supporting a lie. Hate is deteriorating to the soul. I am content with allowing my rewards to come from the truth that I know, the principles that I embrace and loving what, and whom I love. These places are designed to rob one of his soul and mind. It's easy to become a shell of what was a man. If I receive some love in return than that's a blessing, because me loving what I love is not predicated on them loving me. The gift comes from the ability to love after all these years in prison in and of itself.

Dope fiends concede to the euphoria of a semi-conscious existence and in the end getting high will be their reward at the expense of all other human values. The same is true for the pathetic man. His pain runs deep forbidding him from loving anyone. He pretends to be tough, but his soul is shattered. He is still the punk who dropped from his mother's womb crying.

The truth exists in all of us and those who choose to embrace the lowest part of their nature and inhumanity know they ain't worth shit. Being nonprincipled and evil doesn't substantiate worth, or true meaning in the lives of human beings. They know the taste of filth that reeks from their own hearts doesn't make them a better person. They have been running from themselves all their lives, hiding behind whatever masks that are popular at the time. Fearful of being revealed as an imposter. The same childish anxiety they felt as a result of parental discipline they feel in the presence of men. That's why they work so hard to mask their insecurities. Age is not a determinate on what constitutes men. At 30, 40, 50, 60, we can still be boys who reject the principle of being responsible. Death has no criteria, we can leave this world being a boy as many do.

When we start assuming responsibility for those around us without expecting rewards for being human, that validates our manhood. Then you will discover the spirit of a man within you. Children are part of the life cycle and provide you an untainted opportunity to let the man within you grow to full maturity. They justify you taking another breath. If the concept of responsibility and a child frightens you then you shouldn't have them.

It's quiet in the hold and I am waiting on the clambering sounds of breakfast to count another day done. The only thing that disturbed the silence of the night was faulty sinks and the sounds of toilets flushing. From the advantage point of sitting in a dungeon I am absolutely clear about the strength of love. I have no fear of the power of my capturers because love shields me against tormentors. I know that beyond these bars and shackles that I am loved. With that awareness comes dignity.

I tend to believe that pretending and deceiving ourselves bares no fruit. We all have flaws and weaknesses and when we acknowledge those fragilities we empower our self to deal with them. The life we were born into wasn't of our making, but as men we can definitely define who we are. Having a sense of honor is a conscious decision we make for ourselves. It isn't bestowed by others even though it's respected by all.

Enemies of right are great deceivers. Odds are that every human wants to receive full equality in this lifetime. That might not happen. Keep in mind that the powers of this world stop at death's door. We can be rich in spirit with love and can't anybody deny us that. How we live it can last for an eternity. Who is going to be the victor? Those who cherish the ideology of greed and are willing to dehumanize and murder millions through deception and hate or the man who did all he could to protect his family with love.

I had to embrace my pain to find freedom. By man's equations all is lost. Hopefully the judgment of the heavens will vindicate me.

I was in extremely bad shape and life was whipping my ass. The conditions of my existence were deteriorating drastically and expediently. Instead of poverty being the target of the powerful, I found myself in the bull's eye of a get rich scheme that eradicated African American males in the process. It wasn't personal. The conniving had painted a whole culture as ready for annihilation through media misinformation and deliberated manipulation of the truth by those paid to deceive. Everybody who stood to benefit from the economic boom of crime tooted the banner that promoted my doom.

> In accepting this challenge to suffer bravely, Life has a meaning up to the last moment.
>
> ❧ ❧
>
> Viktor Frankl

With the air of moral authority my community has been stripped of educational, employment and drug abuse resources equal to the larger society. Instead of providing potential tools for the upliftment of a people, we received reasons to hate one another, a multitude of weapons, drugs, and deceptive imagery that robbed a culture of self-respect. Unfortunately I was already shackled to the wall as a result of my own ignorance. They can say and do anything to me without fear of recourse, regardless of how mean or vindictive their statement might be. I was no longer locked up to be rehabilitated or come to terms with the human values of a larger society. Now my purpose was to be warehoused and dehumanized beyond any conceivable valuable benefit to mankind.

I felt like this world was eating my flesh one bite at a time. Through rhetoric and mean spirited ideologies that didn't make the California prison system any better than the criminals. The ability to murder, maim and pursue an agenda that destroys other human beings all comes from the same consciousness. Good people don't murder babies, and empower themselves by demoralizing women and the powerless. Yet I am expected to kiss the feet of tyrants. I need to apologize to those who love me for having some remnants of pride. If they kill me or allow me to rot away in these penitentiaries it won't be because I am a threat to others. It will be because they are not unlike what they accuse of being, they're murders which has been proven and validated through history as such.

The realization of my predicament created moments of self-pity filled with loneliness, depression, death longings, and short-lived energy spurts. I thought I just couldn't do the time and was going crazy. My inner-voice drowned out all other sounds, I no longer gave a damn about what came out of the mouths of men. As I was only concerned with the truth that I would hopefully die with. I had to understand that without ceremony, justification or due process hearing my 7 to 13 year sentence had been converted by greed to one that wanted 85 to 95 years out of my life. I wasn't silly enough to believe that I owed anybody that much time, or was capable of doing that kind of time for whatever reason. They would have been more merciful just to drag me into the dayroom and blow my brains out.

Along with the feeling of cynicism, defeatism and helplessness, my inner-being suffered the lost of love and the opportunity to realize meaning and self-worth in this life. My cynicism took the value of the stick of power away from my keepers. Why should I cringe for people I literally don't respect as being anything more that the opposite side of the same coin they persecute me for. The result of evil is evil and one's viewpoints in justifying it only substantiate the presence of evil. The debate over which face best justifies evil became irrelevant to me.

The depths of my pain equaled and countered the depths of the inner-rivers of love that flowed through me. My potential to actualize who I am through deeds and actions amidst those that I rightly owe the best of who I am, was taken away by unemployed and bankrupt politicians without recourse. For me to remember the joys of love, I had to experience the depths of loss. To think of a love and responsibility that a father holds for his daughter, I had to waddle in failure. Being conscious of the heights of love, along with understanding the obligation that humans have to their offspring tormented me and caused the essence of who I am to cry out painfully. I have been shot, stabbed, abused and rejected. My pain over my own shortcoming far exceeded anything that I will allow this world to do to me.

I was content with wallowing in my own pain and rationalized I was deserving of suffering in this manmade hell. Of course I could have accepted inhumane circumstances if I had no concept of what being humane was. There wouldn't have been any love loss if I hadn't truly loved anyone. There wouldn't have been any molestation of principles if I would have existed unprincipled. The rain that showered my life was no longer wet and nourishing. It had become dry, purposeless and often as harmful as being pummeled by a downpour of rain drop sized stones. In the absence of death my days were excruciating. I was expected to shrink to a level of a farm animal and walk the yard asleep to my own reality. I was dismayed that the world thought so little of another human being.

Two paths were available to me in life which were either to allow this world the pleasure of murdering me internally by putting me to sleep consciously with rhetoric and hyperbole. Causing me to become subservient, and complacently allow myself to be dehumanized and ridiculed by enemies. Or I could empower myself with the awareness of man's ability to be motivated by deceit, using treachery as a tool, based upon his own inhumanity. I will accept at judgment day a friend's hatred for me based upon his inability to be fiendish. Those of us, who find comfort in existing in the lowest part of our nature, are submitting blindly to the faces of deception. We all have your own reality to deal with.

When this life is over my truth is what's going to be paramount to the judgment of my existence. How another man journeys through life is his business, as I won't be praised for his accomplishments, nor punished for his shortcomings. I am responsible for being the best I can be, despite the conditions in which I exist. Unfortunately being principled and having values may not coincide with conforming to the existence of chattel.

If I had it my way I would reach the gates of judgment being applauded. I understand fantasy may not be reality. I don't want to have a litany of excuses when it comes my time to be held accountable for who I am. My life is a dismal, tragic existence. I survive in an abyss of misfortune. The nature of suffering means to suffer. I have dwelled in the caves of mistakes made by me. Although I take responsibility for my mistakes they did not happen without the influence of those who ushered me into the fire of hell. Repeatedly trying to analyze how this happened to me. The crime I committed was a symptom of other problems that infancy didn't allow me the insight to deal with, so I suffer. I would have definitely preferred the life of a physician over the life of a convict.

My life may end in the friendless environment of Folsom State Prison surrounded by people I have little regards for on many different levels. Before I was thrown into the darkness of confinement I wasn't an athlete, and I didn't draw or sing well at all. I do know my truth. Obviously I do not stand alone enduring predesigned depravity. The tools I have available to me for redemptive and contributive purposes is the ability to put my truth into words. Hoping that my friends and loved ones will heed to the warning of suffering I have endured and avoid wasting their lives on things that don't really matter. Although these words don't erase loneliness and grief, they do provide some sense of meaning to this tragedy.

Life allows us choices when we are down on the ground being kicked by the world. We can pathetically lie there accepting our plight as some kind of master plan that makes sense to everybody but the person being kicked. Or we have the option of becoming numb and indifferent, submitting to an atrocity, allowing ourselves to be riddled by hatred. Some are fortunate enough to get back up on their feet fearlessly. They vow to comprehend how they allowed themselves to be whipped by impish midgets in the first place.

My stupidity is shameful. I allowed myself to get played from the cradle to the grave. Personally that is interesting to me, because slavery and I don't mix well. This situation may have been different if I would have known coming through the front door how arbitrary and capricious doing time is. They are subject to change the rules based upon temporary moods and entrepreneurial schemes. I can't control the way of man, but my predicament deserves some thought on how I found myself on the ground being kicked in the first place. Regardless of how high my mountain of excuses might be, there is no pride in being manipulated into self-destruction.

Some behavior can be overshadowed or ignored. Other things will play in your conscious throughout your life becoming a witness for or against you at judgment day. I have come to understand the definition of remorse and empathy in a profound way. Unintentionally I have damaged many lives pursuing imagery related to my ego, and not related to who I am. I wanted to be cool, have friends, and enjoy the sense of family. Foolishly, I couldn't discern between the callousness of the streets, and the security of a loving family. Although I can stand on my record in dealing with wolves, that accomplishment is of no value when compared to all the lost opportunities to establish myself as a man through caring for a family. The route my life took may speak to conditions and experiences I have endured but say little about who I am.

Instead of sitting in Folsom I would rather be surrounded by my grandchildren and if you think otherwise you are an idiot.

Evil only provides darkness and there is no inner-joy in accepting that at the core of our being, that we are bad. Education is the god of insight, that provides answers to the origin of a monster. For us that represents a culture of behavior unbecoming of a human being, there may come a time to examine who we are and why self-destructive conduct is acceptable, if not glamourized. It doesn't really matter whether we are free or in the penitentiary after a while the excuses that mask insecurities, self-hatred, addictions, become worthless. Nobody in this world cares anything about your lazy weak ass. There is no value in being irresponsible and a master of excuses. We shouldn't think that we are so clever that the people we have misused don't at some point realize that they would have been better off never knowing you.

Circumstances may prevent friends and family from exiling leeches, who only suck the blood of those who for biological or sympathetic justification allow their worthless existence to remain a part of their life. It's a mistake to bamboozle ourself with the belief that others will always accept our self-deception as truth. The majority of individuals that journey through these penitentiaries come to realize they ain't tough, especially when they are not surrounded by those who love them. A lot of bad boys don't like it in prison because they are not free to deceive themselves that they are more then they actually are. There is always some principled individual who provides an example of what the next man is not. Even those who hide behind the mask of religion and conformity realizes what they are not. If they didn't there would be no cause to hide. They could stand on their own truth and not the tentacles of deception.

I have no sympathy for those who embrace the fallacy of evil. I could careless about men who hate me. It will be a cold day in hell when I am trying to impersonate those who disparage me. It says a lot about the nature of a man who admires and pretends to be those who murdered your parents. They have been whipped and the worshipping of conquerors represent a gallant minstrel show of submission. It's mind boggling that we sacrifice everything to fulfill another man's vision of himself.

Life don't last forever, and many of us won't get the chance to undo a wrong. So why violate someone's ears with things that diminishes us as men? Sacrifices for loved ones is honorable. Sacrifices for enemies is horrendously foolish. In truth, as in death, your existence becomes fruit for late night jokes. Deception gleams when we accept principles and values that are not true to our own nature. The bounty of deception resides in the numbers of lives destroy by its hand. There is no mystery in the results of our actions, either its good or bad. Someday that will be decided.

At some point a man has to be responsible for deciding who he sincerely is. All humans are capable of being deceived, of misjudging the hearts of men around them. That's considered being human, we use to be allowed to make a mistake in judgment. These days they will lock us up for profit for the rest of our natural lives. A child is not allowed to make too many mistakes. If he does he will be chatteled to the benefit of plantation profiteers. We have to learn to discern between mindful words, meant to mislead, and those spoken from the heart.

It's a tragedy, a cause for shame when actors, phonies and fakes are endowed with the ability to steal the words of true men. Mumbling the sounds of honor, while souring its meaning. There is nothing glamorous about my life, nor does pursuing bad reap good. Along the road of being bad, every apparent victory steals something good from you. Enjoying the pleasures of a lot of women is meaningless, if I am incapable of seeing the human in each and enjoying the essence of who they are. The experience of sexual conquests is insignificant when your heart is close to any and all. Sexual gratification can be achieved quite sufficiently without coupling with a shadow created by your own inability to feel. When inspired by falsehood we disconnect ourselves from truly being alive.

Boys aspire to be men and men are constantly defining their manhood through the choices they make. The process of becoming a man is evolutionary and we enter that journey attempting to define the man within us. Satisfying the ego has boundaries, fulfilling the soul has infinite possibilities. If the keepers of this plantation find a market for human flesh, and decide that I must die to laden their pockets today. Love is going to accompany me to judgment day. Making the decision process about my existence easier. Despite all the hardships of my life, I am content with not allowing this world to take away what I deem to be the best of who I am. I do not want to wake up finding myself filled with hatred, jealousy and discontent with the natural order of beauty. Prisoners always want to be free but what good is freedom to those who medicate themselves with drugs and alcohol to deaden inner-voices trying to be heard. They don't see the beauty of the innocence of a child's heart. Nor do we appreciate the wonders of a raindrop that nourishes what one never sees in prison.

To spend our lives attempting to find solace in things outside of ourself is a waste of the energy it took to create us. Personal richness doesn't come from things, it comes from what resides in our hearts. Along with the ability to shoulder a family. The best of actors never own the character they portray because that will always be the property of who performed that role authentically from the depths of his or her soul.

Some people are just goofy and will sleepwalk through their entire life, receiving bits and glimpses of what it is to be a man, but never understand the concept. Frightened by life and death, their personal truth is an adversary. Aligning themselves with groups, manipulatively seeking power through association. Their hearts see only themselves, causing the principles of loyalty to be nonexistence. There is no brotherly love in them. Their only concern is in camouflaging the bitch they witness dancing merrily around in their own soul. Their life energy is devoted to protecting the shattered deviant that resides within them.

I have existed in dungeons and have played in the dark for most of my life. Have accepted friends as friends, only to have to reject them as foes. When the light shines on our souls, those pretending to be our friends will vanish, leaving hate and envy squirming for shelter. The safest route for us meandering in the jungles of the wilderness is to illuminate our own soul. There is nothing in this life to fear when we can see our authentic truth. Death is a promise and all that transpires between now and then I am empowered by my truth to define. My beliefs are mine and my priorities are of my choosing. Why does man pick things to die for that mean nothing at all besides being a folly of life.

Prisons are the ideal soil for loneliness to flourish in all of it's splendor. Loneliness can reach new heights and creating huge voids in the life of prisoners. There is no purpose behind these walls beyond torment and punishment. Weasels who are no better men than I, and in some cases clearly inferior have been kicking my ass for the last 38 years with borrowed power. The strength doesn't belong to them. It belongs to the Justice Department. I no longer believe in the why of this seemingly never ending punishment, where I have experienced no friends, no shared realities, and no logical reason for taking another breathe. Mysteriously, I found compassion and the courage to empathize with others.

The potential for good resides in all of us. Self-respect and dignity isn't a tent of any particular group, creed, or color. Being clueless about life's purpose and allowing yourself ot be deceived is foolish. I don't respect men who willingly deny their families what little they can give of themselves. I don't feel any less of a man to decide to define myself by what little I am fortunate enough to give my family. I am content with allowing another man to be less than a man in the eyesight of those who remember once loving him. He can stomp his feet and shout as loud as he wants to demanding respect. Men command respect through their action, and don't demand it with threats. Any man that fails to stand by his own whenever possible is not much of a man to me. But in death Osirus will be the judge, not me.

I have swam from one oasis to another for the majority of my life seeking to find myself, just to find out that the refuge I was seeking resided in me all along. I needed to realize myself to understand inner-peace. All of my discomforts and rejections of caricatures provided by my environment were shortsightedness and unnecessary if I would have understood myself. I never needed someone else's business to see myself. Their life and journey belonged to them alone. To unwittlingly journey down paths laid by demons has caused me to experience asinine adversity almost all of my life. Today despair and hardship are part of who I am. I know grief well. The problem is that I am not that soft to allow those elements to define me.

When circumstances bite, rip my skin, and cut deep with humiliating tactics designed to separate my being from love, loyalty and dignity, love is what refuses to allow me the degradation of conceding to demons. Weaknesses and lower-self values are not something I want to past on to those I love. I am not going to allow a man to deny me the right of entertaining my truth. If they must I will accept death knowing that I definitely won't be their prostitute on the other side of this existence. I can accept whatever it is when deception is exposed, and the truth is known.

I know emptiness and the sense of having no true purpose for breathing. Defeatism and depression are not foreign to this experience. I am human and would rather be at Magic Mountain than walking a prison yard. At some point I had to accept suffering as a friend. I can't beat back the realities and the powers of this world. For years I viewed suffering as an opponent. One who was kicking my ass, and causing friends to commit suicide to maintain their honor.   There was no doubt that suffering was trying to murder me also.   When there is nothing lost and no pain, nothing is gained.   For those of us who see value in life, our pain runs deep along with the desire to not become imbeciles of the prison system.

Despair has the ability to rob a man of his dreams.   It can steal his voice and whatever purpose he had for wanting to see tomorrow. If it wasn't for the presence of friends and family believing in me, I don't know what insanity may rule me today. Their belief in the concept that how I endured the journey was more significant than any aspects of the journey itself has been in my evolutionary process. They gave me the power to define my walk through snake riddled hostile territories of my life.   Enduring my journey with some dignity became paramount to my existence. It wasn't the suffering that was killing me but how I viewed being helpless in a hopeless situation was wearing me out.   Unbeknownst to me one inch beyond my realm of consciousness existed the power to remove the blinders.   It finally dawned on me that life had already assaulted me with its full arsenal.   Yet I was still standing.

Awareness brought to my attention that fighting the wrong fight, just to be fighting didn't make sense.   Accordingly, my attitude shifted and my pain was redirected to fuel the life energy of my foundation.   What was destroying me now fortifies me in life and death.

These days I don't have a lot of unfinished business, those I love know that I love them.   I'm just in an awful situation that hinders complete expression of that love.   We never know when this ride through life might be up.   Or when the day comes that my path is short stopped by transitioning to the next world.   I don't want those I love to be confused about who I was or who I am today.   I don't believe in waiting on freedom to be the linchpin of love and inner-peace for me.   Those mental faculties are alive and well even as the fires of hell blaze around me.

247

Allowing scoundrels to designate our life course is shameful. That naivety represents a lot of wrongs. Seldom do we take into account the amount of love and pride one witnesses enroute to self-destruction. I sympathize with those who did the right thing for the wrong reasons. I even understand those who did the wrong thing for the right reason. A lot of people claim to be about the business saying that they are one hundred percent true to the game. I don't always believe that proclamation because most people I associated with ended up in the same position as me or dead.

It's been said that a dead man tells no tales, well that's not always true. In this wasteland of human experiences I have been fortunate enough to be accompanied and empowered by a multitude of spirits. Their existence in my consciousness speaks to a lot of different human values, pride and tragedies. I have an inkling of what it is to be those who allow themselves to be ripped a part by dogs. Pride is glorious, when you are willingly to allow yourself to be eaten by sharks, rather than being humiliated by men. Just as evil has its brotherhood, souls that have honor also share a comradery in life and the thereafter.

I may never realize a day in this life without psychological or physical bondage. For those I have harmed, I sincerely apologize for proving to you how inhumane one human being can be to another by acting out learned behavior that wasn't necessarily me at all. To all those individuals in life who befriended me trust that I will carry that friendship into death. I thank you!

To those that await me on the other side of this existence, I want to take the time to acknowledge and pay homage to the essence of the gift your life provided to those who were capable of seeing your spirit....

Timothy "Lil Wag" Rucker

Lil Wag was my Big Homie. He lived like a warrior but was humane. He displayed love without appearing weak. He didn't solely select the strongest or bravest of the community to stand with. He was prepared to protect the entire community, at all costs. I was about six years old when he stood up for me against an older boy that I had offended. Also his sister, Beverly was once prepared to fight for me over childish issues. He instilled a sense of family and pride in those who knew and everybody had their role. He lived like a man and died like a man. Those who claim to be descendants of his legacy by adopting the tribal name of Harlem should strive to be the moral equivalent of the man who gave birth to Harlem 30's. H.I.P.

Ronnie "LightBulb" Fuse

The man was a revolutionary. You felt his sense of Blackness. He was ruthless and brave in providing an example of what we were made of. He made Harlem Crips dangerous and didn't' tolerate the pillaging of your own community. His moral judgment was supported by death. If one didn't like the concept of treating his brothers and sisters as your own, you could definitely be taught a life or death lesson or pack bags and flee the community. LightBulb had a low tolerance for cowards and snakes. He kept his circle small with quality individuals and didn't mind rejecting questionable characters. Today he would be amazed by the numbers. He would also be disappointed by the apparent lapse of values by those claiming to be a descendant of the tribe he was instrumental in establishing with stern love. In a dangerous world he became a dangerous man. He challenged life and any foe he recognized within it. Hopefully in death he knows peace. H.I.P.

Ronnie "Yogi" Miller

I loved this man as a brother. Only a few things have caused me to shed tears in this life. News of him losing his life was one of them. The man lived life on his own terms and his loyalty to me was unparalleled. His death taught me that being right on the wrong road doesn't promise success. The best intentions in the world often fail when confronted by fearful individuals. People tend to allow selfish, unethical behaviors to outweigh the good of the whole. It's sad to witness a child capable of greatness succumb to environmental pressures and become feared by the world he tried to right. He didn't take into account that those pretending to be tough who sought the protection of a tribal identification were capable of pulling a trigger. Just because a man wants to be like you doesn't mean that he's not capable of hating you. I look forward to seeing him on the other side and discussing with sadness the waste of human potential. We trusted the face of deception and was disappointed by it's lack of commitment to it's ideals. We warriored out of ignorance. When principles came into sight, the false hearted shivered in resentment. My love for him is stronger than the fear men felt in his presence. When this ride is over I will be looking to kick it with Yogi. H.I.P.

Jimmy "Cadillac Jim" Shelton

I was always taken aback by the outpouring of love delivered by his mother, Ms. Shelton. He was her baby. She showered all that came into contact with him a love that could be felt deeply. I have sat alone in this world, feeling isolated, but warmed by her presence in

249

my life. He grew to also be a product of the environment but his love and loyalty never faltered and was cemented in his representation of belonging to a family. Love is not always enough to protect us from ourselves. I am sorry that bullets had to find their way into his body extinguishing a vibrant life. I loved him as a brother. In death we will meet again. Hopefully he resides in peace. H.I.P.

James "Big James" Miller

Death before dishonorment was his motto. The man was intelligent and could have been a professional football player. At 15 years of age he weighed 240 pounds and had 19-inch arms. The University of Southern California promised him a football scholarship if he finished high school. At one time he wore the warlord of Harlem title. He promoted and instilled the history of Harlem New York with the heroic's of Bumpy Johnson. Others may have colored our persona with their own personalities but he promoted the name Harlem amongst natives of Denker Park Recreational Center. Life wasn't easy for him at all. He spent years in solitary confinement, drawing the wrath of government officials and their puppets. Externally there was no weaknesses. Internally he chose to commit suicide to relieve his pain. I once read an old Indian folktale that spoke about warriors choosing death at the top of their games instead of waiting until they declined in prowess. I like to think that was his reasoning for killing himself. Whatever the cause I chose to remember his strength and not the way he died. Hopefully on the other side there is no battle and he can rest for once. H.I.P.

Marvin "Bumpy" Johnson

He wasn't' the biggest or baddest dude from Harlem, but he played his role well and assisted others to positions of honor. Bumpy quit school and started working odd jobs at thirteen years old and probably was the smartest of the lot. He loved being part of Harlem. There wasn't anything he wouldn't do to help those he dealt with. He was a hustler, and knew every gambling and bookie joint in West. L.A. Sadly, individuals turned his loyalty against him, which led him to get tortured before his life was ended. We can't always wholeheartedly trust the homies. Jealousy may turn them against one another over frivolous things. I hate that Bumpy is a testament to the fact that everybody who says they love you, doesn't necessarily love you. He stayed true until the end and I hope that gives some comfort in death. H.I.P.

Isom "Beaver" Hall

The man was a brother to me. After being groomed and rough housed by him as a boy, I was confidently ready for the streets from the shoulders. He was truly a decent man. After pregnating his girlfriend in the 9th grade he quit school and got a full time job. He was comfortably taking care of a family when most couldn't fend for themselves. Unfortunately, love took him down the wrong street, murdered his soul and made mockery out of wanting to be a family man. When most boys didn't even know the meaning of fidelity and commitment, he was both, just with the wrong woman. His internal pain drove him away from his truth and into the arms of death, cultivating in his eventual suicide. I wish I would have been more of a friend, wise and mature enough to be that outlet he needed to release his pain. Hopefully in death he finds some peace. H.I.P.

Peter "Pistol Pete" Owens

He played in the dirt, but never got dirty. While being raised in an environment full of vices, prostitution, drug and alcohol addiction he never allowed himself to succumb to those elements. The warrior in him was elegant and he kept his chin up throughout life. When you take a stand based on your own beliefs you are going to be feared by some and loved by others. If I had to pick a man to go to battle with he would be at the top of that list. His memory is a story about what we are missing, pain, and confusion. He fell victim to intentional misleadings but never lost his integrity. His life was cut way to short by a bullet as he slept. I don't know if he lived long enough to realize inner peace in his life. If not I wish him that peace in death. I do hope to see him again on the other side. H.I.P.

Lynette "Pepper" Favors

In those moments when life is still I ponder on what life would have been if we were not in search of ourselves. Could we have found fulfillment in raising a family? We experienced love and friendship while immature. She was a nectar of life forced to be grown while still a child. Wanting love and to belong, caused her to be vulnerable in a world that cared about nobody. There was a beauty in watching her soul realize its own strength. During an era of chaos she gave me a child, a daughter. We loved during a time that I was indifferent to feelings and my ego was travelling fast down the road of death or imprisonment. In my mind, on the other side of this world she is in a feisty stance, proud and feeling insightful about giving me a piece of my own humanity back. I have a multitude of reasons to be indifferent about this life, but she gave me

something that continues to strip away the calluses that shields my heart from living. She has never left my consciousness and I will see her in the next world. H.I.P.

Jede "Q.T." Rodale

This man was the foundation of Harlem. Where others sought fame, he shied away from the spotlight. His principles are what gave the community honor. He deplored weakness and saw little value in talking once someone had already acted out disrespectfully. To associate with him, you understood that getting off first was the rule you were expected to follow. Although violent, he was highly moral, loyal, and loved family. He set the standard of the culture that I embraced. H.I.P. and I hope to see you on the other side.

Deborah Watkins

We were like gas and fire, true young love. She put the actions to what I felt. Together we didn't know fear and didn't understand that life wasn't going to allow us to keep racing at 130 miles an hour, while everyone else is doing 65 miles an hour. Love and friendship were one and the same with us but as in any relationship when the roles become blurred friends have to part ways. The love never diminishes, it just become hurtful. We were our first experience of true love but unfortunately she never lived long enough to realize the gift of love again. There are a lot of what ifs when I reminisce about her. Often I wish I knew then what I know now about life. As a friend I would love to see her happy and alive reflecting on life's perils. As a source of love she'll never die in my heart. Until we meet again. H.I.P.

David Adams

We attended the 7th grade together at Foshay Jr. High School. The girls loved him and he was in love with life. He hadn't lived long enough to hate or to form evil words about anybody. One night we were enroute to a party with several girls and by happenstance I got delayed along the way. By the time I caught back up to the group the Bloods had already beat him to death. They justified murdering this kid by saying he was a Harlem Crip. He did live in the community but gangs were the last thing on his mind. There was no real war before his funeral. After his burial demons were unleashed and the Harlem Crips haven't lost a war yet. Hundreds have died as a direct result of killing this child. Ironically, he has the type of spirit who wouldn't have wished harm to anyone. H.I.P.

Michael Johnson

By the time I came to the penitentiary I already knew the rules to the game because Mike exemplified the model of what my community stood for. Of course, there are things to learn about life and naturally everybody wasn't going to be able to stand by what they claimed to be. He wasn't looking for a squabble but if aggressed upon he was going to give you something that you didn't want. He was a macking gangsta. He stayed dressed and made a vocation out of chasing woman and dollars, and was selective about who he Harlem'd with. He had a lot of wisdom at a young age. It pains me that he didn't live long enough to cultivate his understanding and apply love of family as a community aspiration. I appreciated the encounter and I hope to see him on the other side. H.I.P.

Brandon "Baby Brother" Davis

The man lived loving who he was, pridefully keeping his thumbs up. Behind his actions was love. Sometimes applying ourselves wholeheartedly can lead to unforeseen occurrences. Life sometimes requires that we conform to the unnatural and allow yourselves to be tamed by deception. Baby Brother's spirit never knelt before men. I sometimes question whether it's better to live a short fulfilling life or a long life filled with hardship. It's a mystery why such a bright spirit's shine was put out so early in life, while others who have no legit purpose or contribution to life keep breathing. That will be the subject of his and my conversation on the other side. H.I.P.

Christine "Miss Crissy" Jelks

She challenged the concept that men were somehow superior. Her life was a testament to courage and loyalty. Most men can't honestly claim those personality traits to be part of who they are. What she left in memory is equated to any man's contribution. The lady offered me her friendship not out of obligation, or some selfish desire, she simply loved what she represented and wanted it to be known. She died like a soldier. Hopefully she knows the same peace in death. Until we meet again. H.I.P.

Raymond Washington

He was the founder of the Crips. Before him there was none. The man was reserved and confident. Strong with a keen understanding of people and could make anyone feel comfortable in his presence. I doubt that in his wildest dreams he could have imagined how his knee jerk reaction to tenets of racism could have grown so large, getting twisted way beyond his initial intent. He was definitely a General that commanded respect. I wonder if he is in awe of the capabilities of his enemies. Does he see some the inherent value in being defiant and proud. It's a slippery slope between self-empowerment and self-destruction. I am interested in knowing how he distinguishes the two. In death I salute him and may he rest in peace. H.I.P.

Dontae Marquise Williams

This was a life cut short way too soon for nonsensical reason. His potential was limitless and the love he generated in those who knew him was addictive. He was the son of a true lifelong friend and his birth fertilized a sense of responsibility in him that made me question my shortcomings. Witnessing his life caused childish and self-serving thoughts to dissipate allowing me to understand that this existence isn't about me at all. His obituary has a stringing together of words that effectively denotes his presence saying, "To our son, just to let you know, you were born out of love, was wrapped in love, to be loved. In return you gave love and for that you'll forever be loved. We love you son. Mom and Dad." This would be a better world if we all sincerely felt that love for each other. Dontae, H.I.P.

Bryant "B.B." Black
Contributed By Miss Slim-T

He was from the era of the '80's where true homies were created. We all have our faults but to be a real G' that's not a fault, that's realness. I'm speaking from experience with him. C-Hall is what they called him and he was every bit of it. He was going through a transition to become a man. Meaning putting the street life behind him and discovering himself. I loved him for being real with me and others that crossed his path. We taught each other the value of loyalty on every level. He was a real Harlem and he was a real friend and a real ass brother. It was an honor for me to share life on earth with him. My cmonsta keep it 100 and I will do the same. You will truly be missed Crazy Hall. Loved you then, love you now, until we meet again. Thumbs Up! H.I.P

Terry "Little Fly" Lotter

Little Fly was an old man in a young body. He looked like a pimp and sported a perm that extended almost to his waist. He claimed the family and was shot once defending the family name. Then he fell in love, had a child and gave up youthful pursuits. Unfortunately his struggles to establish himself as a family man dealt him some demons that led him to this death. He was a good man who tried to find peace in the world utilizing the wrong tools. He tried to do the manly thing and failed. I have to respect the effort at being responsible to love. I hope that in death love always accompanies him. H.I.P.

Terrence "Hucabuc" Phillips

The man was a star and shined within his own light. But where there is love, one should expect hate. He did what many wish they could have and smiled where others concealed frowns. His life was shortened unnecessarily but nevertheless he had enough time in his short life to become spiritually rich and that is something death can't take from us. Cutting his life short dimmed the whole community. Hopefully in death he is as rambunctious and high spirited as he was in life. H.I.P.

Donny "Don Don" Hamilton

No matter how hard you try you can't stop me now. He once told me that despite me being gone the community was still unstoppable. There was something about the light in his eyes that made that statement true. Everybody knows that he played by his own rules and did whatever he felt that he was big enough to get away with. Regardless of what prison yard I was walking, or whether it was friend or foe speaking, he was always spoken on in the highest esteem. His spirit was u n b r i d l e d a n d d e m a n d e d acknowledgement. In death I hope that he can look back and see some significance, to the way that he lived his life. He walked through this life the only way that he knew how, defiant, and demanding his respect. I hope in death that he realizes the value of love. H.I.P.

Johnnie "Black Johnnie" Ealy

He built 43rd Street and was the first Crip to ever come to Folsom State Prison. The man was stabbed several times but never put his hands down. Black Johnnie was a few years older than me, but circumstances caused us to be allies way before we had to cope with the realities of incarceration. He was feared yet remained humble, was insightful without really understanding the total situation. He didn't survive the prison experience well at all. He became content with only relying on himself but never allowed his spirit to be broken. I hope on the other side that he see's what he couldn't see in life and experiences peace for eternity. H.I.P.

Tyrone Robinson

I really can't blame the man for wanting to belong somewhere. Unfortunately whatever exiled him from inner peace also got him killed. He came to Harlem and life was rough for him. His skin was too light not to be tested. Proving himself to others became his undoing. While both of us were being housed at San Quentin State Prison his loyalties came into question. You can't be from the community of Harlem and dedicated to a prison gang. Eventually his prison alliances got him killed. Those who followed his path by definition became traitorous. Loyalty was a flimsy concept to him in life. I hope in death he see's the value of it. H.I.P.

Dwayne "Hawk" Capers

The man was rich in spirit, loyal and loved what he loved. Too bad that his life was cut way too short. I would be interested in his opinion about truth. Those we care about are who they are inspite of themselves and we tend to see them in the best light. I hope that in death he realizes things that he didn't know in life. We walk through this life believing what we see, not taking into consideration that our eyes can be deceived. I trust there are no illusions in death, and that what we are is what it is without pretense. I see him and his parents rejoicing. I hope they are experiencing joy on the other side. H.I.P.

Rodney "Big Rod" Green

The man once told me that he had given ten years to the community and that he had to start focusing on his family. I had to admire the choice. He moved away, found a decent job and started giving back to humanity through loving his family and church work. It seems as though he questioned his loyalty. I hope in death that he understands that a man is obligated to himself first, then family, and finally the community. I am glad that he got it right before death claimed him, because his loyalty to his babies and loved ones

254

establishes who he is for eternity. Doing the right thing shouldn't have been a hard choice. H.I.P.

Alfredo "Time Bomb" Flanders

The man danced to his own drummer. The choices that generated his actions were always suspect. His loyalty and bravery never came into doubt. One time I saved him from young children who were collectively mad at him. Their anger was amusing, as was his unbelievable assertion that he had no idea why they wanted to kick his ass. His life was marked by similar conduct. I wasn't really shocked to hear of his death. Hopefully, in death he has found some logical reason for being who he was. H.I.P.

Juan Anthony "Ant Dog" Johnson

Everytime we talked it was about love and responsibility, or the disappointment felt from a lack of each. Many appear to be proud but in their heart it can't be true. I was reading your obituary and the love expressed by those who loved you is priceless. This journey through life becomes a waste of energy if what we leave behind is nothing memorable. Many loved you, and many miss you. You warriored for a community while loving your family. What else can be asked of a man? I hope your journey through eternity finds you with your Thumbs Up, and at peace. H.I.P.

James Edward "Baby Rocc" Roquemere Jr.

As a man he exemplified who we are and there is no real need to step beyond ourselves for examples of what we are supposed to be. His warrioring for the community equals the best of us. In a road laden with quicksand he possessed the strength to pull himself away from vices and pick himself back up when self-destruction loomed. Men who survive the wrath are normally empowered with self-respect and love, and obviously this man had an abundance of both. In death the love and respect that you garnered while on this earth survives. H.I.P.

The words of men can be empty of meaning, but his actions tell the story of who he is. Loving one's self is a virtue that allows us to love others. The souls of all these dead homies talk to me. Any life unnaturally cut short is a loss of precious moments. We who have allowed this life to misdirect us costing us our last breathe. Those who lost their lives to treachery and haters amongst us suffer the violation of love and trust. For that alone, I salute all my dead homies...

Chile, Killa Watt, Peaches, Lil K.F.

Pie-face Reece, Fatty, Pimpin' Nate, me, Devil, Ronnie P., Mark and others at Tehachapi, California State Prison,1988.

Relay for Life, American Cancer Society Fundraiser. Folsom State Prison. 2012 Lil Crazy D., Baby Twin (kneeling), K.D., Baby K.F., Chile, Dee, Baby Cowboy, Baby G-Rocc, Lil G. Black, Lil K.F.

C-Dog, Big Bob, Lil Jimbo, Peaches, Chile, Enfant L, Pie face
Reese, Lil K.F., Crazy-O.
Portrait by Jerome

Big James, Yogi, Watt Nitty, Sad Sack, Chile, D-Mac, Cadillac Jim,
Baby Brother.
Portrait by Jerome
Big James, Yogi, Cadillac Jim, Baby Brother are deceased.

Relay for Life, American Cancer Society. Folsom State Prison. 2014.

Lil D-Macc, Peaches, Slick and others. 2008

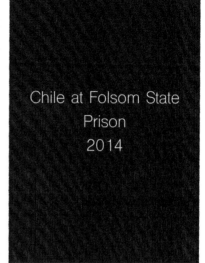

Chile at Folsom State
Prison
2014

Wino, Stacy Bullock, Harlem Roc, Dutch, Kali, and me.
Soledad State Prison, 1985

My brother, Isom Beaver Hall.

Ronnie.

Harlem Rob,
Hawk, E-Roc.
Hawk is
deceased.

D-Mac, G-Roc, and Crazy-O.
D-Mac and G-Roc are deceased.

Me, Baby-T, Ant, Pee-Wee, Slim, Shitty Smitty, Dog, Doss at San Quentin's Coyote Park. Early 1980s.

Killa Watt, Crazy Tom, Wino and others at my fundraiser. 2007

Lil' Den and Killa Watt at Michael Johnson's grave site 30 years after his death.
2007

Baby Rocc, Lil Dave and Cadillac Jim. All are deceased.

Enfant-I, G-Roc and others.

The Dead Society of Harlem's

In Memoriam

Poochie Phillips
Alonzo "Porky" Peterson
Harlan "Big Harlem" Williams
LaDonna "Pumpkin" Bell
Darryl "Lil Dee" Stubberfield Jr.
Ava Williams
Darryl Copes
David "lil Dave" Brown
Steven "Sgt. Carter" Carter
James "Jimbo" Brodnick
Darryl "Bulldog" Reed
Ricky "Big Ricc Rocc" Mooney
Kenny "Don Juan" Jordan
Herman Hall
Gregory "Baboon" Leinear
Bruce "Lil Iceman" Wright
Dean "D. Macc" Hyde
Liston "Big L. Macc" McShields
Eugene "Brother" Sanders
Andre "Casper" Miller
Michael "Mousie" Pullard
Dave "Lil D. Macc" Gentle
Edward "Tiny Iceman" Cook
Melvin "Big Perv" Brown
Kenneth "Ken Bone" Olstien
Shantae "Lady Keta" Blanche
Keith "Lil Crazy Keith" Worhal
Dominque "Domo" Collins
Charles "Warlocc" Wright
Steven "Baby Hilly" Jenkins
Michael Taylor
Derek Brown
Anthony "T-Tone" Hodge
John "Worm" Graham
Josephine "Josie" Sanders
Troy Bernard Stroman
Roosevelt "RoughHouse" Bowden
Otis "Lee Rat" Jenkins
Andre Jordan
Michael "M.C." Chambers
Joseph "Nutty Joe" Brown
Antione "Crafty Nine #3" Marshall
Michael "Mano" Lofton

Damien "Coco" Peoples
Todd "Lil S.A." Jeffries
David "lil Kip" Ware
Michael "Lil Mouse" Williams
Will "Will Dog" Williams
Shannon Dawson
Anthony "Bo-Ya" Boya
Augustus "Doo-Doo" Fields
Lavell "Shark" Hughes
Michael "Nudy" Carr
Donny "D-Dollar" Miller
Caden "Lil K.O." Royce
Grey Hardy
Sandy Harden
Davis Williams
David "Crazy Dee" Green
Melvin "Lil Mel" Burton
Cedric "Big Snake" Roboto
Tip Toe
Tweedy
James Hardy
Harold "Lil Quake" Brown
Darwin "Z-Rocc" Smith
Antione "Baby Popnose" Ewells
Jerry "J.J." Phillips
Larry Hamilton
Michael "M-Rocc" Paige
Shark #3
BK-S.S
Bam
Ce-Ce
Kevin "Rat Bone" Jones
Silk
Dracc
Kee-Kee
Lil Forehead
T-Kevin "Rat Bone" Jones
Bruce "Bogart" Johnson
Derrick "Psycho" Atkins
Brian "Lil Phil" Dago
T-Fly
Baby Den
Ms. Killa Watt

Osie
G-Rocc
James "Bird" Lawrence
Loco Boy
Blue Devil
Tiny Watt
Wynn
Ghost
E.T.
Jimmy
Fiddler
Lil Jackie Girl
Big Dee
Smurf
Shady Blue
Young-Cee
Sherlocc
Gill
Kendel 'Baby Yodie' McGee
Andy Macc-3
T-Boy
Egg-Bone
David-O
A.C.
Holland W.
M.F.
Ricky F.
Price
Tearl
Rerart
Worthy
Tiny Flea
Tiny C-Rag
Son
Norm
Eddie Macc
Harold Macc

Lil Baby Brother
Ms. Baby T.
Lil Mike
S-Rocc
Lil S-Rocc
B.C.
Michael M.
Tiny Heachache
Clifford H. "New Birth" Anderson
Koqweesha Latrice "Ms. Coco" Johnson
Lil Reese
Enfant Popnose
Alcatraz
Lil Rich
Ticc
Jolly 4
Mecca
Gary "Dove" Walker
Ricky Silas
Robert Battle
Keith "Cray Keith" Cole
Ruben "Big Ruben" Watson
Darren "Porky" Weathers
Ricky Reed
Stanley "HalfPint" Buckman
Adori 'Ms. Carzy D.' Johnson
Justin 'Dirt Status' Gary
Enfant Snake
Floyd 'Big Floyd' Willard
Dana 'Dana Dane' Hill
Ruby Lavern Grant
Latrell 'Big Boo' Livingtonly
Jarvis 'Lil Dino' Bradley
Frank 'Nitty' Reed
Eugene 'Brother' Sanders
Bryant 'B.B' Black

CPSIA information can be obtained
at www.ICGtesting.com
Printed in the USA
LVOW13s0621300117

522567LV00009B/67/P